Pathways to Data

PATHWAYS

OBSERVATIONS
A series edited by Howard S. Becker
Northwestern University

TO DATA

**Field Methods
for Studying Ongoing
Social Organizations**

**Edited by
Robert W. Habenstein
University of Missouri**

**Aldine
Publishing Company
Chicago**

DEDICATED TO THE MEMORY OF
ARNOLD M. ROSE

First published 1970 by
Aldine Publishing Company
529 South Wabash Avenue
Chicago, Illinois 60605

Library of Congress Catalog Card Number 74-124403
SBN 202-30173-7
Printed in the United States of America

Contents

Preface

THE DECISION to edit a collection of essays written specifically for those inexperienced in research by craftsmen of the field came about several years ago when Howard Becker and I met in Tulsa, Oklahoma. We had been invited to the University of Tulsa to help open a series of sociology lectures, now a yearly event. After having delivered pronouncements on the theory, method, and ethics of research and kindred matters, we found ourselves wishing there were more literature we could recommend that would be of immediate use to those who needed practical, how-to-go-about it advice on the techniques of field research.

At Becker's suggestion I began to sound out a number of colleagues who had carried out significant field research and who might be persuaded to share their experiences with others. We agreed that I should ask for techniques of a particular sort—those applying to behavior "situated" by virtue of the fact that it took place in organizational contexts. A glance at the table of contents will indicate the range of organizations concerned in the thirteen essays brought together here, and another glance will reveal the names of practitioners whose writings have been grounded in many excursions into the world of persons as they are and organizations as they persist.

I would be remiss indeed if I did not acknowledge the assistance of Jane M. Habenstein, my wife. James McCartney also must be thanked, as well as Daryl Hobbs, an understanding and supportive departmental chairman. Processing of manuscripts was facilitated by the Center for Research in Social Behavior at the University of Missouri. For researchers who specialize in research on research, I shall add that this

work was not supported by any form of grant, and that with one exception—the chapter by the late Robert K. Lamb, which represents a
memorandum he prepared for his students at MIT—all essays were
written specifically for this volume between the winter of 1967 and the
fall of 1969.

Columbia, Missouri
January 1970

ROBERT W. HABENSTEIN

Contributors

Howard Becker was born in Chicago and received three degrees at the University of Chicago including the Ph.D., in 1951. He has divided his time professionally between jazz music and sociology and his residence between San Francisco and Evanston. Author and co-author of four major works dealing primarily with deviance, he is now professor of sociology at Northwestern University and for 1969-70 Fellow at the Center for Advanced Study in the Behavioral Sciences.

Bernard Farber, professor of sociology at the University of Illinois, Urbana, was born in Chicago, attended Roosevelt University, and in 1953 received his Ph.D. from the University of Chicago. His graduate training was under the aegis of Ernest W. Burgess, and he has spent his academic career in family studies. A major area of his research dealt with families with mentally retarded children. His fourth major publication deals with late 18th century family structure and organization in Salem, Mass.

Blanche Geer is an outstanding field worker in the areas of medical sociology and the sociology of education. She received her Ph.D. from Johns Hopkins in 1956 and has collaborated in a number of participant-observer researches with Howard Becker, notably those reported in *Boys in White* and *Making the Grade: The Academic Side of College.* She is now professor of sociology at Northeastern University.

Robert W. Habenstein began a delayed career in sociology after experiences in C.C.C. camps, armed forces, and industrial work in Cleveland, Ohio. His Ph.D. dissertation at the University of Chicago in 1954 dealt with funeral directing, and at the University of Missouri where he has been on the staff since 1950 he has conducted a number of studies in the family and occupations and professions. He is the author or co-author of eight books. Currently he is professor of sociology and research associate in the University's Center for Research in Social Behavior.

Gene Kassebaum completed undergraduate work at the University of Missouri and, following service in the armed forces, received his Ph.D. from Harvard in 1958. He has taught and carried out research on small groups, village life in Egypt and India, crime and medical sociology. His publications include three co-authored works in criminology and deviance. Currently he is chairman of the Department of Sociology at the University of Hawaii.

Robert K. Lamb, a native of Washington D.C., received his Ph.D. in economics from Harvard University in 1935. He taught at Williams College for two years, and from 1938 until 1944 he served as a special investigator for several Senate Committees, staff director of the House Committee on Migration and staff director of the Senate Committee on Problems of American Small Businesses. He then served as legislative representative for the United Steel workers of America until 1947 when he resumed teaching at Harvard. At the time of his death in 1952 he was a lecturer on history and English at the Massachusetts Institute of Technology.

William C. Lawton's undergraduate majors were political science and history, and he received an M.A. in economics at the University of Texas. After several years' experience with large business firms in New York City, he served as captain of an LCI (L) in the Pacific Theatre in World War II. He received his Ph.D. in sociology at the University of Chicago in 1955 and is now professor of sociology at California State at Hayward, California, where he is currently preparing an updated version of his dissertation dealing with the Dupont Family business empire.

Roger W. Little received an A.B. in social relations at Harvard, an M.A. in social work at the University of Chicago, and his Ph.D. in 1955 at Michigan State University. He was a participant observer in a rifle company during the Korean conflict and later taught sociology at West Point. His published works center around the sociology of military establishments, and he is now testing notions reported here by field work in Viet Nam. He has been on the staff of the University of Illinois, Chicago Circle campus since 1960.

Hans O. Mauksch is professor of sociology and of community health and medical practice at the University of Missouri, Columbia, where he serves as Head of the Section of Health Care Studies in the Medical Center and is responsible for a doctoral training program in medical sociology in the Sociology Department. Having received his doctorate in sociology from the University of Chicago, he spent 12 years at Presbyterian-St. Luke's Hospital, first with the School of Nursing, later as director of the Department of Patient Care Research. Before joining the University of Missouri in 1968, he spent six years as Dean of Liberal Arts at Illinois Institute of Technology.

Lee Rainwater received an M.A. in sociology and a Ph.D. in human development in 1954 from the University of Chicago. After a number of years spent in directing researches on working and lower class life styles he became director, in 1963, of the Pruitt-Igoe research described in this volume and which was reported in part in *Behind Ghetto Walls: Black Family Life in a Federal Slum*. He is currently professor of sociology at Harvard University and faculty associate of the Joint Center for Urban Studies of M.I.T. and Harvard.

Arnold Rose received his Ph.D. at the University of Chicago in the era of the "sociological giants" and had a distinguished career at the University of Minnesota. Prolific author, researcher, and applied sociologist who won a term in the Minnesota state legislature, he was preparing to serve as President of the American Sociological Society at the time of his death early in 1968.

William L. Yancey is assistant professor of sociology at Vanderbilt University. Florida born, he received his Ph.D. at Washington University, St. Louis, in 1967 where his experience in ethnographic research was gained in studies of the Pruitt-Igoe housing project and a lower and working class neighborhood in St. Louis. Recent publications include the widely heralded work co-authored with Lee Rainwater, *The Moynihan Report and the Politics of Controversy*.

The Ways of Pathways

"It is much better," observed C. Wright Mills at the beginning of his seminal essay on intellectual craftsmanship, "to have one account by a working student of how he is going about his work than a dozen 'codifications of procedure' by specialists who often as not have never done much work of consequence."[1] Three-quarters of a century earlier Beatrice Webb, the Florence Nightingale of sociological field studies, had jotted in her field diary:

> July 16. Sitting for five or six hours in a stinking room with an open sewer on one side and ill-ventilated urinals on the other, is not an invigorating occupation. But in spite of headache and mental depression I am glad I came. These two days debate have made me better appreciate the sagacity, good temper and fair-mindedness of these miners than I could have by reading endless reports.[2]

These well-taken observations underscore the premise of this book: that there is a need for working students in sociology to communicate the procedures and strategies of field research they have found consequential in their own studies to the less instructed or less experienced. Having become known for their works, the writers of this book now seek to make known their field-developed techniques of research craftsmanship. The pathways to data thus wind in a common direction, toward a concern with research happenings in situations of organization: in agencies, associations, institutions, campaigns, organized demonstra-

1. C. Wright Mills, *The Sociological Imagination* (New York: Oxford University Press, 1959), p. 195.
2. Sidney Webb and Beatrice Webb, *Methods of Social Study* (London, New York, Toronto: Longmans, Green, 1932), p. 172.

1

tions, goal-directed social movements, and other organizing collective endeavors.

Watching the Organization at Work

These essays are neither biographies of research projects nor subjective evaluations of personal experiences written by researchers working at their craft. Rather, the writers stress techniques, operations, and know-how. To use a kinship analogy, the essays in *Pathways to Data* may be seen as collateral cousins of the collection of research biographies found in *Sociologists at Work*.[3] But the lineage, or progression of thought, traces back to the Webbs' *Methods of Social Study*,[4] written in the early thirties, and is most closely related to the recent Glaser and Strauss volume, *The Discovery of Grounded Theory*.[5] In any consideration of the work at hand, then, the endeavors of the Webbs are instructive. Having spent nearly a half century in social surveys and field research, successively studying British trade unionism, consumer cooperation, and local government, the Webbs step aside from substantive reporting to show how one goes about making

> a comparative study of the working of particular social institutions in a single country, made by observations and analysis, through personal participation or watching the organization at work, the taking of evidence from other persons, the scrutiny of all accessible documents and the consultation of general literature.[6]

As investigators who have watched the organization at work, the contributors to this book reflect in their chapters a common concern with organization in the "down home" sense of social bonds opening and closing, of self-involvement, and, importantly but not imperiously, of social structure. Process is stressed above system, becoming over being. When setting is described, as is the social agency in Bernard Beck's chapter, the correctional system in Gene Kassebaum's, and the hospital in Hans Mauksch's, there remains the clear acknowledgment of the importance of persons collectively endeavoring to bring under control the vicissitudes of daily existence within such a setting. The authors point to people with roles to play and selves to sustain as both a source of and a resource for social data. It is for this reason that the problems of access and the questions the researcher asks loom so importantly in the following chapters.

Situations of organization can vary from the large-scale impersonal

---

3. Phillip E. Hammond, ed., *Sociologists at Work* (New York: Basic Books, 1964; also reprinted in 1967 as a Doubleday Anchor Book).

4. Webb and Webb, *Methods of Social Study*.

5. Barney G. Glaser and Anselm L. Strauss, *The Discovery of Grounded Theory* (Chicago: Aldine, 1967).

6. Webb and Webb, *Methods of Social Study*, p. vi.

social artifact, the business corporation, down to the minimally organized encounter of homosexuals in a public toilet. But in almost any attempt to penetrate such milieus, the field researcher will have to interact initially and persistently with the persons who people it. As Howard Becker points out, field research consists primarily in finding certain kinds of people and then getting them to give away the things our concepts, hunches, and sensitivities as practitioners of social research direct us to look for.

Outline Guide for Chapter Content

With this precept in mind we might now turn to the content outline submitted to the authors as a guide for their chapters. The degree to which they were able or willing to follow it not only reflects the degree of applicability of the suggested categories; the obvious variation from chapter to chapter also suggests an independence of spirit and action that makes a shambles of any theory of cultural or structural determinism.

The Research Problem of	*Specifically*
Access	How do you get access? Who are the most important people to contact or clear with? The order of contacts. Sponsored and unsponsored initiation of contacts.
Questions	What kinds of questions, in general, are asked? How phrased? The problem of idiom in question-asking.
Events	What kinds of typical or recurring events should be watched for and observed? (E.g., national conventions, institutes, retreats.) What kinds of things can be learned from them?
Subgroupings	What divisions, status hierarchies, polarizations, schismatic groups, informal, quasi, and formal subgroupings exist? What ecological niches and physical characteristics of the environment make for subgroups? Sampling these groups.
Related groups	Who, outside of members of the group, will know something about it and should be talked to? (E.g., talk to cops about professional criminals; talk to LPN's about registered nurses.)
Records kept	What kinds of records does the organization or group keep, and how can they be used? What likely records or data would be found in special places? (E.g., archives, collections, special libraries, etc.) What cautions must be taken in using them?
Information about	What kind of records do others (police, doctors, government, newspapers, opposition groups, fact-gathering agencies) keep about them?

Literature from	What professional, trade, public relations, human interest, memoirs, diaries and other biographical or descriptive literature — apart from records — are likely to exist and be found?
Investigatory materials	Are they subject to study or investigation by others (e.g., physicians, government agencies, congressional committees, insurance companies, state boards), so that there is a literature available on them in some file or hearing?
Measures	Are there any typical kinds of unobtrusive measures that might be useful?
Participation	How one determines and goes about effective participation. Moral judgments. (Smoke pot? Hide guns? Intimidate finks? Get cut in?) Limitations, fancied and real, in participation.
Linguistics	Opportunities for sociolinguistic analysis. Codes, repertoires, private languages, argots.
Strategies	Specialties of the field, area, or subject. Flexibility, recouping, salvage jobs, crying for help.

A review of the above catalog of field problems and their elaboration into a manifold of specific research questions indicates that almost exclusively they deal with what-to-do and how-go-about-it operations. No broad guage theoretical formulations were asked for and none were offered. Specialized techniques and strategies, tested and developed by the field-experienced, then, constitute the subject matter of the book.

Unanticipated Concepts of Purposive Method

A recently popular song asks, "Is that all there is?" As far as this book is concerned, that's all that was specifically intended: techniques, strategies, and procedures of field research dealing with situations of organization. But there is the happy improbability of prescribing methodological technique without at the same time introducing or fleshing out substantive concepts. These concepts, often clothed in metaphor, may be necessary to help organize, define, or direct techniques, e.g., Roger Little's "echelons of risk," William Yancey and Lee Rainwater's "caretaker contracts," Bernard Beck's "monitoring establishments," Donald Roy's "Ernie Pyling," and my own "holy grailers." Or, in his need to build contexts of understanding for the intelligent application of technique, an author may adduce other, often fresh concepts.

Again, William Lawton finds it necessary to sketch the genesis of the corporation as a social artifact before elaborating on methods for the study of big business; Little tells us a lot about army organization; Beck sets the welfare agency in a context of impinging interest and watchdog groups; and Arnold Rose explains in some detail what makes a legislator tick in order that he may be better studied in his habitat. Some concepts or principles of broader application emerge, such as Hans Mauksch's "decorator syndrome," the "research bargain," described by Howard S. Becker and Blanche Geer, Beck's observation that in organizational study the maintenance of trust has its reciprocal in the demonstration of harmlessness, and Gene Kassebaum's reminder of the tolerance with which ongoing institutional systems accommodate known observers. None of these organizing concepts, elements of description and analysis, and characterizations were specifically asked for by the editor. But the fact that they are found in some profusion throughout the book is good evidence in support of the proposition that one not only needs to know something about what he is going to study in order to subject it to productive research inquiry, but, conversely, must in some measure conceptualize the object of study in order to discuss techniques of field research applicable to a situation of organization.

A different matter of concern to the field researcher is the ethical, pertaining to that which is overtly or implicitly promised, bargained for, or traded, and must as a matter of expectable reciprocity be delivered to those who in some manner have been knowingly implicated in the research. This problem has both immediate and particular as well as more general aspects. That is, what one reciprocates in day-to-day interaction with members of the subject group must be differentiated from the more general bargain with the group itself.[7] In any event, reciprocity becomes an ineluctable problem for the researcher the moment those implicated in field research become in any degree aware of their role. The matter cannot be ignored; like Banquo's ghost, it will return to plague the researcher. In various ways and without editorial direction nearly all the writers take note of this problem of reciprocity.

Another concern, that of value relevance—i.e., the rationale or justification for studying one organizational situation as against another—is not directly dealt with by the writers. From the standpoint of the editor, the effort to get a group of working students who in a general way shared a consensus of research perspectives and values seemed as important as picking out specific organizational situations to serve as subjects for discussion. However, substantial diversity of subjects was attempted; where differences of opinion on related matters occur, the reader for better or worse must fall back on his own resources. If there has been no explicit rationalization of the choices or the need for particular subjects of study, there remains implicit in each author's contribution the judgment that his interest in and study of a particular organizational phenomenon has not been trivial. Finally, in the work of most of the authors there is the further implication that more general theory might well be

7. This idea is elaborated by Blanche Geer in chap. 4 and by me in chap. 5.

built out of a multiplication of studies done comparatively within the unit
of research they have specified.

Conclusion

Seen programatically, field methods deliver data to concepts, and techniques are consequently grounded in the heuristic value such data display. Theory, it would follow, is grounded in the return trip, with
concepts validated by the efficacy with which they apprehend and give
meaning to the data of field technique. Thus the production of social
knowledge is a symmetrical, reciprocal, but analytically divisible affair.
In this work of fourteen writers, the burden of effort has been to move
from experience to prescription, from know-how to tell-how. But in their
efforts to make prescription intelligible the authors have often found
themselves building descriptive contexts and developing explanatory
concepts that tell something about the nature and operations of their
units of study. The student of society will consequently find a holiday
assortment of knowledges in the following pages, sufficient in their own
right to make large portions of our society more understandable; the
variety of techniques and strategies that make up their methodological
scaffoldings are invaluable as initiating guides for field research ventures.
The stride of the giant can always be paced off in baby steps.

Cooking Welfare Stew

> *Recipe for rabbit stew:*
> *First, catch one rabbit.*
>   *– Old cookbook recipe*

It is harder than you think to find a welfare setting to study. It makes a great deal of difference whether you first pick a research setting and then decide it is welfare or first decide to study welfare and then go looking for a situation. The general term "welfare" can refer to several common characteristics, and the procedural advice appropriate for the student will vary accordingly.

Before discussing how to go about studying welfare settings, we should figure out why a discussion of welfare studies might be relevant to your particular project. If you begin with a specific setting, the question is: Why are the methods for studying welfare good methods here? If you start with an interest in welfare, the question is: How do you select a setting where this interest will be satisfied and where the study methods of welfare will work? I have written elsewhere about the difficulties in drawing conceptual lines around welfare as an area of sociological interest.[1] The practical question that has to be answered here is: What are the general characteristics of settings where the advice that follows in this essay will be good? I shall offer some recognition signals that I believe characterize many settings commonly called welfare in the literature. The advice that follows is aimed at studies of settings with these characteristics. For present purposes this will serve as a crude operational definition of welfare.

1. Welfare is an extraordinary activity that is defined as beyond the routinely expectable outcomes available to members of society. It represents an expressed intention to help, provide for, or take care of people who, em-

1. Bernard Beck, "Welfare as a Moral Category," *Social Problems,* 14, no. 3 (Winter 1967): 258–77.

barrassingly, are in less than good shape under the ordinary, automatic workings of the system. Definitionally, benefits from welfare to recipients are not as fully deserved as, say, wages for work done. According to prevailing definitions, welfare is available because someone was considerate enough to provide it, not because he owed it to anyone.

.2. Welfare is dispensed by workers to clients in a formal organizational setting; that is, an agency.

3. Workers and clients are recruited from different segments of society, and from different hierarchical strata. In particular, workers have higher prestige than clients and come from social strata of higher prestige.

4. Whether clients receive welfare benefits and how much they receive depend on how the worker does his job.

5. The agency, operating in a morally suspect area, is continually subject to critical review of its operations by more powerful agencies that are not completely sympathetic with its work.

6. Agency operations consist largely of paperwork, which is carefully scrutinized for correctness.

7. Agency operation is dependent on large-scale decisions made, often for ulterior reasons, by high-level decision-makers.

8. Welfare activities are a matter of general public concern. They are highly constrained by their public reputation. They must continually be justified. Welfare agencies cannot regard resources as secure. Welfare rhetoric is high-flown and is continuously employed in order to maintain the agency's mandate.

Welfare is mainly distinguished by its special moral reputation. Many related or similar institutional areas may share these characteristics, and some of my remarks may be applicable to them as well. Thus hospitals, prisons, employment agencies, schools, certain occupational groups, and certain urban neighborhoods may or may not be labeled as welfare establishments, but this essay undertakes to be useful to studies of them if they conform to the listed characteristics. On the other hand, a health insurance plan, for example, ordinarily listed as a welfare program, may not meet many conditions of the list; a study of such a plan would not necessarily benefit from the suggestions that follow.

Thus, in studying a welfare setting, it is important first to get hold of a welfare setting and to pay attention to how you do it. The old joke depends for its impact on calling attention to the fact that to make a rabbit stew, you have somehow to get a rabbit, a matter taken for granted in most cookbooks. One rabbit is not the same as every other rabbit. Make sure you know what kind of "welfare" you are studying.

Getting In

Getting to study welfare is usually a matter of getting into welfare offices. Although a welfare study may lead you into the streets, into living rooms, hospital wards, custodial institutions, or funeral parlors, and into the haunts of people who have never used or dispensed welfare services, the fact that gives the study a focus is likely to be the existence of a program, incarnate in a block of offices. As a result, most investigators find that the first or second important step they must take to reach the data they want is gaining entry to an office and the cooperation of someone who works there.

The welfare field offers opportunities for research of many varieties. Some of the varieties are methodologically quite dissimilar. Some people have been interested in welfare organizations as cases of bureaucratic structure;[2] some have focused on the life and culture of recipients;[3] some have been interested in the worker-client relationship as an interaction setting;[4] some have studied the occupational careers of caseworkers,[5] or the impact of programs on the labor market,[6] or the shifts in ideological emphasis of public discourse on welfare,[7] or comparisons of welfare and nonwelfare populations.[8] The procedures of study may include participant observation, depth interviewing, statistical analysis of welfare records, surveys, and inspection of historical documents. However heterogeneous the forms of welfare research may be, most of them have their beginnings in the offices of some welfare official, public or private. But not all, as we shall see later on.

For many ordinary purposes, gaining the cooperation of welfare officials is neither difficult at first nor a reputational liability later on. (Compare the cost to an industrial sociologist, who wants candid answers from workers on the assembly line, of coming into the plant under management auspices.[9]) This is particularly true in the case of studies conducted in other societies. Welfare officials often have personal and

2. For example, Peter Blau, *Dynamics of Bureaucracy* (Chicago: University of Chicago Press, 1955).

3. For example, Richard M. Elman, *The Poorhouse State* (New York: Pantheon Books, 1966).

4. For example, Peter Blau, "Orientation Toward Clients in a Public Welfare Agency," *Administrative Science Quarterly*, 5, no. 3 (December 1960): 341–61.

5. For example, Earl Bogdanoff and Arnold Glass, "The Sociology of the Urban Public Aid Caseworker" (unpublished master's thesis, Department of Sociology, University of Chicago, 1954).

6. For example, Gaston V. Rimlinger, "Social Security, Incentives, and Controls in the U.S. and U.S.S.R.," *Comparative Studies in Society and History*, 1961, pp. 104–24.

7. For example, Harold Wilensky and Charles Lebeaux, *Industrial Society and Social Welfare* (New York: Russell Sage Foundation, 1958), especially chap. 6, "Conceptions of Social Welfare."

8. For example, the comparative project on employed and unemployed working-class groups carried out by the Seminar on Social Change, conducted by Arnold S. Feldman, Northwestern University, from 1966 to date. See Phyllis Fox, "A Working Paper on the Effects of Skill Level and Employment Stability" (unpublished paper, Department of Sociology, Northwestern University, 1969).

9. Compare Eli Chinoy, *The Automobile Workers and the American Dream* (Garden City, N.Y.: Doubleday, 1955).

professional backgrounds similar to those of social scientists who come to study them. Politically and ideologically, they are often compatible. Officials are likely to hold favorable opinions of social research and of its potential benefits to the effectiveness of their programs and to the enhancement of their positions in the organization. Finally, they are likely to have more understanding of the role of social researcher that an investigator may choose to invoke for himself.

In certain respects, however, this kind of easy entry is dangerous, and the temptation to avail yourself of it should not be succumbed to uncritically. Whether welfare organizations are more image-conscious than others or only seem to be, the standard cautions against accepting "official versions" from cooperative officials deserve special emphasis. People may be all too willing to explain everything about the program to you because they have compelling private reasons for getting you to believe and pass along their own interpretations. Whatever the purpose of your investigation, those in charge of a program may see your presence as an opportunity to get it recognized as a success or to present reasons why its failure was due to extrinsic factors.

When you are allowed and helped to conduct your study, it is more often a bilateral contract than a unilateral grant of privilege. Getting into the organization is crucial, but equally crucial is the question of how far in you get. The degree of entry is primarily controlled by a factor that distinguishes welfare, though it is not unique to it. This factor is confidentiality.

Welfare agencies often deal with the most intimate facts of clients' personal lives (including the taboo topic of personal income) and transform them into impersonal data controlled only within the organization. Consequently, agencies are likely to have formal rules limiting the access of unauthorized persons to case records and files, as well as direct contact with clients. These rules are institutionalized in a variety of ways and at various levels in the hierarchy. Thus statute law usually controls the availability of information in public agencies. Private agencies may have comparable high-level by-laws from boards of directors. Such rules are legal, formal, and public, and consequently they are officially nonnegotiable. In addition, agencies will have their own internal policies promulgated by high executives. Individual offices build protections of confidence into standard office procedures. Finally, the professional sensibilities of caseworkers may produce strong resistance to divulging information or exposing their clients to social inquiry.

On the other hand, the question of who is an authorized person provides an area of leeway to prospective investigators. Until now, we have assumed that you enter a welfare agency as a free investigator, whose only credentials are those of a social scientist with a research interest. But a good percentage, if not most, of the studies carried out in welfare settings are officially sanctioned at the outset. Such organizations often commission research themselves. Higher levels in large welfare systems will often wish to have specific subprograms investigated. Research is often done in conjunction with evaluations of ongoing programs and experiments with new programs. Many welfare organizations have research operations of their own. A would-be investigator must make an assessment of the costs and rewards of becoming a research employee of an agency. He should take account of the organizational tolerance for expenditure of time, methodological sophistication, and the naked truth. He should also be aware of the limitations that may be placed on the publication of his findings. Finally, he should try to calculate how much of his effort will be devoted to organizational tasks or peripheral interest to him in return for a chance to do otherwise impossible work of his own.

The official welfare bureaucracy is not the only locus of large-scale organizational activity in welfare. There are also independent but influential establishments that monitor welfare systems. In the United States, this role is most prominently played by foundations; in other countries it may fall to national institutes, academies, or parties. These establishments are especially active in the welfare field, where their operations can be diverse and diffuse. They are often in the forefront of attempts to promote new approaches and programs.[10] Consequently, they afford research resources to prospective students of welfare. The resources may consist of little more than a study grant of funds, but sometimes they will provide an organizational umbrella to the student, including magic credentials that open many doors. The quasi-public character of such auspices implies advantages to the researcher without the constraints imposed by a monolithic agency that is itself the subject of study. On the other hand, the long-range plan that a foundation may be boosting can constitute pressure enough to make the costs outweigh the rewards. A related problem arises: since foundation goals may be relatively obscure to the individual researcher, he may find it hard to decide who is manipulating whom.

Many welfare organizations, especially in the private sector, welcome regular arrangements with research-oriented persons. They often operate on minimal funds that force them to be innovative in getting fringe services, like research. Arrangements of "mutual benefit" can often be worked out by social scientists who appear at the right moment. Such an arrangement is more attractive, and therefore more convenient, if a steady stream of colleagues and students can be channeled into it. The

10. Consider the role of the Ford Foundation, for example, in the movement for community control of schools in New York City.

regularity makes an ad hoc agreement into something resembling a regular research department. The longer such an arrangement lasts, the more valuable it becomes to both parties, and the more complex are the mutual expectations. As a result, the hidden constraints that may impinge on a Johnny-come-lately investigator who approaches a welfare agency as the latest in a series of sponsored students can preclude fresh approaches and unorthodox interpretations.[11] The stability of the mutual relationship may outweigh the results of any single study.

Many researchers have felt most comfortable in the role of consultant. As in other fields, the professional who acquires a reputation for competence, discretion, and familiarity with welfare is regarded as a valuable resource. The consultant need not feel the constraints of long-term identification with a single organization, but he can present himself as something of an insider. Consultation can be managed as a long-term career; oppressive limitations may be accepted in the early states for the sake of developing the kind of credentials that allow independence later on. The consultant also retains great flexibility in dealing with a variety of audiences. He can combine general or academic publication with commissioned services in such a way that he is neither a dependent of the agencies he studies nor a rank outsider who can be rebuffed at whim. It is possible for a consultant to gain access, not because he is liked, but because his stamp of approval is necessary to the agency. (Compare the power of some nationally syndicated newspaper columnists.) In addition, in the highly political and factional field of welfare planning, a consultant is an available resource for any faction in its attempts to discredit another.

With some felicitous exceptions, the price of inside status is usually the discretion required of insiders. Investigators who are sufficiently attractive, slippery, or independently powerful may be able to get well inside without honoring debts of kindness, but this strategy is advised only for experts and crusaders. There is, however, sufficient access available across the welfare spectrum for ordinary, unsponsored social scientists so that it is rarely necessary to surrender the freedom to inquire and publish according to your own professional judgment. Note well that many people who do research on welfare have other interests besides pure research. In particular, many who want to study welfare also want to influence planning and decision-making or otherwise directly affect outcomes. For such projects, the balance sheet of costs and rewards associated with various degrees of involvement in the organization may be markedly different. The price in restriction of publi-

11. A comparable situation results from the arrangements between local schools and colleges of education for placement of student teachers. The activities of any student teacher are constrained by the college's desire to maintain the arrangement.

cation that is unacceptable to a university sociologist may be of little concern to an investigator who wants most to influence the decisions of the higher administrators in the agency, or is only interested in bringing its operations to an end.

Whatever the official or unofficial status of the would-be investigator, confidentiality is a norm that is invokable by officials, rather than one that is automatically and strictly enforced. Thus an administrator who does not like your looks for any reason may refuse you access to part or all of his agency operations on the grounds that the material is confidential. If, on the other hand, he is willing or anxious to allow you in, exceptions to the rules can usually be made. Note that relaxation of confidentiality provides the agency with a control over your research activities. If you become obnoxious at any point, your permission to study can be revoked or limited under the rubric of protecting confidences. This places the student on indefinite probation and makes each new privilege dependent on past good behavior. It also allows the official to change his mind about you without ever having to say so or appearing to censor your work.

The practical questions that arise reduce to two important ones: Who should you approach first? How should you present yourself to him? The general principles for answering the first question are these:

1. Approach someone high enough in the hierarchy to empower you (formally or informally) to enter the places you want to observe, to interview the people you want answers from, and to read the documents you want to analyze.

2. Approach someone low enough in the hierarchy to have working knowledge or routine operations and material impact on those operations.

In all probability, the first official you contact will not be the most appropriate one, and your first few days will be spent following a chain of referrals until you find the right office. It is wise not to be more communicative than necessary until you are sure you are talking to the right person. Otherwise, you will maximize the chance of giving offense to someone who is not in a position to do you much good anyway.

If you have an idea of the specific kind of project you want to carry out or the specific kind of program you want to study, then there are two most likely appropriate officials, the director of such programs in the local area and the director of some office carrying out the program (e.g., the director of job-training programs for the city and the director of a job-training center in a ghetto neighborhood). If you do not have such a specific focus at the outset, you may conduct a two-stage exploration. First you will speak to a high-level official with jurisdiction over a wide variety of programs (e.g., someone in the office of the welfare commissioner), who can acquaint you with the range of programs and refer you to the appropriate offices of the ones that interest you. Second, you will find the appropriate official in some particular program, as above.

While you are trying to find the best setting and the right contacts for your study, the people you talk to first will be screening you or referring you to the screeners. These first impressions will affect your access to the setting, but are not likely to affect your subsequent work if you are admitted. This brings us to the second question: How do you present yourself? Your interviewers will be looking for certain basic reassurances and insurances and will be testing you against sensitivities that they may or may not be aware of having. They will be posing two questions to themselves: Do they want you? Do they mind having you? Of the two, a favorable answer to the second is more important than a favorable answer to the first. It is not wise to try so hard to be wanted that you risk being found intolerable. Favorable answers are those that lead the official to feel that you are not the sort of *person* who would do something dangerous or unacceptable or that you are not in a *position* to get away with it. Desirable personal characteristics include seriousness, sympathy for organizational goals and procedures, sympathy for the perspective of the official, but also not having an ax to grind and not assuming you already know the answers. Desirable positional characteristics include being at the mercy of persons or organizations that can be influenced by the agency personnel and not having access to media for broadcasting embarrassing findings.

There is no easy formula for finding your way through such interviews. One of the most important sources of difficulty should be specifically mentioned. The talk must be conducted in the official vocabulary and rhetoric of the program, but the questions in the mind of the official will often be related to unofficial interests involving the practicalities of the agency's career or his own. The prospective researcher must show sufficient homage to organizational rhetoric without appearing so zealous about it that he would reject the privately negotiated, self-serving interpretations of the rhetoric that agency personnel have developed.

Unless you are clever or fortunate enough to have personal values that coincide with those of the official, your position as a social scientist and your commitment to social research are the best possible credentials, as expressed in the evolved rhetoric of the social sciences.[12] It is very likely that this rhetoric has evolved in its particular form because it works in such situations. In other words, coming on straight is the best approach. It has the added virtue of not leading you to make promises you have no intention of keeping. It is worth noting here that the

12. In this and later discussions of the social scientist role and its invocation in fieldwork I lean heavily on ideas of Howard S. Becker.

appearance of social science propriety is not necessarily associated with the reality. I have known students who were committed investigators but were not perceived as such and therefore were denied access, as well as those with ulterior purposes who presented an image of scientific respectability and were given the run of the place.

The social science role, it should be noted, includes a quid pro quo, as well. The magical invocation of science affords opportunities to do unbought research, but also commits the researcher to conduct himself in a certain way. In particular, it will often be necessary to make explicit to the person you are dealing with the terms of the bargain you want him to make with you. As a rule, do not try to gain access without making a full disclosure. The advantage you hope to gain all unnoticed will probably come back to haunt you in later days. Prior agreement on these points is not only fair to your subjects, it is also a protection for you. You may find it necessary to give assurances about anonymity and you may have to promise to make your results available to the agency, usually before general publication. You may be invited to take a confidant role on certain issues; that is, you will be tempted by pieces of information that you can have if you promise not to tell. It is wise to hold these to a minimum, if you allow this arrangement at all. It is crucial to make it absolutely clear that you will not promise to withhold from publication anything you may learn. "Classified" research may present a moral dilemma to only a few, but too often the secrecy rules make it just plain bad research.[13]

Reliance on the social scientist role to gain access may tempt you into a basic error of fieldwork procedure, giving the appearance of already knowing a lot. It is not wise to depart too much from a basic posture of requiring to be told *everything*. If you claim to know something, then (1) you may be required to prove the claim, which can at least be embarrassing and at most destroy the legitimacy of your position in the organization, and (2) you will make it far more difficult for yourself ever to find it out. This point is true in most fieldwork settings, but especially so in welfare, where there are so many levels of real stories underlying apparent stories.

I mentioned earlier that while most investigators must and do gain access through official channels, there are alternatives. What these alternatives lack in frequency of use they more than make up in power and validity when they are used. The two major categories are (1) intensive and imaginative use of data that are publicly available and (2) noninstitutional approaches to people and places involved in the institutions of welfare. The first category consists of secondary analysis of published

13. See the discussion of the fate of Project Camelot in Irving Louis Horowitz, *The Rise and Fall of Project Camelot* (Cambridge: MIT Press, 1967).

material, in the tradition of what good reporters used to do. In the welfare field, in spite of the endemic security precautions, there is still a great deal of material susceptible to such analysis, as I shall indicate below in the section on sources and documents.

In the second category of noninstitutional approaches, I include all the forms of reaching welfare settings without getting permission from welfare officials. There are as many ways of doing this as there are kind of people and places involved in welfare. Welfare clients and their families, friends, and associates can be reached directly by the same methods used in reaching other informal categories of persons, e.g., deviants.[14] Welfare workers can be reached by the kinds of techniques used in reaching nonorganizational workers in the study of occupations. Obviously, personal contacts that antedate the decision to do a study help greatly.

In addition, one can take the phrase "participant observation" quite seriously and become a welfare client or welfare worker in order to gain access. Once again, it is much easier if you are one already when you decide to do your study.[15] Finally, the recent growth of countervailing organizations in the welfare field, such as public aid employees' unions and welfare clients' unions (e.g., the National Welfare Rights Organization), provide alternative routes. Enterprising researchers have used the classical informant-referral method of ethnography to find clients, workers, or settings on a personal basis and to develop a usable sample of respondents by being passed along through a network of acquaintances. One student frequented public gathering places, such as bars and laudromats, in a neighborhood with many ADC clients. Through casual conversations, he was able to meet a few veteran recipients who had extensive contacts with other recipients whom he was able to interview and observe. As a result, interviews between clients and caseworkers, which would probably have been denied him under the rules of confidentiality of the agency, were open to his observation as a friend of the clients.[16] Another student was able to get data on caseworkers because his wife was one and introduced him into her network of acquaintanceship. One final interesting possibility is afforded by the

14. See chap. 2 of this volume, "Practitioners of Vice and Crime," by Howard S. Becker.

15. The data collected by Bogdanoff and Glass in "Sociology of the Urban Public Aid Caseworker" show the unique value of this approach. Also compare the study by an outside investigator, Blau, *Dynamics of Bureaucracy,* with a study in a similar setting by an employee of the agency, Harry Cohen, *The Demonics of Bureaucracy* (Ames: Iowa State University Press, 1965).

16. This approach was used by Lawrence Felt for his Ph.D. dissertation in preparation, Department of Sociology, Northwestern University, provisionally entitled "The Relative Importance of 'Welfare Participation' and 'Mother-Headedness' upon Social Mobility: Intergenerational Mobility Among 'Welfare' and 'Non-Welfare' Families."

intimate contacts between semi-insider consultants and research employees in welfare and the unconstrained academic social researchers. Professional colleagueship makes available a wealth of inside dope on an informal basis which the source is prevented from publishing himself by the constraints of his position in the system of mutual obligations among welfare personnel.[17]

As countervailing organizations grow in the welfare field, the convenience they may provide to an investigator who wants to get inside will increasingly be offset by the development of organizational reticence of the kind discussed earlier in connection with officials. As community organizations, caseworker unions, and professional associations achieve power, they will recognize both the need and the desirability for demanding quid pro quo. In other words, as the unorganized segments of welfare get organized, they produce institutional protections. Organization is an asset. It can be improved or blighted by events; it can achieve a better or worse bargaining position with its competitors. Leaders in such organizations will seriously scrutinize any proposed research project in the light of their own goals and tactics. An outraged community leader can be as effective an obstacle to your study as a hostile administrator.

An example may make this point clearer. Fieldworkers have developed a set of conventional protections for the anonymity of informants. These may serve to protect one among thousands of recipients from repercussions; they will hardly suffice to protect what may be the only or one of a very few welfare rights unions. Thus the bargain in the second case is likely to be more complex and demanding than in the first case. Likewise, since the individual recipient is unlikely to have much bargaining room with the agency, cooperation with an investigation will not affect his personal economy beyond the expenditure of time and talk. Since organizations are presumably in existence to create the possibility of effective bargaining, the decision to cooperate in research is an investment or organizational capital and hence a matter of some moment.

In general, the same kinds of considerations should guide you in dealing with community, union, and other hierarchies as in dealing with agency structures. The specific content, of course, will most likely be different. The sensitivities, ulterior motives, and ideological climates will vary, and the best advice is to remain open to cues in the individual setting rather than to rely on any all-purpose characterization of the players. The variations in space and time require that you use antennae rather than a gyroscope. There is help, however. Because of the intimate connections between the currently live issues in the social sciences and the action in the welfare field, even the most insensitive researcher can

17. I am indebted for this insight to James W. Carper and Lawrence Sherwood.

find clues to the sore spots in his own professional (or counter-professional) literature.[18]

One final word on access: The study of welfare is not necessarily limited to welfare settings. A great deal can be learned through study of nonwelfare populations and scenes, particularly in a comparative design. Thus one study instructively commented on welfare clients' careers by comparing them with the careers of "similar" nonwelfare people (blue-collar factory workers).[19] Furthermore, since welfare occurs within and is strongly shaped by the prevailing political and economic institutions of general society, especially in their moral aspects, an investigator may find it most useful to turn his attention completely away from the settings discussed here.[20] Finally, significant welfare issues may come to light in areas no one has ever identified as related to welfare before. In such a case, the study of "welfare" will be best informed by the wisdom appropriate to that scene as it is ordinarily labeled.[21]

The foregoing remarks have dwelt on the numerous impediments to welfare studies that can arise. People who undertake such studies occasionally find themselves frustrated, embarrassed, humiliated, or even physically abused. Nevertheless, most people who want to learn about welfare can do so without great difficulty. Almost any approach, if taken honestly and inquisitively, will yield rich results. To repeat, the most generally effective method is to *be* and *appear* to be a social scientist. This role has evolved over time in response to the typical constraints on research activity. At any given time, however, the fortunes of the social science reputation vary. In our own time, the social sciences are both more respected and more seriously criticized than they were in the recent past. In particular, searching questions have been raised about the value-free stance, about the covert idelogical biases of "disinterested" research, about the auspices under which it is carried out, and about the personal integrity of investigators. Such criticism has come from inside and outside the disciplines.[22] Under such conditions, a

18. See, for example, Irving Louis Horowitz, ed., *The New Sociology* (New York: Oxford University Press, 1965); Arthur Vidich, Joseph Bensman, and Maurice Stein, eds., *Reflections on Community Studies* (New York: Wiley, 1964); and issues of *The Subterranean Sociology Newsletter* and *The Insurgent Sociologist*.

19. Phyllis Fox, "Working Paper," and the work of the Feldman seminar.

20. Wilensky and Lebeaux, *Industrial Society and Social Welfare;* Beck, "Welfare as a Moral Category."

21. See Bernard Beck, "The Military as a Welfare Institution" *Inter-University Seminar on Armed Forces and Society,* 1969. (mimeo).

22. See C. Wright Mills, *The Sociological Imagination* (New York: Oxford University Press, 1959); Alvin Gouldner, "Anti-Minotaur: The Myth of a Value-Free Sociology," *Social Problems,* 9, no. 3 (Winter 1962); Arthur Vidich and Maurice Stein, eds., *Sociology on Trial* (Englewood Cliffs, N.J.: Prentice-Hall, 1963); Howard S. Becker, "Whose Side Are We On?," *Social Problems,* 14, no. 3 (Winter 1967): 239–47; Alvin Gouldner, "The

more convincing performance may be required of you, along with a more complex set of credentials, than formerly. While this makes our work harder, it is probably for the best in keeping us honest.

Asking, Looking, and Acting

Once you have won the opportunity to ask around, look around, or hang around, you will have to figure out how to ask and what to look for. Asking questions is in itself a significant step in research. It greatly increases both the power and the risk or error and contamination of research. As much as possible should be gleaned from the setting non-reactively.[23] A question put to a respondent is a deliberate disturbance of the situation. The principles of environment conservation are a handy guide: Don't tamper with the balance of nature more than you have to. There is an opposite source of difficulty as well. Virtually all veteran welfare participants, on either side of the counter, are question-wise. Welfare is an arena of strife over scarce vital resources; the form of combat is question-and-answer and the arena floor is covered with paper. The controlling official work in welfare is "help," but most participants actually operate so as to avoid being put at a disadvantage. Recipients have to cool out negative decisions by caseworkers, caseworkers have to cool out burdensome demands of recipients. Workers and supervisors within agencies have to disarm one another. These negotiations must all be couched in official agency rhetoric, which is about other things, deriving mostly from the most benign social reform ideologies and the most parsimonious fiscal policies. Welfare people survive by learning to use public languages to pursue private ulterior ends. Many of them will apply this technology to answering research questions, prudently trying to psych out and con their questioner. Whether they do it well or badly, their responses cannot be taken at face value; they require sophisticated analysis. On the other hand, they may furnish good data about respondents' question-answering technology, an important aspect of the situation.[24]

In addition to the instrumental manipulation of questions and answers, welfare respondents are likely to be sensitive to hidden implications and slurs on their character. Most welfare people operate in a

Sociologist as Partisan: Sociology and the Welfare State," *American Sociologist,* 3, no. 2 (May 1968): 103–17; Eric Hoffer, "Doubts Impartiality of Some Sociologists," *Chicago Tribune,* August 3, 1969.

23. See especially Eugene J. Webb, Donald T. Campbell, Richard D. Schwartz, and Lee Sechrest, *Unobtrusive Measures: A Survey of Unconventional and Non-Reactive Measures for Social Research* (Chicago: Rand McNally, 1966).

24. See Aaron V. Cicourel, *Method and Measurement in Sociology* (New York: Free Press, Macmillan, 1964); and Harold Garfinkel, *Studies in Ethnomethodology* (Englewood Cliffs, N.J.: Prentice-Hall, 1967).

climate of public suspicion and disreputability and work out personal defenses against it. They may flare up, launch into long harangues, diatribes, apologies, recriminations, and lectures. These too are good data. But they are often tedious and irrelevant. If you really need a straight answer to that particular question, you may have to go elsewhere for it. Remember, though, that heavy answers to light questions are an excellent tip-off that something important is concealed beneath that answer and should be explored. Light answers to heavy questions may be a good clue as well, but may also mean that the question was poorly phrased or irrelevant.

In the beginning, a few general rules may be helpful. By the time you are well into your study you should become sufficiently familiar with the local conditions to gear your questions to what is happening. Concrete questions are better than abstract ones, and specific ones are better than general. Never ask questions in the early stages that are based on assumptions you are not dead sure of. This may reduce to asking only about the most basic human chacteristics. You can get a lot of volunteered information by asking about local geography, timetables, numbers, histories, and routine activities. Be on the watch for unexplained resistance to a harmless question. It may indicate an important adaptation of real life to formal rules. For instance, if you ask a woman who is a recipient of Aid to Dependent Children how many people live at home with her and who they are, you may be coming dangerously close to the fact that she has a male consort whose presence in the household, if it were known to the agency, would get her dropped from welfare rolls. However, anyone who survives on welfare for long under those conditions will have developed an impressive poker face. Similarly, if you ask a caseworker how he spends his days when he is making field visits, he may have to conceal from you the fact that on those days he goes home at noon to work in his father's business. Once again, he is likely to be adept at not giving you the clue you need to figure out that something out of the ordinary is going on.

The goodness of a question may depend on details of phrasing. Simplest is best. In the early stages it is important not to make your way of expressing yourself an issue between you and your respondents. In the world or welfare this rule is complicated by the several intersecting universes of discourse, not excluding the most obvious problem of informants who are not native speakers of English. Spanish is the most likely other language you will encounter, but not the only one. It will not hurt if you bring proficiency in the local language with you as a research tool. Most investigators, however, have to make do without it. There are additional complications of dialect, variations in inflection, slang, patois, technical jargon, and the peculiar lingo of bureaucracy, half made up of numbers and initials in indecipherable patterns. Whether you are dealing with a ghetto resident of rural origin or a college-graduate caseworker whose speech is peppered with code designations for agency forms and talismanic incantations like "putative father," "eligibility," and "basic ed," you will be faced with new lexicons in a strange syntax. Many veterans shift back and forth between these vernaculars with dazzling ease. These days you will also hear leftover War on Poverty shibboleths and late-model Movement rhetoric.

There is a great temptation to come on as an insider, as a form of protective coloration and as a way of achieving rapport. Unless you speak these languages naturally and easily already, resist this temptation. If you bring it off, you will certainly be in good shape, but if you fail, you will look like a fool, and no one in the welfare business can afford to trust a fool. If your language shows you to be an outsider, you can still operate effectively by asking straightforward questions that are not patronizing or pugnacious. Remember that if you present yourself as knowing the insider's language you will waste an opportunity to be taught it by real speakers. Do not rely too heavily on proficiency in a language you have not used for a few years. The welfare scene is in constant change from all directions and language evolves to suit. If you sprinkle your talk with archaisms, the effect will be the opposite of what you want. Ultimately, you should learn how the locals speak, and your progress in learning is a good measure of your success in the field. But it is better to learn it in public than to make believe you already know it. Since speech reveals something about social reality, the learning process will give you opportunities to ask strategic questions about the referents of the words and phrases you learn. If you manage to demonstrate that you are trustworthy and harmless, no one will mind your difficulties with local usage. In fact, the dependency of the novice role you assume may do more to maintain rapport than presenting yourself as a smart ass. Finally, using your own language may allow you to avoid taking sides in public by chossing one local style of talk in preference to the others available. How you talk is commonly used as a measure of whom you prefer to talk to. It is a mistake to get yourself committed in this way without a good research reason. In some studies or in situations where research is an adjunct of an action posture, this warning may be irrelevant. But unless identification with a particular welfare party is a deliberate choice, there is no point in wasting your neutrality. On the other hand, you should be prepared to find that you cannot operate at all in the situation without taking sides, whatever your original intention. Note that I do not advise against making personal value choices or seeking involvement as a whole human being. But commitment as self-indulgence is unproductive and uninteresting. No one will congratulate you for failing to learn the truth because you insist on flaunting your ritual purity. All the standard cautions against ego trips apply.

In addition to asking questions, you will be observing. This requires that you go somewhere at some time and observe something. Many welfare activities occur as routines. The most basic understanding to be sought initially is the pattern of these routines in the agency you are studying. The simplest way is to sit in the offices (in the general case) where workers deal with clients. The volume of required paperwork in most welfare agencies virtually dictates this arrangement. These office activities are crucial to everyone's career in welfare because the payoffs of the system depend mostly on the care and correctness with which forms are prepared. Being in the office affords you the opportunity to ask about how this work is done and under what constraints.

From the office as a center you can move out to other settings. Among the important ones to look for are clients' homes, where periodic or ad hoc visits of the caseworker may occur; regulatory and custodial institutions, such as hospitals, police stations, and schools, where welfare agency jurisdiction overlaps with the work of the caretakers, in the form of either counseling, settling the bill, or auxiliary service (notifying family members, bringing changes of underwear, acting as interpreter or spokesman); inner offices, where staff meetings occur, inspectors general look at the books, and research and development go on; legislative halls, where decisions are made that may drastically alter agency operations; the streets and gathering places of communities, where recipients may find a common life. The career of the welfare client, as well as the worker, may revolve around a set of outposts of service-dispensing organizations: the local welfare office, hospital clinic, school, church, settlement house, community organization, political club, etc. Look for patterns of clustering. If the people who show up in one place at a certain time can usually be found in a specific other place at a specific other time, you may be on the track of a complex pattern of operation by means of which the client survives, but which would remain unknown if you stuck with only one agency location.

At least as important as the stable pattern of places is the regularity of time organization. Beyond the essentials of daily routines are the cycles of longer periods, such as seasonal events, life-cycle patterns, and histories of changes in the system. One of the easiest errors to make is to overlook the fact that some pattern you observe is specific to that time of year or to a certain welfare commissioner who has been in office for three months.

You will find that the welfare timetables are highly dependent on two types of events: the disbursement of funds and deadlines of required paperwork. Thus the days of the month on which welfare checks are mailed to recipients affect the personal budgets of all participants in a marked way. Stores in the ghetto may raise their prices on these days to take advantage of the availability of funds.[25] Caseworkers may find the pace of office work more demanding and their personal lives more encroached upon at these times. Similarly, the common requirements for periodic review of the eligibility of clients imposes an ineluctable time-table on the visits of workers and clients. Whatever else is happening on the case, those reports must go in on time.

Although the standard welfare workday may be like that of other jobs, many welfare operations have arrangements for emergency service at any time. These arrangements should be studied as well. On a larger time scale, there are regular events that determine peaks and troughs of activity. The opening of school in the fall and the end of school for the summer are such strategic periods, since many welfare cases involve school-age children whose careers in school or summer programs demand attention. Seasonal pressures also come from the organization itself, in the form of annual budget recommendations, periodic field visits by high executives, audits of accounts, and the like. Some agencies may also have a seasonal schedule of additional activities like professional conventions, staff conferences, in-service training programs, etc.

Finally, and very importantly, comes change in the institution on a linear rather than a cyclical basis. Such change can occur because of alteration in high-level administration, in general policy in the organization, in the broader context within which the agency operates (such as a change of the party in power through local elections). Welfare is one of the most vulnerable bureaucratic activities in public life. The strains toward conservatism in complex organizations are often offset by the dependence of welfare agencies on the policy decisions of outsiders. It is common for workers in welfare to find entire programs turned upside down every few years because some legislator, expensive consultant, or agency power broker has finagled a strategic position to try his own pet theory of what needs to be done. Since so few such programs ever get a long enough trial, most agencies work out patterns of accommodation that allow them to get their basic work done in much the same way, whatever the shifts of rhetoric and paperwork may be. This will be reported as resistance and conservatism by administrators, but here as elsewhere the official version is not necessarily correct. Often you may find that such major shifts in orientation are not a result of new thinking on welfare, but merely the back wash in welfare activity of decisions made for other reasons. Thus if the governor, as an economy move, wants to cut down drastically on the institutional population of the state,

25. See David Caplovitz, *The Poor Pay More* (New York: Free Press Macmillan, 1963).

he may promulgate new treatment guidelines that are unrelated to any program successes or failures.[26] While these events are arbitrary from the viewpoint of insiders, they occur frequently and have major effects on all participants. Therefore, it is important to be aware of the specific microhistory of the agency you study, lest you describe as a structural necessity some way of doing things that is due to the lieutenant governor's dyspepsia last summer.

The participants in welfare institutions are themselves highly differentiated. An adequate account should consider the role of each type. The major distinction invoked by participants and by the general public is between clients and workers. This cleavage is usually treated as though it marked the boundary between different species of life. You may find, however, that the difference exists more in social reputation than in structural dissimilarity.[27] Clients come in many varieties, depending on the kind of service they use and how they use it. Many participants who are sometimes overlooked are indirect clients of welfare in the sense that while they are not registered with the agency, they have a stable connection with someone who is. The most obvious and easiest case is a family member, since he is likely to be listed as an official appurtenance of the client (though not necessarily, as in the case of the bootleg male consort of the ADC mother). Others to look for are networks of friends and associates, and people whose own subsistence is dependent on the dispensing of welfare services. Examples of the last are storekeepers and landlords whose clienteles are largely made up of welfare clients, and entrepreneurs of businesses of more dubious legality, such as usurers. Other people deserve mention as adjuncts of either clients or workers, such as organizers for autonomous programs, political or religious, governmental or independent, revolutionary or charitable. Such activities have been largely ignored in past treatments of welfare, but increasingly demand our attention since the birth of the New Left, the black movement, and the War on Poverty. Whatever the fate of these movements, the new organizational consciousness will probably remain an important component of the welfare scene.

On the workers' side of the counter, we find the usual variations in bureaucratic hierarchy, with numbers of vertical layers and relations among them determined by so many different rationalities that a reasonable investigator needs months to get them straight. Never expect your first few collected accounts of the formal organization to be anything more than a very rough, partial sketch. They are likely to be attempts at

26. For example, the decision by Governor Ogilvie of Illinois to discharge 10,000 mental patients from state mental hospitals.

27. See Bernard Beck, "Welfare Careers and Manpower Problems" (unpublished paper, Northwestern University, 1967, presented at meetings of the Society for the Study of Social Problems, San Francisco, 1967).

doing the impossible: describing the indescribable. You will have to start with a simplified picture that is interesting only because everything you see can be interpreted as a deviation from it. Investigators in welfare hierarchies often throw up their hands and say they cannot make sense of it. There is too much going on and none of it seems to have a good reason. This usually works out to be a situation in which "good reasons" have been unduly narrow in specification and based on formal rhetoric. As soon as you dispense with the notion that the place is about what it says it is about, you have a fair chance of seeing what really makes things run as they do. Formal rhetoric is rarely irrelevant to what happens, but it is just as rarely an adequate account.

Once you get past the combat squads of caseworkers, you can usually go as high up as you can bear. Local structures articulate with state, national, and even international structures. Furthermore, there is a good deal of lateral connectedness, since many welfare agencies find their work overlapping though the same clients or the same locations. A good list or organizations relevant to your agency operations will include every caretaker or dispensing operation in the area that is run by people considered to be different from and in better shape than the people they minister to.

While all the standard sociological forms of differentiation make a difference in welfare, two deserve special mention: age and experience. The variation between old and young, veteran and novice are crucial among all participants in welfare, ranging from subjective and ideological matters to objective characteristics like income and security.

Resources

It often helps to have access to some people who are not directly involved in your study who can comment on the scene. The general rule is to look for someone who occupies a role that is interdependent with the roles you are focusing on. Thus, if you concentrate on clients, you will look for any outsiders who routinely deal with them on the basis of their clienthood, like policemen, school counselors, storekeepers. If you are studying workers, then clients, teachers of social work, state accountants, or political precinct captains may help. If your subjects are high-level welfare administrators, your best sources may be independent social science consultatnts who work with or for them and know lots of dirt. The welfare field and the social sciences occupy more or less the same universe of gossip, which is invaluable to you. You may as well use it, since your welfare informants will probably be using it on you. Your most annoying problem may be the tendency of your subjects to try to creep into your research role with you, by giving helpful suggestions or second-guessing your design. Everyone in welfare would like to be Doc in *Street Corner Society*.[28] On the whole, this eagerness is helpful, but it can become overbearing. It is often only an informant's copout.

The major resource available to you is the paper that is the life force of most welfare agencies. In fact, you will face an embarrassment of riches. In addition to the files and case records themselves, assuming you are permitted to see them, there are many summary reports to superiors, results of studies and investigations commissioned by superiors, legislative investigating committee reports, blue-ribbon commission inquiries, articles in house organs of the agency (usually self-congratulatory, occasionally self-flagellatory), and the huge quasi-professional literature in the social welfare and social work fields. Furthermore, much of the work social scientists have done on poverty and social problems has at least indirect relevance to welfare. And nowadays a great deal of general magazine and book writing focuses on welfare. Finally, welfare is a favorite area for journalistic exposés. All the bibliographic resources of a large library will be needed to use this literature. A lot of it is published in odd forms, such as special monograph series, government documents,[29] and United Nations reports. Unfortunately, even more of it is not published, but circulates internally in large organizations in technical report binders. A good inside dopester who makes his living by being available to the welfare system, as a consultant, for example, is worth his weight in maintenance checks for referring you to or providing you with copies of this quasi-secret documentation.

In addition to sources strictly within the welfare field, there is also the voluminous literature in the fields of medicine and hospitals, psychology and mental hospitals, the police and courts, and the labor market. They are all very relevant. The proceedings of legislatures and their committees are also revealing, and in most cases are available as public documents. Tracking down what you want, however, demands special bibliographic skills. Finally, a major exception to confidentiality requirements in public welfare is the statutory requirement that the welfare rolls, like the real estate tax rolls and the voter lists, be public documents. You may need days of free time and the patience of Job, however, to find anything systematic in them, such as a geographically based sample.

The most basic kinds of information to be had from such sources are

28. William F. Whyte, *Street Corner Society* (Chicago: University of Chicago Press, 1955).

29. It is a good idea to keep abreast of the list of current publications from the U.S. Government Printing Office in the areas of relevance to your study. Apply to Superintendent of Documents, U.S. Government Printing Office, Washington, D.C.

easy to list, but many more specific items can be gleaned, depending on the specific nature of your study. Basic information consists of numbers of people and amounts of money, together with their distribution patterns. These may be translated into information on services or other measures of activity, and you may have to spend some time learning how to infer figures you are interested in from figures available. This process is not as easy as it may appear, and certain obvious errors, such as ecological correlations, are common. In any case, most of these officially and semiofficially generated statistics are untrustworthy and misleading in the ways that have been indicated in the literature on the abuses of official statistics (or good organizational reasons for bad records).[30] The most common frustration you will encounter is lack of or unknown degree of comparability.

If you accept the standard, and on the whole wise, recommendation of treating record-keeping as the subject of study rather than the tools of studying it, you can have a field day in welfare. There is a vast amount of productive work to be done in analyzing how paper is produced and filed in welfare agencies. In fact, the major cooperative project of all welfare participants is the production of an acceptable record on paper. While all modern bureaucratic establishments face similar problems of reconciling practice with paper records, welfare is a setting where this problem is raised to paramount and central concern.

Similarly interesting is the large body of internal writing of a self-justifying, hortatory kind, especially as found in newsletters and monthly trade journals put out by agencies, unions, professional associations, and action projects. As in the case of records, you should be suspicious of these as accounts, but interested in them as social products. They will tell you a great deal about the terms in which people think or are permitted to express themselves before others in the area of welfare.

Playing a Part and Shooting Trouble

It should be clear by now that the student of welfare must be aware of his own effect on the balance of forces he encounters. There are virtually no one-way mirrors that allow you to see and not be seen. The results of studies feed back very quickly to the field of study itself, since the social science literature is also the social welfare literature and the general public literature on welfare. Welfare is a prime example of an

---

30. See Garfinkel, *Studies in Ethnomethodology,* chap. 6, "Good Organizational Reasons for 'Bad' Clinic Records"; John I. Kitsuse and Aaron V. Cicourel, "A Note on the Use of Official Statistics," *Social Problems,* 11, no. 2 (Fall 1963): 131–39; and Jack Douglas, *The Social Meaning of Suicide* (Princeton: Princeton University Press, 1967).

area in which all action is political and nothing is inconsequential.[31] This means that your role as an investigator cannot be fixed once and for all at the outset. To maintain a given version of your participation requires constant effort and is always vulnerable to changes of circumstance that change the meaning of your presence and your activity. Long-term platitudinous promises may not be enough to assure you of unlimited access indefinitely. You will be expected to make short-term assurances as well, and you will be checked to see that you have lived up to them. Do not be surprised if you have to renegotiate your bargain several times, with different parties and different attendant costs. You original plans may suddenly become impossible, while new opportunities present themselves.

The ideal situation is to have a clear and reciprocal arrangement with all the relevant parties who can affect your study or veto it. But the profile of factional interests does not always remain the same. Some of your friends may suddenly disappear from the picture, while new interest groups arise with whom you have no connections. A varied collection of powerful protectors is always handy. If you can have both the local commissioner and the local welfare rights organizer, the local Democratic club and the local Black Panthers, the local public aid union leader and the local research coordinator of Community Systems, Inc., in your corner, you can weather most crises. It is entirely possible, however, that most of these will refuse to deal with you if they know you are friendly with the others. Then you may have to make a choice and hope you are with a winner. Or you may have to see if you can change allegiances at a crucial point. One useful strategy, if your circumstances permit, is to have several investigators, each of whom caters to a different segment of the situation.[32] This can backfire, however, if the involvement of any of you with a certain faction taints all of you in the eyes of the other factions.

The basic issues underlying these problems are the maintenance of trust and the demonstration of harmlessness. Once an official has decided that you may cost him his job or his promotion, once a community leader has suspected that you are informing on him to his Establishment oppressors, it is difficult to give sufficient assurance that you are up to something more benign. In fact, most of the time those assurances will

31. See Lee Rainwater and William Yancey, *The Moynihan Report and the Politics of Controversy* (Cambridge: MIT Press, 1967).

32. *For example*, Howard S. Becker, Blanche Geer, Everett C. Hughes, and Anselm L. Strauss, *Boys in White* (Chicago: University of Chicago Press, 1961); Becker, Geer and Hughes, *Making the Grade: The Academic Side of College Life* (New York: Wiley, 1968); and Gerald D. Berreman, *Behind Many Masks: Ethnography and Impression Management in a Himalayan Village* (Ithaca, N.Y.:Society for Applied Anthropology, 1962).

not be true, in the sense that the protection of your subjects is of secondary importance to the discovery and publication of the truth. In other words, some studies cannot be done honestly. On the other hand, research in only one of the human values, and you can console yourself with the thought that a phenomenon that is really important will manage to get studied somewhere and sometime, if not here and now.

In spite of all the things that might go wrong with the welfare study, most studies in most settings are still routinely manageable. Welfare people are still very likely to view the social scientist as a sympathetic friend or a useful ally and spokesman. In a field as understudied as welfare you should be able to find a research setting that has not been fouled by a previous bad research experience. Furthermore, welfare people have many burdens; even a blundering investigator doing an embarrassing study is the least of their problems. The major question to be resolved is not how to cool out their resistance to study, but how to temper our own ambition.

People involved in welfare typically lead lives full of frustration and grief. Our basic attitude should be to carry on our studies in an open, honest way, and we should avoid visiting additional trouble on our brother- and sister-subjects gratuitously.

Practitioners of Vice
and Crime

Ideally, we would gather data on deviants by observing them as they go about their characteristic activities or by interviewing them about their experiences.[1] But in studying deviants we face all the problems that observation and interview occasion in any social group, and additional ones as well; or perhaps it is only that those problems are exaggerated. We must find people who engage in the behavior we want to study. We must assess the degree to which the people we find resemble the ones we have not been able to find. We must persuade, manipulate, coerce, or trick the people we find into furnishing us with the data we need for our analyses.

But the feature that makes deviance of interest to us (or at least one of the features) is precisely what makes the job so difficult. Because the activity in question is ordinarily stigmatized and is very likely to be legally punishable as well, those who engage in it do not make that face publicly known or easily available. We may have trouble locating practitioners of the vices we are interested in, or locating them in such a way as to allow us to get any information about their deviance, because they will not engage in it in our presence or because they will not admit to us that they engage in it. Still, studies of deviance have been made, so the task is not impossible.

1. I have refrained from any complicated definitional discussions of what deviance is. In general, I shall be talking about the problems of studying people who engage in conventionally (and, usually, legally) disapproved forms of behavior and the patterns of collective action — the worlds — they move in. I focus primarily on such traditional vices as sexual misbehavior and the use of forbidden drugs, but occasionally refer to various forms of more ordinary crime as well.

30

Gathering Data Directly

ACCESS AND SAMPLING

Factories do not give lists of employees, complete with names, address-es, and phone numbers, to anyone who asks for them; nor do unions readily give out lists of their members. Many colleges sell lists of students publicly (largely for the convenience of other students, to be sure), but no hospital makes a list of patients so easily available (though new mothers sometimes wonder how else all those salesmen found them so soon). In all these cases, however, the list exists, or could be com-piled. A researcher, with proper credentials and justifications, might persuade the proprietors of the list to make it available to him for purposes of drawing a sample from which data might be gathered. Alternatively, since the locations where characteristic activities take place are known to some specific official, a researcher can similarly learn and use them as a sampling universe.

No such officially complete list of participants in any deviant act exists. I suppose that, in some sense, none could, since the acts are unofficial. In any event, the researcher must draw his sample from a universe whose limits, units, and locales are known to him fragmentarily. Conventional sampling theory has unfortunately ignored this problem; but a conventionally mathematical approach might not be of great help. Strategies of sampling based on the sociological characteristics of the population that interests the researcher are likely to be much more fruitful in the study of deviants.

1. If the researcher, in his own private life, has achieved access to circles in which the deviant activity occurs, he can use that access for research purposes. I made use of my contacts among dance musicians (I had been a musician before I was a sociologist) to get interviews about marijuana use, an activity then relatively more common and more open among musicians than among others.[2] Similarly, Ned Polsky used his established position as a billiards buff and amateur hustler to gather data on pool hustlers and their activities.[3]

This strategy solves the access problem conveniently; you at least know someone to observe and interview, and can attempt to have them introduce you to others and vouch for you, thus setting up a kind of snowball sampling. Since you are known, and known of, in your prior capacity, few doubts as to your trustworthiness arise. It is probably wise to reveal your research purposes, because your questions probably re-quire explanation. In addition, such openness will explain your other-wise unaccountable desire to meet more and more practitioners of the

2. See Howard S. Becker, *Outsiders: Studies in the Sociology of Deviance* (New York: Free Press, Macmillan, 1963), p. 45.

3. Ned Polsky, *Hustlers, Beats, and Others* (Chicago: Aldine, 1967), pp. 44–46.

vice under study. If it can be said that, by consenting to be interviewed, deviants are helping you (as one of them) to earn an academic degree or a scientific living, they may be very willing to cooperate. Deviants who know your purposes may cooperate so that the "true story," which they feel they can trust you to tell, can get to the public through your research report. Your participation will, of course, be limited both by what is conventional among the group under study and by what you are willing to do yourself; more researchers, presumably, will be willing to participate in after-work crap games than to engage in prostitution, even though the arguments in favor of completeness of data are equally compelling in the two cases.[4]

The representativeness of your data will depend on the degree to which all those you might want to study belong to a connected network. If, at one extreme, the activity is a solitary one (embezzling, klepto-mania, masturbation), there are no circles to belong to that would give access to subjects of study. If everyone involved knew everyone else, to know one would be to know all and participation at all would solve the problem. If (as was probably true of marihuana smoking when I did my original study) a number of worlds where the activity is carried on overlap only slightly, this strategy may afford you good coverage of one subgroup, but only beginning leads or none at all to other groups. This may be the case in studies of homosexuality, where there seems to be little overlap of the quiet and respectable homosexuals studied by Eve-lyn Hooker,[5] the teenage hustlers studied by Albert Reiss,[6] and the participants in encounters in public toilets studied by Laud Humphreys.[7]

2. When you believe that you know nothing and have no contacts, the only sure method of getting at least some beginning information is to interview deviants who have been legally processed as a result of appre-hension for a deviant act. This usually means interviewing incarcerated deviants, a strategy that has much to recommend it. For one thing, there is probably no quicker way to accumulate a large sample. No other

4. I do not mean to argue that one way is better than the other, for that judgment depends on what one wants to study. Nevertheless, the choice of methods constrains what one *can* talk about. Compare, for example, James Henslin, "Craps and Magic," *American Journal of Sociology,* 73 (November 1967): 316–30, and its detailed dissection of the smallest features of gambling behavior, with the necessarily more macroscopic analysis in James H. Bryan, "Apprenticeships in Prostitution," *Social Problems,* 12 (Winter 1965): 287–97.

5. Evelyn T. Hooker, "Male Homosexuals and Their 'Worlds,' " in *Sexual Inversion,* ed. Judd Marmor (New York: Basic Books, 1965), pp. 83–105, and "The Homosexual Community," in *Sexual Deviance,* ed. John H. Gagnon and William Simon, (New York: Harper & Row, 1967), pp. 168–84.

6. Albert J. Reiss, Jr., "The Social Integration of Peers and Queers," *Social Problems,* 9 (Fall 1961): 102–19.

7. R. A. Laud Humphreys, *The Tearoom Trade: Impersonal Sex in Public Places* (Chicago: Aldine, 1970).

location has so many deviants whose deviance is publicly known and who thus might as well talk to you as not. In addition, some activities occur in so private and solitary a way that subjects could not otherwise be found. How else, for instance, could Donald Cressey have found embezzlers to interview?[8] Successful embezzlers disappear, as do successful "missing persons." You can find only the failures who are caught.

That, of course, is a chief criticism of studies based on imprisoned populations: they use samples that are unrepresentative in a peculiarly bad way, for there is reason to suppose that, with respect to many forms of deviance, those caught differ in skill, in mode of operation, or in some other important way that is tied to their failure. Professional criminals, it is said, arrange for the "fix," and so amateurs are vastly overrepresented in prison populations; and amateurs, it might be argued, are more likely to have psychological difficulties, with obvious consequences for the validity of etiological theories of deviance based on such samples.

A second major criticism suggests that imprisoned deviants do not talk or act as they might in their native habitats, any more than animals in a zoo behave as they would in the wild. No longer operating in their normal circumstances, they now respond to vastly different controls, and in particular may think that by telling their story in one way or another they can use the researcher to influence the authorities on whom their fate depends. They may tell only "sad stories," self-justifying tales of how they got where they are. Clearly, studies using imprisoned populations should recognize the limitations this stratagem introduces. It should not be used simply because it is convenient, but only when some more compelling reason of structurally restricted accessibility requires it.[9]

3. If deviance were common enough, rather than being a rare occurrence, one might study it by questioning random samples of the total population or some approximation thereof, relying on this screening procedure to produce a sufficient number of cases for intensive study. For relatively rare activities — heroin addiction or incest, for example — this is an incredibly wasteful method. But some studies have found quite justifiable the assumption that particular deviant activities are common. This is a particularly useful device when you have some other research reason for the larger interviewing program. Thus, Kinsey and his associates wanted to study sexual activity in human adults and

8. Donald R. Cressey, *Other People's Money* (New York: Free Press, Macmillan, 1953).

9. Polsky argues this position forcefully in *Hustlers, Beats, and Others*, pp. 117–49. D. W. Maurer takes strong exception in a review of Polsky's book; see Maurer, "How to Consort with Con Men," *Psychiatric and Social Science Review*, 2 (February 1968): 26–31.

interviewed normal populations (as well as others) on the assumption, proven correct, that they would find large numbers who had engaged in various deviant sexual activities as well as the "normal" ones presumably more widespread. Self-report studies of delinquency rely on essentially the same device,[10] and Reiss discovered teenage "queer hustlers" by routinely asking boys interviewed in a larger delinquency study whether they had ever engaged in the activity.[11]

This approach is probably most useful when you are interested in the distribution of a great variety of deviant activities in the general population. It becomes progressively less useful as you focus in detail on some specific deviant activity, subculture, or world. To study the perspectives and structures characteristic of such worlds, you need detailed information on other people with whom the interviewee interacts. But while an interviewee who volunteers for a Kinsey-style interview in effect agrees in advance to regard questions about himself as legitimate, he may draw the line when asked to "incriminate" others, never having agreed to that as a fit topic for discussion. And the requirements of the larger study may interfere with such specialized inquiries (although they need not, as the Reiss study demonstrates).

In any event, this strategy produces a population of subjects if, but only if, the activity occurs commonly. Then Kinsey-like procedures will generate much information and care should be taken to allow for specialized inquiries into particular topics, making use of informants and contacts produced by the larger screening.

4. A variant of the preceding approach likewise assumes that deviant activities, though hidden, occur quite frequently. Instead of contacting large numbers of people and inquiring directly about their activities, however, one advertises for volunteers in places where the sought-after deviants would be likely to hear of one's research interest and then waits for them to turn up. Nancy Lee used this strategy in her study of women who had had illegal abortions.[12] She first inquired among her own acquaintances and then asked doctors, birth-control clinics, and other likely sources to spread the word that she wanted to hear from women who had had the experience and were willing to be interviewed about it. She ultimately achieved contact with over one hundred women, who either granted her personal interviews or completed a questionnaire for her. One can advertise in this informal way or even use more public media to make known one's research.

10. Such studies are reviewed in Robert H. Hardt and George E. Bodine, *Development of Self-Report Instruments in Delinquency Research* (Syracuse, N.Y.: Syracuse University Youth Development Center, 1965).

11. Reiss, "Peers and Queers."

12. Nancy Howell Lee, *The Search for an Abortionist* (Chicago: University of Chicago Press, 1969). Clark E. Vincent used similar procedures in his study of illegitimate births, *Unmarried Mothers* (New York: Free Press, Macmillan, 1961).

This device produces willing volunteers who speak freely of their experiences and activities. Interaction with them is no problem, but sampling becomes difficult. You end up only with volunteers, so you can expect, as the debate over Kinsey's research suggested, that they will not represent the full range of experiences and social types to be found in the universe. It probably works best when one is investigating activities that can be expected to be fairly common in the general population or, alternatively, when one has some knowledge as to the specialized population within which it might be profitable to advertise. It may be the only feasible approach with activities, like abortion, in which each participant engages only once or a few times, which generate no subculture or continuing organization unique to those who have had the experience, but which are of at least potential interest to some much larger group (as abortion is likely to be to women in general).

5. You can induce deviants to reveal themselves by offering some service they desire and perhaps cannot get elsewhere, then taking advantage of your knowledge of them to ask for research data. James Bryan, for example, began his study of call girls[13] when he discovered that a patient to whom he was giving psychotherapy was in that profession, and interviewed her. Not surprisingly, other call girls she knew felt they needed the same therapeutic services, and Bryan got part of his sample that way. Deviants frequently look for unconventional sources of medical, legal, and psychiatric services, either because they cannot afford what is conventionally available or, as is often true with regard to medical services, because they do not like the embarrassment and harassment they experience from conventional practitioners. Anyone who provides these services free or in a more neutral fashion will have plenty of people to study.[14] The advantages and disadvantages of this approach resemble very closely those of the preceding one.

6. Finally, the researcher can locate himself in those areas or places where the deviants he is interested in habitually or occasionally congregate and then either simply observe them or take the opportunity to interact with them and gather information in a more direct and purposive way. This strategy in some ways solves the problem of sampling very neatly. If you regard as your universe all those who engage in the collective activity under observation, then those who do not show up to be observed by definition do not belong to the group to be studied; problems arise only in considering whether there are other places that could have been observed, and assessing how the observed activity fits

13. Bryan, "Apprenticeships in Prostitution."

14. Dr. David Smith and his colleagues at the Haight-Ashbury Medical Clinic have achieved such a relationship with the hippie population of that San Francisco community and have been able to gather a great deal of important information on drug use and other medical problems. For early reports on this material, see articles by Smith and others in the *Journal of Psychedelic Drugs,* published at the clinic.

into some larger pattern of related activities. For example, you may study gay bars but wonder how the activities observed there fit into some larger pattern of homosexual activities in the community.

Other problems of this strategy include finding the proper locations for observation and choosing and playing an appropriate role once you are there. Locations can often be easily discovered with the help of a knowledgeable informant. An experienced cab driver can often tell you where homosexual bars may be found, or where pimps and prostitutes or thieves and gamblers hang out. Newspaper reporters may have similar kinds of information, as may bartenders, policemen, or a lone member of the deviant group with whom one already has made contact.

Supposing you have found your observation post, what role will you play once you are there? The chief choices are to disguise yourself as one of the deviants (we have earlier considered the case where one comes by this role honestly), to be one of the service personnel associated with the location (a waitress in a homosexual bar, for example), or to make yourself known as a researcher. The latter choice gives you great freedom to pursue your scientific interest, for you need not tailor your words or actions to what would be appropriate to an occupant of either of the other roles, but can instead ask and do a great variety of things, offering science as the justification. Furthermore, you can avoid incriminating or distasteful participation in deviant activities on the reasonable grounds that, while you are perhaps sympathetic, your personal inclinations run in another direction. Many researchers feel, however, that to be known as an outsider will severely limit the amount of information one can get. I know of no definitive evidence on the point, but informative studies have been accomplished by this method, suggesting that the limitation can be overcome.

If the social scientist wants to study settings in which there is no opportunity to introduce himself as a researcher, he probably has no choice and must pass as a deviant. If he is not seen by others as a deviant in these situations he will be seen as a tourist, policeman, or something else unwanted, and the people he wants to study will simply refrain from the activity he has come to observe while he is there, or perhaps drive him out so that the activity may resume (Sherri Cavan has described the way habitués of a gay bar get rid of sightseers).[15] To avoid these unpleasant results, the researcher must discover some role in the deviant world he can comfortably play that will allow him to get the information he needs.[16]

15. Sherri Cavan, *Liquor License: An Ethnography of Bar Behavior* (Chicago: Aldine, 1966), pp. 216–26.

16. See Donald J. Black and Maureen A. Mileski, "Passing as Deviant: Methodological Problems and Tactics" (Ann Arbor: Center for Research on Social Organization, University of Michigan, 1967, mimeo).

Humphreys used this strategy with great success in his study of homosexual activity in public toilets.[17] These activities, of considerable sociological interest, take place without conversation between men who have very likely never seen one another before, but they will not take place in the presence of anyone suspected of being a policeman or a "straight" person. How then can one observe them? Humphreys discovered that a role existed for voyeurs, who simply watched and also assisted in the action by looking out for intrusions by dangerous outsiders. By performing as lookout, he was able to observe a large number of homosexual acts and develop an ethnography of this behavior. He also observed the license numbers of the cars men drove up in and used these to discover names and addresses of men he had personally observed engage in homosexual acts. He then interviewed these men, using a standard interview from a contemporary health survey, and so acquired a great deal of information on aspects of their lives other than sexual, which he then compared with similar information from a control group included in the larger survey.

It should be clear that no one of these strategies solves all the problems; each has its advantages, each costs something. The nature of the topic under study constrains the choice of method; you cannot use methods that assume the existence of an organized deviant world, for instance, where none exists. The nature of your social connections and experience constrains the kinds of roles you can play and will be willing to play. The deviant world one wants to study may be divided into several somewhat separate segments, such that various methods will be necessary for each; any study of homosexuality must reckon with this. In general, the situation calls for methodological flexibility; a researcher may use several approaches to the same topic as time, his resources and capabilities, and the situation allow.[18]

I have spoken of participant observation and interviewing as though they were almost interchangeable, largely for convenience in discussing problems of sampling and access. Although most deviant activities can be studied by either method, the results differ, each limiting you in a different way. The choice depends on the relation between the character and frequency of the activity, the goal of your research, and the costs and difficulties of each method. Take abortion as an example. Given the way the activity is carried on, you probably cannot get much information on the experiences of the women involved if you choose, as Donald Ball

17. Humphreys, *Tearoom Trade.*
18. There are limiting cases in which it appears impossible to locate any kind of sample. See the account of an attempt to study a mildly deviant activity, the use of health foods, in Peter Kong-ming New and Rhea Pendergrass Priest, "Problems of Obtaining a Sample in a Study of Deviancy: A Case of Failure," *Social Science and Medicine,* 1 (1968): 250–54. For examples of various approaches to another problem (drug use), see *Journal of Health and Social Behavior,* 9 (June 1968), a special issue on recreational drug use.

did, to observe an abortion mill in operation.[19] You can get that information by interviews after the fact, as Lee did, but you then sacrifice knowledge of the professional side of the activity. Where people engage more continuously in the activity, or where there is not such great social distance between the various categories of participants, observation may allow you to get both kinds of data.

WHAT TO ASK; WHAT TO OBSERVE

Ask "How?" — not "Why" I think it a good idea in research on any topic to avoid asking people *why* they have done something when you really want to find out *how* it came about that they did it. When you ask why you are asking for, and will receive, given the conventions of our common speech, a justification, an explanation, a selection from the currently available vocabulary of motives. We very often want just that, but we should never mistake it for an account of how something came to pass.[20]

This caution applies with exceptional force to studies of deviants. If their unusual activities have come to the attention of friends, relatives, colleagues, or enforcement officials, they will have been asked repeatedly why they did what they did. In thinking of the difficulties they have had, they may even ask themselves the same question. And so they are likely to have stock answers and sad stories prepared for the researcher's version of the same old question.

It is much more effective, if one wants to learn the sequence of events leading to some pattern of deviant activity, to ask *how* the thing happened. "When did you first do X?" "How did you happen to do that?" "Then what happened?" "How did that work out?" Questions that probe for the concrete details of events and their sequence produce answers that are less ideological and mythological and more useful for the reconstruction of past events and experiences. Such an interrogation can and should include questions on the subjective aspects of events: "What did you think when that happened?" "How did you feel about that?" But the answers to such questions should be interpreted with respect to the historical context of events elicited by the other questions. If the interviewing is carried on as part of a program of field observation, the researcher can focus his questions on current events, asking simply for descriptions of what is going on and explanations in the form of descriptions of further phenomena likely to be of interest. Though general doctrinal discussions have some interest, you need specific, situation-bound data for detailed analysis of social structures and individual careers.

19. Donald Ball, "An Abortion Clinic Ethnography," *Social Problems,* 14 (Winter 1967): 293–301.

20. See C. Wright Mills, "Situated Actions and Vocabularies of Motives," *American Sociological Review,* 5 (December 1940): 904–13.

In general, to ask why something happened shifts to the interviewee the analytic job that the researcher himself should be doing. An interview should elicit the concrete descriptions from which such an analysis can be made, rather than the amateur analysis the interviewee might be able to provide.

Argot. Deviant activities tend to generate a special language, at the least to describe the esoteric events, people, and objects involved, and perhaps as a matter of symbolic differentiation from nondeviants as well. How should the researcher take account of this language?

He must, of course, eventually learn to understand it. But he need not be too quick to demonstrate that he does, for he can get very good information by insisting that his informants and interviewees explain the special language to him. In so doing, they will have to make the explanations and provide the examples he needs for his analysis. Many researchers find it hard to feign ignorance or admit it when it is real, wanting to appear knowledgeable, either to make themselves feel good or to assure the interviewee that he can talk safely and that what is said will be understood. The latter reason may apply, but the other alternative should be considered. (If the researcher is passing as a member of the deviant society, then he must, of course, exhibit the necessary degree of linguistic ability.)

However the researcher resolves this dilemma, he will as he would in the study of any form of collective action, want to pay close attention to nuances of language. Unusual terms or unusual uses of conventional words signal areas of central concern to the people under study and provide an opening analytic wedge, as the term "square" did in studying musicians or "crock" did in studying medical students.[21] Differences in the use of deviant argot may serve as useful indicators of generational differences among members of the group, of differences in degree of involvement in its activities, or of differences in the segment of the deviant world one belongs to.[22]

Organizational variation. Deviant activities, as the discussion of access will have made clear, may take place in a solitary fashion, each deviant constituting a private world unto himself, or they may, at the other extreme, occur in a complex and segmented world. In the latter case, the researcher should make the structure of that world a topic for study, using that knowledge, as it accumulates, for sampling purposes as well.

In more complex worlds, a typical axis of differentiation for which the researcher should look centers on the relation of the deviant activities to

21. See Becker, *Outsiders,* pp. 85–91, and Howard S. Becker and Blanche Geer, "Participant Observation and Interviewing: A Comparison," *Human Organization,* 16 (1957): 28–32.

22. See Paul Lerman, "Argot, Symbolic Deviance, and Subcultural Delinquency," *American Sociological Review,* 32 (April 1967): 209–24.

the conventional world. One group will believe secrecy the best policy and act accordingly. The "closet queens" of the homosexual world, the quiet pot smokers, recognize that, at some price in spontaneity and fun, they can carry on deviant activities without ever revealing to outsiders that they do so. Another segment frequently opposes such prudence, insists on "flaunting" their deviance publicly, has a lot of trouble as a result, fights for "equal rights" for their brand of deviance, may support "defense" organizations (such as LEMAR and the Mattachine Society), and are in general much more visible to researchers as well as to the public than the first group.

In addition, the researcher may discover segments defined by the differing degree of involvement of their members in the characteristic activities of that deviant world. Some persons might reasonably be called professionals: purveyors of necessary items used by members, proprietors of locations and establishments where the activities take place, or sellers of specialized services. Drug wholesalers, proprietors of gambling casinos or gay bars, and homosexual prostitutes exemplify this segment. Another segment consists of ordinary members deeply involved, people who participate frequently in characteristically deviant activities: "drag queens," addicts, and the like. Still others partake only occasionally, are much less committed to "the life," and have a correspondingly complex life in the conventional world, and one more important to them: the occasional drug user, the part-time whore. Finally, there are the sightseers, experimenters, and novices, who, even while they investigate the deviant world, still retain for themselves the option of having nothing to do with it after all.

The researcher should look for these typical forms of differentiation and organize his work so as to gain some kind of access to each of the parts. Alternatively, he should learn at least enough about the matter to know how what he has observed or been told about stands in relation to the rest of that world he has not been able to explore fully. For many sociological purposes, he need not have samples of all segments in representative numbers; i.e., the members of the various segments in his sample need not constitute the same proportions of his total sample that they do of the universe. His first order of business should usually be to discover the full range of social types, roles, adaptations, and styles of life that surround the deviant activity he is studying, for the discovery of a new type is likely to have great theoretical import.[23]

Typical situations. Certain typical situations and events arise in relation to most deviant activities; look for them and make them the focus of

23. A general perspective on the development of theory from research data is presented by Barney G. Glaser and Anselm L. Strauss, *The Discovery of Grounded Theory* (Chicago: Aldine, 1967).

study. It pays, first of all, to get a good understanding of the deviant activity itself, insofar as it occurs publicly enough to be observed or is talked about freely enough to allow such understanding. By learning about the activity, one comes to appreciate the contingencies for action it creates and the effects these have on other aspects of collective action in the deviant community. Since lay people have many unfounded beliefs about deviant activities, which the sociologist for lack of any better knowledge will probably share, one should observe them simply to get rid of those conceptions; to learn, for instance, that drug users do not typically engage in sexual orgies following ingestion of drugs. In addition, the activity itself may be of great theoretical interest. Humphreys' study of homosexual activities in public toilets, for example, represents an extreme case of coordinated activity occurring on the basis of tacit bargaining, a topic Thomas Schelling has treated on a much more abstract level.[24]

Other typical situations worthy of special attention include the process by which novices are introduced to the deviant activity and taught how to carry it out, and the concomitant process by which they are inducted into whatever community may exist around the activity. The "coming-out" parties given some homosexuals are an extreme and formalized instance of this, but more informal analogues are common, except of course where the activity is carried on in a solitary fashion; even then, the person may invent such occasions for himself, as transvestites do when they appear in public in the clothing of the opposite sex.

In more organized deviant communities, look for the more or less formal educational situations in which the novice learns the culture of the deviant community. Bryan describes the elaborate procedure by which a call girl is taught her trade and the ideology associated with it; but he also shows — an important caution for sociologists who take the notion of deviant subculture as given rather than as something to be discovered empirically in each case — that girls learn the ideology but neither believe it, act by it, or permit it to influence their other ideas.[25]

Since deviant activity is sometimes illegal and always stigmatized, deviants discovered by the conventional community can expect to be publicly labeled as deviant, to suffer various sanctions, and to have the normal order of their lives grossly interrupted and changed. Make a point of observing or asking people about the situations in which deviants are apprehended, the consequences of apprehension, and its effects on other aspects of their lives. In addition, look for the effect of

24. Thomas C. Schelling, *The Strategy of Conflict* (Cambridge: Harvard University Press, 1963).

25. James H. Bryan, "Occupational Ideologies and Individual Attitudes of Call Girls," *Social Problems,* 13 (Spring 1966): 441–50.

this constant element of danger on the organization of the deviant community, and for differential attitudes toward it and actions with respect to it on the part of community segments.

Indirect Approaches

In addition to the direct methods just discussed (or, in rare cases, instead of them) the researcher may employ various indirect ways of getting at his subject. He can ask about and observe the operations of related people, groups, and organizations, and he can also search several relevant kinds of literature and archival records for useful material.

OTHER PEOPLE

We can learn about the contingencies of deviant lives and organizations by studying the operations of the professionals who come into contact with them. Who these people are will depend on the kind of deviance we study, but likely candidates for our attention include doctors (especially psychiatrists), who may be called on to provide diagnostic or treatment services; lawyers, who serve as prosecutors, defenders, or counselors; and police, public and private, who may be officially charged with enforcing laws prohibiting the deviant activity or may have decided themselves that they ought to. What these people do needs to be taken into account because of its immediate effects on the people we study, and we sometimes find it easier to observe certain key activities by participating as one of them or in their company. For example, it is probably easier, at least for a male researcher, to discover some things about the operations of prostitutes by observing, as Jerome Skolnick did, members of the vice squad as they go about their daily work of regulating and arresting whores.[26]

In addition, specialists accumulate a great deal of practical experience and lore. They know what kinds of things go on, who is who in the deviant community and where he may be found, relevant local history, and a host of other things a researcher can use. Judicious cultivation of informants in these ancillary groups is sound practice.

We may also wish to study the activities of nonspecialist nondeviants, of ordinary lay people whose own actions on occasion figure importantly in the lives and experience of deviants. The most important lay people to observe are family members, work colleagues, and members of the general public. A number of studies have investigated the reactions of family members to the fact or suspicion of mental illness in a family member.[27] Edwin Lemert's remarkable study of paranoia used data

26. Jerome Skolnick, *Justice Without Trial* (New York: Wiley, 1966), pp. 96–109.

27. See, as an example, Harold Sampson, Sheldon L. Messinger, and Robert D. Towne, *Schizophrenic Women* (New York: Atherton Press, 1965).

gathered from family members and work colleagues to demonstrate that paranoid delusions of persecution were not delusions, that these others, on their own testimony, actually did the things the putative paranoid complained of.[28] Richard Schwartz and Jerome Skolnick used an ingenious field experimental technique to show that employers were less likely to offer jobs to applicants who had been tried or convicted of a criminal offense.[29]

Studies of the attitudes and actions of the general public can be quite revealing, especially with respect to questions of when deviant labels are applied and what the consequences of the application are. John I. Kitsuse queried lay people about their contacts with homosexuals, discovering that there was both little consensus about what kind of behavior identified someone as homosexual and great variation in responses to such an identification, from violent assault to complete disregard.[30]

OFFICIAL STATISTICS

Sociologists' past reliance on officially gathered statistics about deviance has provoked a number of severe and telling criticisms. I think it is now clear, though some may disagree, that police statistics, for example, tell us more about police than about criminals or delinquents, reflecting the degree to which officials decide to act against potential deviants in the community. But when we study deviance we may want to know about police behavior, so that the same statistics, so interpreted, become a valuable resource, telling us about levels of enforcement activity and suggesting possible variations in such activity with respect to subgroups in the deviant community.[31]

While it is doubtful that police statistics can be used uncritically to learn about the etiology or causes of deviance, they can be used in conjunction with other information to learn many things of value, especially when there is no other practical way of gathering information. Mary Owen Cameron's study of shoplifting compared police and court records with the much more complete records kept by the store detectives who originally apprehended the thieves, and the comments of the detectives themselves on their own detection procedures, to arrive at

28. Edwin M. Lemert, "Paranoia and the Dynamics of Exclusion," *Sociometry*, 26 (March 1962): 1–20.
29. Richard D. Schwartz and Jerome H. Skolnick, "Two Studies of Legal Stigma," *Social Problems*, 10 (Fall 1962): 133–42.
30. John I. Kitsuse, "Societal Reaction to Deviant Behavior: Problems of Theory and Method," *Social Problems*, 9 (Winter 1962): 247–56.
31. See John I. Kitsuse and Aaron V. Cicourel, "A Note on the Use of Official Statistics," *Social Problems*, 11 (Fall 1963): 131–39; Aaron V. Cicourel, *The Social Organization of Juvenile Justice* (New York: Wiley, 1967), pp. 58–110; and Albert D. Biderman and Albert J. Reiss, Jr., "On Exploring the 'Dark Figure' of Crime," *Annals of the American Academy of Political and Social Science*, 374 (November 1967): 1–15.

estimates of the social class, age, and ethnic distributions of shop-lifters.[32]

As the above example suggests, police are not the only ones who keep potentially useful records. Many forms of deviance never come to police attention, being dealt with either by private policing agencies, as in industrial theft and embezzling, or by laymen in a more informal way. Agencies offering services to deviants sometimes keep useful records and may even collect data for research of their own that can be adapted for sociological use. The researcher should scout around for potential depositories of such records. Once he has located them, he will have to inquire carefully into how they were compiled — who gathered the information, under what circumstances, from whom, using what questions or data-gathering forms — before deciding to what use they can be put. No agency's records should be accepted as accurate on faith; likewise, no agency's records should be dismissed as worthless without careful inspection and inquiry into how they are made up.

PUBLISHED SOURCES

A variety of published sources may contain useful information, depending on the form of deviance. Professional and scientific journals often contain articles on forms of deviance and related topics. If one is interested in drug use or sexual misbehavior, for instance, medical, pharmacological, psychiatric, legal, and police journals are likely to be useful. Most forms of deviance provoke diagnoses of mental illness from somebody, so that psychiatric journals are especially fruitful sources. One should routinely consult the *Quarterly Index Medicus* and *Psychological Abstracts* for leads to this literature, and their appropriate counterpart in law for law-review notes, discussions of public policy, and the like. In using this literature, keep in mind that the facts it reports were not gathered by sociologists for sociological purposes. Quite the contrary. You will have to distinguish carefully between the facts reported (keeping in mind that important facts may not have been reported) and the theories and opinions advanced. The former may be used to test your own theories. The latter may provide profitable material for an analysis of ideologies about the "problem" aspects of the deviant activity. Alfred Lindesmith's work on opiate addiction provides a classic model of both uses of available literature.[33] He uses cases reported by physicians to test his own theory, reinterprets older findings, and uses the theories of physicians and enforcement officials as data for an interpretation of the social problem of addiction.

Another important source of data consists of legislative hearings.

32. Mary Owen Cameron, *The Booster and the Snitch* (New York: Free Press, Macmillan, 1964).
33. Alfred R. Lindesmith, *Addiction and Opiates* (Chicago: Aldine, 1968).

State, city, and federal hearings often deal with problems of deviance, since legislative action is frequently thought necessary to deal with the problems caused by the deviant activity. Legislators and their committee staffs interrogate witnesses of many kinds; police, proponents of changes in the laws, alleged lawbreakers, and so on. They do not always ask the questions we should like asked, but often enough they do; and sometimes they ask questions we might not have thought of. When the witnesses have been subpoenaed, investigators may get answers to questions, under oath, that sociologists might like to ask if they had the nerve. Some of the material in the hearings of Estes Kefauver's Senate committee on organized crime provides invaluable material for an analysis of that elusive topic.

Many forms of popular literature — newspapers, magazines, books — contain material that can be used for analyses of popular stereotypes of deviants and for analyses of propaganda designed to shape those stereotypes. Thomas Scheff analyzed comic strips, jokes, and other forms of popular culture to show how their treatment of residual deviance teaches members of our society the categories of "sane" and "insane."[34] I used the incidence of popular articles about marihuana as a measure of the propaganda activity related to passage of the federal law banning its use,[35] and Jerry Mandel traced the history of the stereotype of the assassin related to the use of hashish.[36] Very little work of this kind has been done, and many possibilities remain to be explored.

Finally, organized deviant groups often produce a self-justifying literature that may also serve some of the functions of a trade magazine: autobiographical documents, reports on legal, medical, and scientific aspects of the deviance, editorials denouncing discrimination and repression, news of important events, and advertisements for other magazines and books of interest to practitioners of that particular activity.[37] This material serves, as I have suggested with respect to other published sources, both as a storehouse of fact for testing your own theories and as raw material for an analysis of ideology. In addition, such magazines can be used to advertise for possible subjects of study; Taylor Buckner, for example, reached some tranvestites in this fashion.[38]

Ethical Problems

Every conceivable topic of sociological study is probably a matter of

34. Thomas J. Scheff, *Being Mentally Ill* (Chicago: Aldine, 1966), pp. 55–101.

35. Becker, *Outsiders,* p. 141.

36. Jerry Mandel, "Hashish, Assassins, and the Love of God," *Issues in Criminology,* 2 (1966): 149–56.

37. As examples see the easily available magazines published by nudist and homosexual groups.

38. H. Taylor Buckner, "Deviant Group Organizations" (unpublished master's thesis, University of California, Berkeley, 1964).

moral concern to someone and thus poses moral and ethical problems for the researcher. Deviance certainly does, and, like the technical problems already considered, the moral problems center on the deviant status of the activities and people studied. What attitude should we take toward that deviant status? How should we respond to those activities?

GUILTY KNOWLEDGE

Unless we study apprehended deviants, we will inevitably know things that, under some strict construction of the law, should be reported to the police. If we do report what we know, we will probably not be able to continue our research. More to the point, we will probably have explicitly or implicitly violated a bargain we have made with the people under study, an agreement not to use the information we get to injure the people who give it to us. If the people studied know we are doing research, they will necessarily have assumed such a bargain on our part.[39] If we have been studying them secretly, then we have gathered information in a way another citizen might, and I see no directive that applies to the sociologist *qua* sociologist. I think it repugnant and dishonorable to use information so gained to destroy people's characters and lives, though I do not know any scientific basis for that judgment. But none is needed; one's personal ethic should be enough. I do not mean to imply that the use of secretly gathered data in ways that do not harm the respondent is immoral. On the contrary, such data may be used for profoundly moral ends, as when Humphreys uses his analysis of homosexual encounters in public toilets to show how police victimize participants in those encounters.[40]

What if law-enforcement officials demand access to our data? To my knowledge, this has not happened yet, but it probably will soon, as deviance and political marginality become more intertwined, both in fact and in the minds of enforcement officials. Lewis Yablonsky has suggested that we arrange in advance with relevant officials for immunity and that we seek legislative relief from these contingencies. But advance arrangements may require us to make bargains we would rather not make (though that is not necessarily so); legislatively granted immunity seems to me unlikely to come about soon. At present, I think we must be willing, if the occasion arises, to shield our informants as some journalists have done, even at the expense of legal sanctions.[41]

39. On the research bargain and related problems, see Everett C. Hughes, "The Relation of Industrial to General Sociology," *Sociology and Social Research*, 41 (March–April 1957): 25–56.

40. Humphreys, *Tearoom Trade*.

41. Lewis Yablonsky, "On Crime, Violence, LSD, and Legal Immunity for Social Scientists," *American Sociologist*, 3 (May 1968): 148–49. See also Polsky, *Hustlers, Beats, and Others* and the letters by Oromaner and Symonds responding to Yablonsky in *American Sociologist*, 3 (August 1968): 254.

TO PARTICIPATE OR NOT?

Researchers often feel that if they want fully to understand the deviants they study they should partake themselves of the forbidden activity. They want to share the experience itself, and the feeling of illegality as well, in order better to frame hypotheses and interpret data. But the activity may seem to them distasteful, frightening, immoral, disgusting, or any combination of these. What should they do?

I think it indisputable that one need not engage in an activity to understand it. If not indisputable, the proposition is at least a necessary assumption if we are to have a communicable social science. Otherwise, no white sociologist could write about blacks or blacks about whites; men could not write about women or women about men. In spite of the romantic yearnings of researchers and the earnest ideiological assurances of some deviants, scientific requirements do not force us to join in deviant activities.

But our scientific purposes often require us to hear about and on occasion to observe activities we may personally disapprove of. I think it equally indisputable that one cannot study deviants without forgoing a simple-minded moralism that requires us to denounce openly any such activity on every occasion. Indeed, the researcher should cultivate a deliberately tolerant attitude, attempting to understand the point of view from which his subjects undertake the activities he finds distasteful. A moralism that forecloses empirical investigation by deciding questions of fact *a priori* is scientifically immoral.

WHO PROFITS?

A final ethical question arises because investigation of any area of deviance ordinarily discredits some portion of the general body of conventional belief. Major institutions, having either promulgated the discredited views or tacitly condoned them, find themselves under attack because the investigation shows them to have been wrong. To be sure, an investigation may be equally likely to discredit antiestablishment views of the matter; but then, no one of any established importance has supported those views or stands to lose when they are discredited. Thus research might show that, contrary to the claims found in some homophile literature, homosexuals are no more sensitive than normal males. This will not occasion the outcry that might arise if research showed that they were less neurotic than normal males, for that would discredit the views of important spokesmen of medicine, psychiatry, and the law.

This is not the place to rehearse this argument in detail.[42] The re-

42. I have considered these questions at greater length in "Problems of Publication of Field Studies," in *Reflections on Community Studies,* ed. Arthur Vidich, Joseph Bensman, and Maurice Stein (New York: Wiley, 1964), pp. 267–84; and in "Whose Side Are We On?," *Social Problems,* 14 (Winter 1967): 239–47.

searcher, briefly, must take into account the consequences of making his research public. Will his findings support popular views that he nevertheless feels morally unjustified, as might occur if a libertarian sociologist discovered that drug use actually caused brain damage? Or will they support unconventional views he feels morally unjustified, as when a more conformist sociologist might discover that drug use could be good for people? I think personally that the scientist must report his findings. I can also understand why one might suppress an obviously misinterpretable finding in situations where it will be misused for immoral ends, though I would not be happy to do so.

Conclusion

Technical problems of research reflect the peculiarities of the social groups we study.[43] In solving them, we simultaneously learn something about the social structure under observation and something about the methods we use. When we adapt our "ordinary" methods to a specific research setting, we do so because something about the setting is organized so differently from what we expect that we cannot ignore its effect on our techniques. The adaptation also shows us what we have been taking for granted in applying the method in "ordinary" situations and makes us aware that even there our routine technical assumptions may be incorrect.

Since we stigmatize and punish deviant activities, the people who engage in them usually take care not to be discovered. Their secretiveness takes a variety of organizational forms, and each variation complicates the technical problems of sampling, for instance, in a special way that requires us to find special solutions. We learn how the activity is organized by finding out what we must do to locate its practitioners: an activity carried on in a solitary way may require us to advertise, while one carried on collectively allows us to gather cases by observing likely settings. We learn which category any particular case falls into by seeing what we have to do to accumulate a sample.

The problem of sampling deviants also shows us that conventional sampling techniques assume, as a condition of their effective use, that we have enough information about the location of the elements of the universe to construct a sampling frame properly. Alternatively, they assume that what we want to study occurs so frequently that sampling

43. See, for example, E. E. Evans-Pritchard, *The Nuer* (New York: Oxford University Press, 1940), p. 15: "Azande would not allow me to live as one of themselves; Nuer would not allow me to live otherwise. Among Azande I was compelled to live outside the community; among Nuer I was compelled to be a member of it. Azande treated me as a superior; Nuer as an equal." See also the discussion of possible legal problems associated with studies of campus disturbances in *Science,* 165 (July 11, 1969): 157–61.

on conventional criteria will turn up sufficient instances of what we want to study. By studying deviance, we learn how badly we need new theories and techniques adequate to the general problem of sampling hidden universes of rare items.

Similarly, to take another instance, because we think deviant activities wrong, they become matters of interest to persons deputized to catch wrongdoers or to treat, cure, and rehabilitate them once they are caught. For this reason, we can find useful information in the hearings of legislatures, the records of police agencies, and the archives of the helping professions. But deviance is controversial, and the arguments over the validity of such material alert us to the general problems of using material gathered by others for their own purposes. It is no wonder that the most penetrating critiques of official records come from the field of criminology, critiques relevant to every research enterprise relying on such materials.[44]

The study of deviance is risky business, studded with traps and pitfalls. It is perhaps comforting to know that our very troubles, seen properly, can help us learn.

44. See Oskar Morganstern, *On the Accuracy of Economic Observations* (Princeton: Princeton University Press, 1963).

Studying Family and Kinship

Although numerous studies of family and kinship have been made, the literature on field methods is sparse. Most of the literature pertaining to family research methodology deals with scales and indices rather than such topics as interviewing or participant observation. Apparently the ubiquitous presence of family groups with somewhat similar composition — parents and children — throughout society facilitates the use of quantitative techniques and simplifies data gathering.

One of the obvious dangers in the use of previously existing scales and indices (such as the Burgess-Cottrell-Wallin marital adjustment scale) is possible unreliability when they are applied to a new population. Customarily scales and indices representing significant dimensions of family life are difficult and time-consuming to construct and test. Small, convenient samples are generally used as a basis for their development and evaluation. It is therefore incumbent upon any researcher who wishes to apply existing scales and indices to another population to test their validity and reliability again. To do so, the researcher should gain an intimate knowledge of the new population. Hence it seems advisable, even when the final research design is based on quantitative techniques, to initiate a preliminary field study using qualitative techniques.

Access to Population

Participation of subjects in research on family and kinship may derive from individual decisions or through the efforts of organized groups. Not everyone will cooperate with this sort of research, and these hindrances likewise may come about through individual refusals or through organized resistance to research efforts.

INDIVIDUALS AS OBSTACLES

When Ernest Burgess and Paul Wallin analyzed the persons who were reluctant to participate in their prediction study, they found that people with anti-scientific and politically conservative attitudes, those who regarded social science as useless, older couples, and Catholics were more likely to refuse or to limit their participation than were others. Low socioeconomic position and low education were also associated with non-participation.[1] Robert Blood and Donald Wolfe, however, found in their Detroit study that respondents did not differ from non-respondents significantly on characteristics of race, urban versus suburban residence, or median value of other houses in the block.[2]

Studies requiring the participation of both husbands and wives have indicated that men are generally more reluctant than women to take part in family research. In investigations of families with retarded children (as well as those relating to kinship), sometimes the wife would initially agree to participate but would later refuse, after consultation with her husband. When both participated, the wife would usually provide fuller and more intimate details of their family life (regardless of the sex of the interviewer). The greater opposition to family research by men is illustrated by an incident in the marriage study by Blood and Wolfe:

> One wife was being pretested while feeding her baby about 9:30 in the morning. Soon her husband, a shiftworker, wandered into the livingroom in his pajamas. He made a running series of critical and sarcastic remarks about the questions and his wife's answers, yet made no effort to terminate the interview. Only when the question of total family income arose did he react more strongly, jumping from his chair with clenched fists to yell, "You get the hell out of here." The interviewer left.[3]

One problem frequently encountered in family studies is refusal to discuss the personal and intimate life normally associated with the family. One of Burgess and Wallin's male respondents scrawled across the page dealing with sex relations, "None of your damned business!" Kinship studies, on the other hand, encounter little resistance, since in

1. Paul Wallin, "Volunteer Subjects as a Source of Sampling Bias," *American Journal of Sociology,* 54 (1949): 539–44. See also Ernest W. Burgess and Paul Wallin, *Engagement and Marriage* (Philadelphia: Lippincott, 1953), p. 46.

2. Robert O. Blood, Jr., and Donald M. Wolfe, *Husbands and Wives* (New York: Free Press, Macmillan, 1960), p. 270.

3. *Ibid*, p. 274.

our society kinship does not have these personal connotations. Bert Adams reports:

> Kinship is not a difficult subject on which to interview. Once the individual was convinced that the interview did not pertain to intimate aspects of his personal life, a frequently overt reaction went something like this: "Well, what are relatives for if you can't talk about them?" Another part of the interviewers' impression was that the great majority of young married Greensboroites, regardless of positive or negative feelings toward specific kin, considered themselves experts on such matters. This "expertise" and the accompanying frankness of response was noted by each of the six interviewers as a definite asset to the study.[4]

Sometimes even in the study of kinship, where intimacy is of little concern, the time demands on the respondent may preclude participation. In a study I conducted which required three or four two-hour sessions, the time pressures were the most frequent reason for refusal. The interviewers made such reports as these:

> Is working three jobs and had only a day and a half off each month. Is unwilling to give up this time for interviewing.

> Not participating because husband is writing his dissertation and is very busy. Interviewer returned three additional times over a period of several months. Husband was still busy on his doctoral dissertation.

> I first contacted Mrs. K. in March. She said that she thought she could do the study but her husband did not have the time. Her little girl was sick and she said she could not set a time for an interview. I checked back in a few days. Mrs. K. said her child had the mumps and she asked that I wait until the following month. When I called again, she said that she would not participate in the study. I asked her why and she told me she did not have the time.

> On my first contact, no adult was at home. I talked to the oldest child and he suggested a Saturday visit. When I came back, I found that Mrs. A. works on the swing-shift. She said she had nine children living at home and was always busy. There is no husband in the home.[5]

In families with special problems, selectivity associated with these problems affects access to the population. For example, in studies of families with handicapped children, an investigator often has to rely on the mailing lists of special-interest organizations and may have to work with parents' groups. These groups are selective in that they may under-represent the very high socioeconomic and the very low socioeconomic

4. Bert N. Adams, *Kinship in an Urban Setting* (Chicago: Markham, 1968), p. 10.
5. Unpublished material.

groups. There are fewer Negroes among them than might be expected on the basis of prevalence figures and epidemiological studies. Moreover, the participation of the families in parents' associations may be a factor in their taking part in the research. Parents who have retained their membership in the group over a long period of time and those who attend meetings regularly are more likely to participate in research dealing with parental reactions to retarded children than are those who have recently joined the group or who attend meetings infrequently. In addition, parents who are having marital difficulties appear to participate in family research less frequently than others. However, the major factor for refusing to participate in family research involving retarded children is a dislike of dwelling upon a situation fraught with frustration, guilt, and anxiety. Parents may refuse to participate because they would "rather not bring the subject up," or because their own child will not be helped.

Sometimes families with retarded children may agree to be interviewed but later find they are unable to face the interview situation. They repeatedly postpone appointments, plead illness, promise to call back, stay away from home at times arranged for interviews; sometimes they even turn out the lights when interviewers approach the house.[6]

ORGANIZATIONAL OPPOSITION

A sizable segment in every community opposes research on family or phychiatric problems. Ordinarily these are the ultraconservative organizations whose members regard social science as a tool used by radicals, principally communists. They view social scientists with suspicion and distrust. In the past, this opposition has taken the form of having the school authorities burn answer sheets to sociopsychometric measures, linking the investigation to socialist or communist aims and goals, and creating a public sentiment against research on mental health.[7]

During the previously mentioned investigation of families with retarded children, one parents' association was sufficiently suspicious of the research to send one of its members 130 miles to determine whether the study was actually connected with the state university as it was represented to be, and whether there would be "highly personal" information discussed in the interview. The member also notified the study director that the association would not take part if there were Negro interviewers. Specific prejudices and auxiliary interests not read-

6. Bernard Farber, "Effects of a Severely Mentally Retarded Child on Family Integration," *Monographs of the Society for Research in Child Development* (serial no. 71), 24, no. 2 (1959): 95–102.

7. Leonard D. Eron and Leopold Walters, "Test Burning: II," *American Psychologist.* 16 (May 1961): 237–244; Gwynn Nettler, "Test Burning in Texas," *American Psychologist,* 14 (November 1959): 682–683; and John Cummings and Elaine Cummings, *Closed Ranks* (Cambridge: Harvard University Press, 1957).

ily apparent in the stated purposes of the organization may thus affect participation of its members in family research.

ACCESS TO INDIVIDUALS

Both personal and altruistic inducements can be offered to individuals to obtain their cooperation in research. The most general inducement is the possibility of contribution to science. In families with mentally retarded children, many of the parents volunteered for an interview:

> 1. To promote the welfare of mentally retarded children and their families. Many parents indicated that they were participating so that other parents could avoid the difficulties they themselves had endured.
> 2. To advance scientific understanding of the mentally retarded, with the vague hope that in some unspecified way the research might help their child or themselves.[8]

In the study of kinship, many families who disclaim any interest in the topic will participate on the promise of a copy of their genealogy. In trying to obtain the cooperation of families with emotionally disturbed children, as well as a control sample of families whose children were considered normal, I discovered that the attitude of prospective participants in the study might change when this inducement was offered.[9]

Sometimes copies of the report describing the results are offered as inducements to prospective participants. However, since the results may be the sort that the respondent might consider threatening, the writing may be highly technical, and the period of time between the interview and the preparation of the report may be extensive, there is a high risk that the respondent will be disappointed.

ORGANIZATIONAL FACILITATION

Just as some organizations that feel themselves threatened by social research can place obstacles in its ways, other organizations that consider their interests would be furthered by research can be used to facilitate the cooperation of potential participants. In one community with many ultraconservative groups, three researchers carefully courted various groups in the community to act as sponsors for their study.[10] The investigation was a family study focusing upon mental retardation and

8. Farber, "Effects of a Severely Mentally Retarded Child on Family Integration," p. 101.

9. For a description of this study see Bernard Farber, "Kinship Laterality and Emotionally Disturbed Child," in *Kinship and Family Organization*, ed. Farber (New York: Wiley, 1966), pp. 69–78.

10. Jane R. Mercer, Harvey F. Dingman, and George Tarjan, "Involvement, Feedback, and Mutuality: Principles for Conducting Mental Health Research in the Community," *American Journal of Psychiatry*, 121 (September 1964): 228–37.

involved the administration of intelligence tests. The investigators first secured sponsorship of the project by local officials, newspapers, and school personnel. Then they kept community leaders informed of problems faced by their staff. An advisory group was formed, consisting of consultants from community social agencies and prominent social scientists. The project staff addressed school personnel and parents' groups, sent introductory letters to parents, and provided the newspapers with material for articles that kept the public informed of the progress of the study. Finally, the researchers agreed to make available to the schools the data secured by their assistance. Since their data would deal with the mentally retarded, a group in which the schools had more than a casual interest, the schools actively supported the project and the researchers got the cooperation they needed.

Often membership in special-interest groups may act as a sufficient lever to induce participation in family studies. Parents' groups urged their members to take part in my own study of families with retarded children. Generally, the decision to participate was made by a motion passed at one of the meetings. Some of the parents participated because they felt that one of the aims of the parents' association was to take part in research projects. Several parents who gave this reason (before being interviewed) felt that survey-type studies would not help families with retarded children. Some parents were uncertain of the nature or purpose of the study but were under the impression that it had to do with keeping their children in a state institution. Others regarded any research connected with the Institute for Research on Exceptional Children as a worthwhile project.

After the study was under way, a competition developed among parents' associations. Officers of associations not yet contacted felt slighted. One association even took the initiative and got in touch with me. There was some pressure for the associations to make a "good showing." Parents who belonged to more than one association indicated the association they would like credited with their interview. At least one association regarded the interviews as a game. The rule seemed to be that if the parents were contacted, they had to participate; otherwise, they were to lie low. Parents would say to each other, "Have you been tagged yet?" or "You'll probably have to lie low only a little while longer. I heard they'll finish their interviewing soon." In any event, participation in the parents' associations facilitated participation in the study by the parents.[11]

Informal constraints such as these may be of importance to the researcher in gaining access to a population. The reputation of the research institute, willingness to provide information or research findings

11. Farber, "Effects of a Severely Mentally Retarded Child on Family Integration," p. 101.

in return for participation, and personal reputation may affect participation. In a smaller community, residents may be helpful. Michael Young and Peter Willmott reported that one of them lived in Bethnal Green, the borough they studied in East London, and he and the other members of his family became well acquainted with the area.

> As a result of this close connection with the district, we came to know well a number of local residents who gave us full accounts of their family relationships which helped us to understand and assess the information given to us in the formal interviews. We also did what we could to check what people told us verbally by personal observation in homes, churches, clubs, schools, parks, public houses, and street markets.[12]

Hierarchy of Questions

A research project can be viewed as an attempt to answer a hierarchy of questions. Ideally, at the apex of the hierarchy is a theoretical question whose elaboration leads to a second order of theoretical problems and so on, until at the base of this hierarchy are the questions asked of the subjects themselves in the fieldwork. In its most general from the theoretical question may deal with the relationship between kinship organization and such matters as socialization, interaction within the nuclear family, the nature of social stratification in the society, and attributes of other institutions in the society (such as industry or religion).

ASKING A SIGNIFICANT QUESTION

Since the value of the research rests ultimately on the basic theoretical question that organizes the research, the first point that must be discussed is: How do you ask a significant question? In the physical sciences significant questions seem to emerge when two theoretical propositions are contradictory. In the social sciences, however, the theoretical paradigms are numerous and points of conflict cannot be so easily identified. Rather, in the social sciences questions have to do with how certain properties or events that are not readily observable influence relationships among people.

Some aspects of family and kinship relations are "structured by explicit principles directly applicable to the behavior of kinsmen vis-à-vis one another," other aspects by principles that only indirectly affect the behavior of kinsmen, and still others by principles "that operate covertly and are identified only by analysis."[13] In the study of family and kinship in American society, the significant questions of research deal primarily with covert principles.

12. Michael Young and Peter Willmott, *Family and Kinship in East London* (Baltimore: Penguin Books, 1962), p. 14.
13. See Allan D. Coult and Robert W. Habenstein, "Exogamy and American Kinship," *Social Forces*, 43 (1964): 174–80.

One procedure for the development of significant questions is to apply an analogy and to suggest that the characteristics of this model are applicable in many situations beyond their obvious relevance. In the study of kinship, the analogy may be drawn between the models established by anthropologists for small primitive societies and kinship organization in modern urban society. Here the model of the kinship group in primitive societies is imposed upon relationships among kin in modern society. For example, Hope Leichter and William Mitchell studied cousins' clubs as corporate kinship structures.[14] The investigator may also ask about the distinction between jural and domestic factors in kinship organization in modern society. Jural factors include normative and legal obligations and rights; by domestic factors I mean the influences of living in the same territory. Questions that might be asked include:

1. When there is little residential mobility, is there a tendency for consanguineal kinship relations to be strong and marital ties to be weak? (Conversely, when residential mobility is extensive, are kinship ties weak and marital ties strong?)

2. In a society with an equalitarian value system, are affinal kinship ties relatively weak as compared with societies whose stratification scheme is imbedded in elaborate justifications?

3. To what extent are ideal and actual characteristics of kinship organization related to religion?

Another illustration is provided by Talcott Parsons' and Robert Bales' study of the family as a small experimental group.[15] In that work, the authors attempt to indicate the correspondence between instrumental and social-emotional leadership in the family and the leadership found in ad hoc experimental groups intended to study interaction processes.

Still another procedure is to take a concept that is already in vogue in the study of the family and apply it in a different context. This was the basic analogy applied in my study of families with mentally retarded children. In that study I tried to apply the family life-cycle concept to a crisis situation. The basic question was how an arrest in the family life cycle affected family integration. Elements in lower orders of the hierarchy of questioning were then derived, at least in part, from this analogy.

The existence of various alternatives in asking a significant question still does not resolve the issue: How does the researcher choose the basic question to ask? Although this question may precede all fieldwork by the researcher, it may also emerge during the course of the fieldwork.

14. Hope Jensen Leichter and William E. Mitchell, *Kinship and Case Work* (New York: Russell Sage Foundation, 1967).

15. Talcott Parsons and Robert Freed Bales, *Family Socialization and Interaction Process* (Glencoe, Ill.: Free Press, 1955).

Perhaps the essential point is that the researcher must be familiar with a variety of analogies. His initial fieldwork can then suggest to him which of the possible analogies are most appropriate. In my studies of families with mentally retarded children, the exploratory interviews and observations revealed that parents equated the retarded child with someone who was chronologically younger. Possibly this equation grew out of the concept of mental age, which has become familiar through intelligence testing. However, the custom among those who deal with the mentally retarded of using the word "child" for a mentally retarded person of any age suggests an interactional base rather than borrowing of the intelligence test conception. Moreover, parents reported their twenty-year-old retarded children out playing with eight- and nine-year-olds in the neighborhood. They generally used similes of younger children or infants when they talked about their own retarded children. Finally, numerous parents indicated that they simply had to treat their children as though they lived in a perpetual childhood. Thus the use of the analogy of an arrest in the family life cycle was not far removed from the conceptualization of the parents themselves.

A different kind of problem emerges in the study of kinship patterns among families with emotionally disturbed children. The families themselves have no common analogies or similies to organize their own thinking and conduct. In fact, they consider the study of kinship to be remote from the problem of emotional distrubance. Here the use of an analogy to provide significance to the study has to be drawn not from the conceptualization of the parents themselves, but from anthropological literature, and especially from ideas on reciprocity and equilibrium in kinship relations. In my study of kinship and emotional disturbance, contrary to the expectations of psychiatrists, the initial exploratory interviews revealed that the parents of the disturbed children were not uniformly isolated from their kin. A review of kinship literature suggested that the crucial relatives in a bilateral system are not ego's parents, but his siblings and his cousins. The questioning then referred to the influences of the adult respondent's siblings and cousins on his family life. An analogy was then formulated on the relationship between unilineal tendencies and authoritarianism in family relationships. Presumably authoritarianism in turn would be related to emotional disturbance in children.

DERIVED QUESTIONS

A second order of questions requires greater specification of the terms in the theoretical question. In the second-order questioning the arrays of alternatives in definition are introduced. For example, in my study of the effects of a severely mentally retarded child on family integration, the basic question was whether the retarded child did in fact have an effect on the integration of the family. The second-order question had to do with the specification of the terms retarded child, effect, and family integration. Thus second-order questions that had to be answered were:

1. Do normal children affect the marital integration of their parents? To answer this question, we examined the composition of families without retarded children. How many children did they have? How many boys, how many girls?

2. How closely were the parents integrated with each other? Did the retarded child's siblings exhibit any mental health problems? The assumption was that if mental health problems of the siblings or marital problems of the parents could not be handled, something had happened to the integration of the family.

3. Did the family with the severely mentally retarded child show characteristics of crisis?

4. How are family effects of the severely retarded child dependent on the parents' definition of the child? In early interviews with parents, it was discovered that before parents had defined their child as severely retarded, they might have been somewhat anxious or apprehensive, but at the time they finally realized their child was severely retarded they were likely to have undergone a profound emotional upheaval.

The third order of questions in the hierarchy pertained to the conditions under which a severely mentally retarded child affects family integration. Here questions were raised about residence of the retarded child (at home or in an institution), socioeconomic status of the family, religion, family integration prior to the birth of the retarded child, extent of interaction between the retarded child and siblings, and the quality of family organization. As a criterion for selecting each of these conditions for study, the question was asked: Why should this condition affect the relationship between the retarded child and the rest of the family? The array of conditions was developed through exploratory interviewing as well as a review of the literature relevant to family crisis and community organization.

The fourth order of questions in the hierarchy pertained to the array of alternative conditions relevant to the effect of the retarded child upon family integration. Coordinate with these questions on possible alternative conditions was the greater specification of family integration, which was defined in terms of consensus on values and coordination of family roles (or lack of tension in the role system). Questions had to be asked about the extent of specification of these alternatives. Should socioeconomic status be refined in terms of deciles, or was a simple lower-class and middle-class dichotomy sufficient? Were specific religious beliefs important, or would the general categories of Protestant, Jewish, and

Catholic serve just as well? Was the retarded child's length of residence in an institution more significant than the mere fact of institutionalization itself? Was the age of the retarded child to be specified? Comparable questions were applied to all conditions. If there was doubt about the degree of specification, the decision was made in the direction of greater specificity. Finally, the questions to be asked of the respondents were formulated. These questions were derived from the alternatives regarding the conditions, the various interpretations of "effects," and measures of family integration. This process of refinement and specificity of questions is applicable to a variety of research problems related to family and kinship organization.

FIELDWORK AND THE QUESTION HIERARCHY

When the questions are asked, there is generally an alternation between theoretical formulation and exploratory fieldwork. The fieldwork may be used to help to refine the questions at each level of the hierarchy. Accordingly, the nature of the fieldwork changes as the project advances. In the final phase data may be gathered in formal interviews for quantitative analysis. In the study of parents with retarded children, the initial interviews were more or less informal conversations with parents and social workers. The final interviews consisted of some precoded and open-ended questions in an interview designed to last about two hours. The open-ended questions were included as leads to further identification of conditions influencing the effects of the retarded child on family relationships.

Events

Interaction between relatives takes place in a variety of gatherings or assemblages. Leichter and Mitchell enumerate these assemblages as "(1) informal social meetings and formal family reunions, (2) calendrical ceremonies, that is, those occurring at particular times in the calendar year such as Thanksgiving and Passover, (3) life-cycle ceremonials such as weddings, bar mitzvahs, funerals, and (4) crisis gatherings where kin meet to help solve a particular problem such as illnesses and feuds."[16]

The extent to which individuals participate in these assemblages offers a clue to the degree to which these individuals are integrated into the kin group. Their participation in these assemblages provides them with an opportunity to interact with the entire group of kin rather than with specific relatives (as they might in providing assistance or in visiting). Taking part in these assemblages creates obligations for reciprocation.

Assemblages may provide many kinds of data. First of all, the gen-

16. Leichter and Mitchell, *Kinship and Case Work*, p. 128.

ealogical ties, age and sex, and socioeconomic characteristics of the relatives assembled can be noted. Secondly, the topics of conversation may reveal the manner in which respect is paid, patronage given, and conviviality maintained. Various persons in the assemblage may specialize in one or more of these activities. (It may be equally important to find out which of the relatives were absent from the assemblage.) Third, it may be of interest to determine the extent to which gossip and information about kin are passed from one nuclear family to another. Inasmuch as most kin do not interact frequently, the assemblages keep alive the images of relatives as personages. At these assemblages family heroes may be acclaimed and family villains defiled in conversation. Fourth, the assemblages may also provide an occasion for gathering data on terms of address and terms of reference.[17] Variations in the usage of terminology can be readily observed in an assemblage. These terms can then be related to kinds of interaction at the gathering and feelings of closeness.

Like the assemblage, a family business provides an opportunity to view relatives engaged in collective action. According to Leichter and Mitchell, "Most husbands reported negative feelings about the experiences of working with kin." Yet they continued to engage in business ventures with various relatives.[18] There were complaints of excessive demands and possible exploitation by relatives with whom respondents did business. Perhaps the precarious financial status of these businesses required a greater commitment than would be possible if the business partners were not relatives. It might be useful to study comparable businesses in which the partners are relatives and those in which they are not related to determine the nature of the interaction of the families with one another, the extent of conflict between the businessmen engaged in a common venture, and the financial state of the business. Leichter and Mitchell suggest that engaging in a common business tends to intensify contacts between kin, and their study suggests that the families of relatives engaged in a common business tend to become a closed group despite the conflicts that may ensue. If the use of kin terms in addressing relatives denotes an affirmation of kinship status in interaction, then related business partners who are in conflict may use kin terms to permit the relationship to persist.

Cousins' clubs and family circles, as well as more informal family reunions, serve to sustain kinship solidarity. Leichter and Mitchell distinguish between family circles and cousins' clubs. The family circles

17. A term of reference describes an individual to whom the respondent refers in talking with someone else (e.g., "I saw Uncle Charlie today"). A term of address is one that the individual uses in talking with the person himself (e.g., "Thanks, Uncle Charlie!"—which is of course quite different from both "Thanks, Uncle!" and "Thanks, Charlie!")

18. Leichter and Mitchell, *Kinship and Case Work*, p. 137.

emphasize the lineal descendants of a common ancestor. They therefore emphasize relationships between generations. Cousins' clubs, on the other hand, are usually organized by individuals of the same generation. It might be of interest to note the different kinds of interaction occurring in these two types of organization. Acts of deference, opportunities for sponsorship, and more formal use of kinship terminology may be more characteristic of family circles than of cousins' clubs. Meetings of these organizations may yield information about participation in the formal meetings as well as in the eating and social activities afterward.

Also productive of information regarding relationships between kin are vacation visits. Many people return to their hometown occasionally, and they may visit distant relatives either on a weekend trip or for a more extended stay. Under these circumstances, interaction between kin may be reflected in the answers to such questions as these: On such visits, which relatives do the individuals consider it imperative to see? Which relatives do they prefer to spend time with? What activities are undertaken during the visit? What are the topics of conversation? What obligations are created to foster reciprocity?

Subgroupings of Kin

The investigator conducting a kinship study must find out from a respondent just who his relatives are—their names and relationships to him. This information provides the basic genealogy. Studies have been made of the extensiveness of genealogies—the relative fullness of the mother's side versus the father's side, males versus females, married versus single adults, the number of generations for which the informant has information, and the range of relatives in the informant's own generation.

Next, a series of questions can be asked about age and sex of relatives, their occupations, their places of residence, and their marital status. These questions can be asked of consanguineal relatives (related by blood) or affinal relatives (related to the respondent by marriage). Additional questions can be asked about extent of education, religious preference, and terms of reference as well as terms of address. The intercorrelation of these factors would reveal (*a*) the extent of ethnic heterogeneity in the kinship group, (*b*) differences between kin groups related by marriage, (*c*) the scatter of kin by occupation, religion, and residence, and (*d*) deviant terminology.

The next set of questions may pertain to detailed personal and occupational histories of relatives. Questions in this category may elicit information on previous marriages, previous places of residence, and work history. These questions may be useful in the study of social mobility in the kin group, family or kinship group disorganization, or traditions of divorce.

The next category of questions has to do with interaction among relatives. The investigator can ask how often the respondent sees each of the relatives and then which relatives visit one another. By learning whether these relatives are regarded as close friends, whether certain favors are exchanged, and whether assistance is given either on a routine basis or in time of emergency, the researcher can discover the quality of the interaction. Specific questions may ask: What do the relatives gossip about? Are there any relatives that other kin do not talk with? Which relatives are in business together (or work closely together)? Which relatives are regarded as deviants or eccentrics or simply as those with whom the whole family has lost contact? These questions enable the investigator to classify relatives into intimate, effective, and nominal kin. In addition, the interaction variables can be related to questions on extensiveness of the genealogy, heterogeneity of the kin group, consanguineal and affinal differences, and social and residential mobility.

Finally, questions on relatives can be related to characteristics of the informant's own family of procreation and his ideas about marriage: (*a*) authority patterns, (*b*) the degree of intimacy or close feeling between husband and wife, (*c*) division of labor in the family, (*d*) fertility, (*e*) membership in formal associations, (*f*) interaction with friends and neighbors, (*g*) effectiveness of social-emotional and instrumental leadership of husband and wife, (*h*) the social competence of husband and wife, and (*i*) their marital adjustment (or integration). The questions on relatives can also be analyzed in association with variables pertaining to the socialization of children—child-rearing practices, deviant behavior, tendencies toward withdrawn or aggressive behavior, internalization of parental values, authoritarianism, life goals, occupational aspirations, educational achievement. In addition, the questions on relatives can be compared with the respondent's views on (*a*) the permissibility of marriage between first cousins, (*b*) discretion over the disposition of property at death, (*c*) appropriate conduct with grandparents, siblings, and uncles and aunts, and (*d*) permissibility of remarriage to former affines in case of divorce or widowhood. These views, in turn, can be related to other variables such as political opinions, religion, socioeconomic status, and race or ethnic group.

Related Groups

Various groups of people who deal with family problems may be informative. On the one hand, these individuals may provide valuable insights into the workings of family and kinship relations; and on the other, they may reveal a mythology—and sometimes scientific understanding—which they·utilize in dealing with families. At any rate, their broad experience and interest may provide many valuable data toward the understanding of the family and kinship organization.

Four groups of persons interested in the family who may be usefully contacted are (a) professional students of the family, such family sociologists, anthropologists, home economics specialists in child development and family relationships, and sometimes zoologists interested in group behavior; (b) professional therapists and advisers, such as clinical psychologists, social workers, marriage counselors, and psychiatrists; (c) religious leaders—priests, rabbis, ministers; and (d) the leaders of ethnic-group associations, both on college campuses and in the community.

For the most part, investigations into the family values held by professional persons indicate a strong tendency to uphold conformity to the ideal of the nuclear family as independent from the extended family, residentially, financially, and emotionally. Caseworkers are less likely than their clients to look favorably upon strong ties with kin.[19] Moreover, these professional persons often emphasize conformity and adjustment to current conventions in either preventing or remedying family problems.[20]

The institutional setting in which the professional person operates may also influence his perspective on family problems. In the pilot study of families with mentally retarded children (in preparation for a more extensive and systematic investigation), social workers connected with residential institutions for the mentally retarded regarded placing the retarded child in an institution as the most sensible solution to family problems. They regarded parents who kept their retarded child at home as displaying evidence of self-punishment, and considered this self-punishment as expiation for the guilt feelings they suffered. Social workers in community agencies, however, often perceived parents who institutionalized their retarded child as showing a rejection of the child. They sometimes considered these parents as abrogating their obligations when conditions did not clearly demand the child's institutionalization. In both institutional and community settings, the social workers' perceptions provided a justification for decisions made by their clients. However, when parents were uncertain about institutionalization, and were in contact with social workers in both settings, the conflict in perception heightened their anxieties.

19. *Ibid.*, pp. 231–32.

20. See William L. Kolb, "Family Sociology, Marriage Education, and the Romantic Complex: A Critique," *Social Forces*, 29 (October 1950): 65–72, and, "Sociologically Established Family Norms and Democratic Values," *Social Forces,* 26 (May 1948): 451–56.

The effects of the institutional setting may also be observed in views on family life by religious and ethnic-group leaders. Often these leaders perceive changes in family and kinship organization as the consequences of a decline in religious or ethnic identity. Being sensitive to deviations from ethnic and religious ideals, they may be able to provide a detailed description of the modifications in family and kin relations that are taking place.

Records of Families

Two kinds of records about family members can be distinguished. First, there are the records kept in relation to households, family businesses, and genealogies. Second, the investigator can ask the family members to keep records for the study. The latter form of record keeping probably produces more relevant data but entails a considerable amount of effort and time by family members.

EXISTING RECORDS

An analysis of existing family records, such as household accounts, records of business transactions with relatives, and both published and unpublished genealogies, may provide many insights into family and kinship organization and interaction. These records may be used to indicate status hierarchy.

Household records of various kinds may be useful. Inasmuch as payment by check has become a major way of transacting business in society, allocations of funds in families can be observed through an analysis of the amounts and payees of checks. Written budgets may also yield useful information. While neither the written budget nor the checking account may be sufficient to describe the activities of family members, they may provide important clues in the analysis. Two other kinds of household records may be of interest: personal and business letters that may be kept in the family file, and diaries and photograph albums. The use of photograph albums as a basis for an interview may evoke much information that might otherwise not be forthcoming.

Family businesses and transactions with relatives may also provide records of high utility. A longitudinal study of transactions and salaries may reveal interesting facets of family relationships over time.

Genealogical information may provide important data for analysis in family studies. Aside from anthropological references, there are various guides on the gathering and use of genealogical material.[21] In addition to

21. Ernest L. Schusky, *Manual for Kinship Analysis* (New York: Holt, Rinehart, & Winston, 1965); Archibald F. Bennett, *A Guide for Genealogical Research* (Salt Lake City: Genealogical Society of the Church of Jesus Christ of Latter-Day Saints, 1956); George B. Everton, *Book for Genealogists,* 4th ed. (Logan, Utah: Everton Publishers, 1962); E. Kay Kirkham, *How to Read the Handwriting and Records of Early America* (Salt Lake City: Kay Publishing Co., 1961).

books on the preparation of genealogies, there are genealogical collections in state and local libraries, in state and county historical associations, and in the National Archives.[22] Various associations in which genealogy affects membership may provide sources for biographical information. Especially prominent are those organizations pertaining to descendants of participants in the American Revolution and members of the Mormon church.[23] Many organizations publish periodicals specializing in genealogical information.[24] Numerous periodicals are published for a short time and are then discontinued.[25] In addition, many county societies publish local genealogical records.[26] Individual families may publish their genealogical records privately. These may be difficult to obtain, but are sometimes to be found in the collections of local libraries and historical societies, or distributed widely among members of the family.

RECORDS RELATED TO THE STUDY

Participants in the study of family relationships may be asked to record their own activities. These records may involve keeping track of persons with whom the participant interacts during the day or a log of specific contacts with family or kin over a longer period of time. Leichter and Mitchell asked the participants in their study to maintain a "kin contact log," in which they were to record all contacts with kin over a period of a week. The log included information on (*a*) the day of the week; (*b*) the relatives involved; (*c*) if the contact was by telephone, whether the participant or the relative called; (*d*) if by visit, whether the visit occurred at the participant's home, the relative's homes, or another location; (*e*) a record of the time during which the contact occurred (e.g., 5:40–5:50); and (*f*) the reason for the contact. Perhaps the most significant information pertained to the reasons for the kin contact. Reasons

22. Meredith B. Colket, Jr., and Frank E. Bridgers, *Guide to Genealogical Records in the National Archives*, pub. no. 64-8 (Washington, D.C.: U.S. Government Printing Office, 1964): *Genealogical Research, Methods, and Sources* (Washington, D.C.: American Society of Genealogists, 1960).

23. For example, see Gilbert H. Doane, *Searching for Your Ancestors: The How and Why of Genealogy*, 3rd ed. (Minneapolis: University of Minnesota Press, 1960). For rosters of Revolutionary War soldiers, see Leslie G. Pine, *American Origin* (Garden City, N.Y.: Doubleday, 1960).

24. For example, *National Geographical Society Quarterly* (Washington, D.C.) and *Utah Genealogical and Historical Magazine*, published quarterly by the Genealogical Society of Utah.

25. For example, *The Genealogical Advertiser: A Quarterly Magazine of Family History*, published in Cambridge, Mass. by Lucy H. Greenlow from 1898 to 1901.

26. For instance, *Genealogical and Biographical Record of Cook County, Illinois, Containing Biographical Sketches of Prominent and Representative Citizens of the Community* (Chicago: Lake City Publishing Co., 1894). Frequently these local genealogical records are compiled to commemorate an event such as the founding of the city or an anniversary of a business institution in the community.

for contact with relatives outside the immediate family included the borrowing of money, a daily chat, and emotional catharsis, whereas contacts with members of the participant's own family (particularly with the mother) were limited to chatting and social visiting.[27]

Information About Families

The investigator can seek information about families from either official or unofficial sources. For the most part, the official sources consist of records pertaining to birth, marriage, divorce, and death. Unofficial records of family events can sometimes be found in newspapers.

RECORD LINKAGE[28]

Linking together several official records about an individual or family has proved to be a useful technique for the analysis of family relationships. The investigator can start with the marriage of the parents, proceed to birth records, then to divorce records involving the same family, and finally to death records. In this way, he can procure a picture of the family as it proceeds through its life cycle. In the course of his investigation he might also have access to school records pertaining to the family.

Various topics can be examined through the method of record linkage. The research can investigate the relationship between socioeconomic status, length of marriage, the performance of a religious ceremony, and the timing of births. Record linkage can also be used to determine premarital pregnancies in relation to divorce, and the effect of age on premarital pregnancy, and as a check upon the veracity of information provided by informants. Record linkage can indicate matrilocal and patrilocal tendencies and the extent of community endogamy. Age may be a factor in residential tendencies: younger couples are more often matrilocal than older ones. Finally, the investigator can use the record-linkage technique to determine the relationship between factors related to marriage and the timing of births to determine effects on school performance of children.

The record-linkage technique has several advantages. First, record data are relatively uniform from community to community and from state to state. Record linkage makes possible internal check on reliability. Both conscious and unconscious errors can be investigated. (There is a small tendency for persons to falsify their age at marriage—about 4 or 5 percent—and to modify birth records to cover up premarital preg-

27. Leichter and Mitchell, *Kinship and Case Work*, pp. 106–107.

28. This discussion draws heavily on Harold T. Christensen, "I. The Method of Record Linkage Applied to Family Data," *Journal of Marriage and the Family*, 20 (February 1958): 38–43.

nancies.) The technique also permits the study of behavior in sensitive areas such as premarital pregnancies and pregnancy timing. Perhaps its major advantage accrues through longitudinal analysis. Ordinarily, researchers conducting panel studies encounter many logistic problems in finding couples to participate and engaging their cooperation over a long period of time. Records, on the other hand, are endlessly patient, require no tact in handling (though their archivist may), and never decide in the middle of a project that they just can't spare any more time. Studies involving a historical analysis of family life will find them admirable subjects in many ways.

At the same time, there are certain disadvantages encountered in record linkage that must not be overlooked. First of all, inaccuracies and incompleteness of data cannot be rectified. Secondly, cases may be lost through migration, misplacing in the files, and the performance of ceremonies (weddings or funerals) and the births of children in other localities. Finally, record data are limited in their scope to the purposes for which they were obtained. Their usefulness may therefore be somewhat less than we may wish.

When record-linkage techniques are applied to historical documents, more problems are encountered: unrelated persons with similar names, different spellings of the same name, the use of baptism dates rather than birth dates in church records, and sometimes illegibility.

In spite of these deficiencies, the record-linkage technique can be usefully applied to the study of family life cycles under a variety of historical circumstances, and to the study of cycles of prosperity and depression in the history of a particular family.

NEWSPAPER ANALYSIS

Newspaper analysis can provide data on assemblages of family and kin as well as on critical events in the lives of individual family members. Robert Janes, in his analysis of newspaper reports of assemblages. found that deaths and funerals were most widely covered, followed by parties and luncheons, weddings, and dinners and dances. Other family events reported by the press included visits by house guests, bridal and baby showers, christenings or baby-namings, birthday parties, wedding anniversaries, and teas.[29]

Events critical in the lives of individuals and reported in newspapers can sometimes be very dramatic — murder, suicide, housebreaking. The family members may be either victims or perpetrators, or related to either. Then there are fires, unusual illnesses, possibly some good fortune (winning a lottery). The publicity afforded by the newspaper ac-

29. Robert W. Janes, "A Technique for Describing Community Structure Through Newspaper Analysis," *Social Forces*, 37 (December 1958): 102–109.

counts may affect the status of the family in the community as well as relationships among its members. Hence the researcher may want to investigate not only the events leading up to the newspaper article, but also its consequences.

Janes has developed a technique for the analysis of newspaper articles:

1. A master listing of events was established in which each event was chronologically numbered.

2. The content of each event was abstracted and included in the master list.

3. The page and date of the newspaper were noted on the list.

4. A separate card was set up for each household for which any family member was reported as a participant in an event, and a separate card was made for each association. Each card was given a code number based on the page in the Illini City telephone directory where the family name or associational name would appear. If there was no telephone listing, the name was inserted on the page where it would have appeared if listed.

5. Each family card included notations on events in which family members participated, the type of events, the roles played by family members in the events and occasional information such as age, place of birth, educational and occupational history whenever this information was contained in newspaper items, and the address of the family.

6. Each associational card showed events involving the association, names of officers and members, if known, and code classification of the type of association based on its function.[30]

Several problems may be encountered in newspaper analysis. One problem is that assemblages and ceremonials tend to have their seasons, so that the researcher is frequently faced with glut or famine. The marriage rate may be low during Lent, high in June. Family reunions and visits by relatives will mushromm in July and August, then dwindle to nothing after Labor Day. A second source of difficulty is biased sampling. The assemblages of prominent families in the community are more likely to be reported than those of poor or isolated families. On the other hand, the critical events of disreputable families may be described in greater detail and with greater frequency than those of respected families in the community. Prominent families may make great efforts to keep their scandals out of the newspaper. Yet critical events in these families (such as murder) may be given unusually broad coverage.

A third problem is that kinds of kinship and family assemblages covered vary widely by community size. According to Janes, "the smaller the community, the greater the range of activities about members of the community reported,"[31] Moreover, much more detailed information

30. *Ibid.*, pp. 102–103.
31. *Ibid.*, p. 108.

about the family is likely to be given in small communities than in large ones. Obituary notices in smaller communities often describe in some detail the spatial distribution of the family as well as the social mobility of its members, and reports on weddings may provide some detail about the locations and occupations not only of the bridal couple and their parents, but those of attending relatives. While city papers seldom go into such detail, newspaper reports in general will often present enough background information so that the investigator gains familiarity with the families he is studying.

Unobtrusive Observations

In the study of the family, the use of unobtrusive observations has somewhat different implications than it might have in other areas of investigation. In studies of workers, the problems of unobtrusive measures depend on the extent to which the employees' activities on the job (regardless of their role in productivity) are open to scrutiny by an outsider. In the study of behavior in public places, the question is whether all behavior exhibited there is *ipso facto* public. In the study of political behavior, there is a question as to which aspects of political belief and activities are private and which are public. In contrast to these areas, the family is considered a private arena.

Various proposals have been made with regard to the use of unobtrusive observations of family behavior (such as decision-making). Suggestions have been made that (with the family's knowledge) various rooms in the house be wired with microphones or TV cameras so that researchers can determine what actually goes on. Other suggestions have included an observer who would keep the house under surveillance to determine entrance and departure times of household members and visitors.

Another sort of unobtrusive measure is the evocation of certain responses that are relevant to purposes other than those communicated to the respondent. For instance, the respondent and his family may be asked to come to a decision regarding a certain product, or to reach a consensus on some political issue, when in fact the investigator has little or no interest in the content of that decision, but is interested only in the procedure by which the family arrives at it.

The important question in the use of unobtrusive observations is whether the family actually has been asked to participate with full knowledge of the conditions. The argument has been made that people who interact never give full information on their motives and intentions. Society would be impossible if everyone had complete information about everyone else. It is the withholding of information that generates and directs interaction. This argument implies that the extent to which an investigator withholds information regarding the study is only a matter of degree, and therefore he is justified in withholding as much information as is necessary to pursue his research successfully. Under this interpretation, unobtrusive observation of family life is justifiable.

There is, however, another interpretation of the use of unobtrusive measures and observations. The code adopted in the report of the Nuremberg trials specifies:

> The voluntary consent of the human subject is absolutely essential. This means that the person involved should have legal capacity to give consent; should be so situated as to be able to exercise free power of choice, without intervention of any element of force, fraud, deceit, duress, over-reaching, or other ulterior form of constraint, or coercion; and should have sufficient knowledge and comprehension of the elements of the subject matter involved as to enable him to make an understanding and enlightened decision. This latter element requires that before the acceptance of an affirmative decision by the experimental subject, there should be made known to him as much of the nature, duration, and purpose of the experiment as will not invalidate the results; the method and means by which it is to be conducted; all inconveniences and hazards reasonably to be expected; and the effect upon his health or person which may possibly come from his participation in the experiment. The duty and responsibility for ascertaining the quality of consent rests upon each individual who initiates, directs or engages in the experiment. It is a personal duty and responsibility which may not be delegated to another with impunity.[32]

Participation

Most studies of family and kinship relations seem to focus upon children. Possibly the relationship between husband and wife is considered too intimate to provide the major focus of the investigation. The immediate reaction to a study of marriage is that it implies a discussion of sex behavior.[33] In some family studies the emphasis on children does provide the impetus for investigation. In others, however, this emphasis merely provides a basis for interaction between the investigator and family members. Common concerns of the investigator and respondent as parents are less threatening than their common concerns as married persons. By virtue of the adult status of the respondent and the investigator, the investigator is immediately a potential interloper in the marriage. John R. Seeley notes that:

32. *Trials of War Criminals Before the Nuermberg Military Tribunals* (Washington, D.C.: U.S. Government Printing Office) 1946-1949, Vol. 2, pp. 181-182.

33. This interpretation may be made by respondents even when only a few items involve sex. See, for example, F. Ivan Nye, "Field Research," in *Hanbook of Marriage and the Family*, ed. Harold T. Christensen (Chicago: Rand McNally, 1964), p. 269.

Given the cultural atmosphere of North America — or at least of middle-class North America — the only scheme which would have any chancè of deeply involving parents, or adults generally, was a scheme which at least ostensibly addressed itself to children. A scheme addressed ostensibly to adults would, it was thought, arouse all the defensive anxieties organized to protect, for the adult individual, the extremely important value implied in such terms as "adequacy," "independence," "self-sufficiency." A scheme ostensibly addressed to children, on the other hand, would appeal precisely to this value, would permit direct dealing with the children, and would in the course of its unfolding inevitably involve the relevant adults, but with a minimum of initial resistance.[34]

The role of the investigator as a participant in his respondent-family life cannot, however, be sustained on a manipulative basis. Even in the course of an interview, the investigator comes to recognize his respondent (especially in family studies) as a human being like himself, with foibles, fears, ideals, and aspirations for himself and his children. Unlike the anthropologist, who must guard against going native, the sociologist is a member of the culture he is studying. The respondents are frequently people he would like to have as his friends, and indeed in an extended study such friendships can hardly be avoided. "People do not — indeed cannot — tell some things except in a context of mutual warmth and support."[35] Yet this relationship may be maintained with full knowledge by the subject that the investigator is an observer trying to understand some things about family life and therefore requires this information. The combination of friend and observer makes the investigator simultaneously a stranger and yet a person to be trusted.

Frequently the researcher relies upon a small and probably unrepresentative sample to gain his major insights into the family phenomenon he is investigating. Sometimes this sample provides the data during the exploratory phases of the investigation, when the observer is trying to specify questions about the phenomenon. At other times he may retain this sample for repeated questioning about topics that puzzle him. In his Oxford study, John M. Mogey reported:

> In each region a small panel of informants was built up outside the random interviewing program: each person provided information of a similar kind to that produced in a typical "free" interview and in addition was called upon very frequently for observations on specific points as they arose. These were not necessarily experts but were individuals whom we got to know exceptionally well and whose opinions we could judge against a rich fund of background material which they themselves had provided and against many informal tests to which they were exposed. In such "check" interviews,

34. John R. Seeley, R. Alexander Sim, and Elizabeth W. Loosley, *Crestwood Heights* (New York: Basic Books, 1956), p. 493.
35. *Ibid.*, p. 440.

problems of personality, group attachments, situational analysis, and cultural milieu could be overtly distinguished.[36]

The close acquaintanceship (and sometimes friendship) developed in fieldwork can be illustrated by the decision of Oscar Lewis to study intensively the family of Jesús Sánchez. Lewis interviewed the Sánchez family in the course of gathering data from a sample of families living in a Mexican slum. He reports that he gathered the required data from the Sánchez family after four interviews, but that he continued to stop frequently at the Sánchez house to chat casually with the members of the family, "all of whom were friendly and offered useful information on *vecindad* life." As he got to know the family members intimately, he "became aware that this single family seemed to illustrate many of the social and psychological problems of lower-class Mexican life." At this point, Lewis decided to study the family in depth.[37]

The reliance upon a small and perhaps unrepresentative sample to gain insights into family life suggests that participation with families to be investigared may precede the development of a clearly defined hierarchy of questions. Participation may then be used by the investigator to refine his questioning and to draw upon the folk models of family life and the subjects' perceptions of problems faced in their families.

Linguistics: Kinship Terminology

Traditionally, linguistic problems associated with kinship have focused upon what relatives call one another and the terms they use in referring to each other. In describing relationships between kin, the terms they use in talking with one another are particularly useful. Families generally have traditions about calling relatives by name or by kin term (e.g., Uncle Bill, Auntie, Grandma). Often the older person or the one with higher status will inform a younger relative what to call him. If that term is agreeable to the younger relative, the terms of address in that relationship are established. If not, however, some compromise must be reached. The nature of this compromise may be (*a*) that the individual will not call his relative by any name or kin term, but will use an introductory phrase or word to catch his attention (e.g., "My goodness!" "Say!" "Hey!"), (*b*) choose a nickname that has been attached to the relative by a small child, or (*c*) negotiate a mutually agreeable name.[38]

36. John M. Mogey, *Family and Neighborhood* (New York: Oxford University Press, 1956), p. 38.

37. Oscar Lewis, *The Children of Sánchez* (New York: Vintage Books, Random House, 1961), p. xix.

38. Brown has an extensive discussion on the relationship between the avoidance of terms of address and ambiguity of the relative status of the speaker and the person

In studies of kinship two aspects of terms of address may provide useful data: (1) the relationship between the use of kin terms and the character of the relationship between relatives, and (2) the misapplication of kin terms, so that an aunt, for instance, is called "mother."

Several studies of American kinship illustrate the usefulness of investigating the relationship between the use of kin terms of address and the character of the relationship. A study of college students revealed that strong personal affect was associated with a tendency to dispense with kin terms of address.[39] Another college sample indicated that "with the exception of an intensely negative category for females, there tends to be a positive relationship between liking and addressing uncles and aunts by their first names."[40] Presumably personal sentiment has greater valence in interaction than does kinship in most middle-class families. On the other hand, investigators have reported that in nuclear families, members resort to formal kinship terminology in periods of stress. Although college women usually call their mothers "mom" in casual conversation, in periods of conflict they often resort to "mother."[41] In these situations the kinship status may be used to reprimand relatives or to avoid punishment. My study of lower-class kinship in Illinois, however, revealed that calling an aunt or uncle or in-law by his or her first name may indicate a feeling of distance between the speaker and the relative.[42] Lower-class persons may instead use the kin terms in addressing relatives to whom they feel particularly close. The use of kin terms of address by lower-class women may be analogous to the way middle-class girls use these terms to affirm a relationship at times of conflict with their parents. The use of kin terms may therefore symbolize the need for a recognition of the unity of the kin group when stress occurs. The lower-class family group (often characterized as the matrifocal family) is particularly unstable.

The misuse of kin terms can be equally revealing of the quality of relationships among kin. One study of Negro women has shown that when both grandmothers are known to ego, she tends to call the maternal grandmother "mother" and the paternal grandmother by the appropriate kin term. However, when ego has known only the maternal grandmother, she calls her "grandmother." The use of kinship termi-

addressed. See Roger Brown, *Social Psychology*(New York: Free Press, Macmillan, 1965).

39. David M. Schneider and George C. Homans, "Kinship Terminology and the American Kinship System," *American Anthropologist*, 57 (1955): 1194–1208.

40. Warren O. Hagstrom and Jeffrey K. Hadden, "Sentiment and Kinship Terminology in American Society," *Journal of Marriage and the Family*, 27 (August 1964): 330.

41. Lionell S. Lewis, "Kinship Terminology for the American Parent," *American Anthropologist,* 65 (June 1963): 649–52.

42. Bernard Farber, "Kinship Terminology in Midwestern Families" (unpublished paper).

nology to bring a relative closer genealogically may denote a special relationship. When this genealogical translocation occurs, the kin term refers only to the particular individual and not to a class of relatives. It confers an honorary kinship status (or sometimes a dishonorable one) upon the relative, and does not affect the rights and obligations normally associated with that status. After all, ego is aware that disavowing an individual as kin or bringing him closer genealogically does not really change the genealogical tie. It is the lack of fit between real and terminological kinship status that symbolizes the special relationship that exists. Sentiment seems to use kinship terms to relocate people in genealogical space rather than to change the organization of kinship statuses themselves.

Allied to kinship terminology is the choice of names. What is the source of names given to children? In her study of naming patterns among middle-class women, Alice Rossi found that the practice of naming boys after paternal relatives and girls after maternal relatives is declining.[43] She has suggested that this is indicative of a trend away from sex differentiation in American society. Boys are no longer considered to belong to the father's family and girls to the mother's as they used to be.[44] Other elements in naming can also be investigated: To what extent do women use their maiden names as middle names? Do families remember family heroes by naming many of his relatives after him? Are there trends in giving the names of celebrities to children? What is the significance of the use of nicknames in the assignment of special statuses in the family or kinship group?

Strategies

INTERVIEWING HUSBANDS AND WIVES

One of the difficulties in interviewing husbands and wives is the management of the logistics of minimizing the amount of communication between them so that their answers are independent. There are several ways of handling this situation. One of them is described by Young and Willmott:

> We would have preferred to see husband and wife separately, but we found it in practice impossible to do this. What we were able to do was to call in the day times and, if the wife was at home and willing to be interviewed, interview her then, calling back to see her husband, usually in her presence also, one evening. . . . Such an approach requires flexibility in conducting the

43. Alice Rossi, "Naming Children in Middle-Class Families," *American Sociological Review,* 30 (1965): 499–513.
44. See Farber, "Kinship Terminology."

interview. Some questions were specifically addressed to the wife or to the husband, while others we felt could be answered by either or both.[45]

Another way of handling interviews with husbands and wives is for two interviewers to visit the family at an appointed time. One interviewer can then meet with the husband while the other interviews the wife. This procedure prevents discussion of responses by husband and wife, as is likely to occur when one of them is interviewed earlier than the other. By piecing together the separate interviews of husband and wife, the case analysist can form his own interpretation. Each may be willing to disclose different aspects of their family life. Sometimes when the home is not large enough for the husband and wife to be interviewed beyond earshot of each other, one of them (usually the husband) can be interviewed in a nearby bar or restaurant. Sometimes one can be interviewed in the home while the other is seen simultaneously at the investigator's office.

OBSERVATION IN THE HOME

Robert O. Blood has also reported on the use of observational techniques in family research. He was concerned with the development of procedures to enable observers to participate actively in the family, and has reported on problems in the recruitment of objects, defining the observer's role, sampling of behavior, recording methods, and the impact of the observer on interaction.[46]

Blood encountered some resistance to the presence of an observer in the home for a two-hour period once a week for three weeks. Most of the women responded negatively to having a "stranger" in the house. However, the more children there were in the household, the more agreeable most of the women were to the presence of an observer. Apparently the observer seemed less intrusive under these conditions.

Various kinds of roles have been suggested for observers in the family. Charlotte Buhler played the role of the mother's helper.[47] The family defined her as the "maiden aunt," and included her in much of the family interaction. As much as half the children's conversations were directed toward her. Other suggested roles have included public health nurse, graduate student rooming with the family, and cleaning lady.

In the Blood study, the observers played the roles of guests on their first visit with each family, and during succeeding visits shifted to more explicit observer roles. The observers gathered their data in the eve-

45. Young and Willmott, *Family and Kinship in East London,* p. 207.
46. Robert O. Blood, "III. The Use of Observational Methods in Family Research," *Journal of Marriage and the Family,* 20 (February 1958): 47–52.
47. Charlotte Buhler, *The Child and His Family,* (London: Routledge & Kegan Paul, 1940).

nings, after the father came home from work. They noted that in the course of the evening the family members were seldom in the same room. Their greatest problem was observing simultaneous but separate activities. Although not all families ate dinner together, the majority did so. Dinnertime therefore provided for many families the single event in which all of them participated.[48] Blood reported that note-taking during the course of the evening presented few problems. In fact, this activity by the observer served to reinforce his role as defined by the family members. Although Blood did not use tape recordings, the families in his sample would not have objected to them. The impact of the observers on family interaction seemed to decline as time went on. The observer tended to become part of the scenery. Generally the families reported that they had "forgotten" the observer's presence. Similar treatment of the observer as a nonperson appears in many reports of observers in schools.

PSYCHOLOGICAL ECOLOGY TECHNIQUES

Closely allied to the observational techniques suggested by Blood are the techniques of psychological ecology developed by Roger Barker and Herbert Wright,[49] who followed children about during the course of a day. Their study was concerned with the kinds of interaction and the psychological environments impinging upon the individual in his daily life, and the relationships between them.

Barker and Wright found that in the midwestern city they studied, people spent five times as much of their time in family settings as in community settings. There was a "regular decline from infancy to adolescence in the temporal dominance of the family, and the return to the family in adulthood and old age." Their data indicated "that males, white citizens, and members of Group I [high social class], respectively, spent more time in community settings and less time in family settings than females, Negro citizens, and members of social Groups II and III."[50]

The Interviewer as Craftsman

Interviewing has long been considered unskilled dirty work in empirical research. The individual ethnographer who both develops his interviewing procedure and carries out lengthy field observations has looked with disdain upon the survey interviewer. Organizations carrying on survey research have perpetuated the assembly-line conception of

48. See James H. S. Bossard, *Sociology of Child Development* (New York: Harper, 1954), chap. 8, "Family Table Talk."
49. Roger G. Barker and Herbert F. Wright, *The Midwest and Its Children* (Evanston: Row, Peterson, 1954).
50. *Ibid.*, pp. 98–99.

interviewing by giving interviewers low pay, irregular work, and little voice in the design or interpretation of research. Somehow the interviewer is supposed to obtain reliable and complete data without any special competence, pride in his work, or apprenticeship training. Some guidelines on the training, duties, and supervision of journeyman interviewers in family research are badly needed. Although the suggestions I have to offer are focused on the training and supervision of employed interviewers, most of them may be applied also by the investigator who does his own interviewing. His role as investigator may be regarded as distinct from his role as interviewer.

INTERVIEWER TRAINING

In organizing a research project requiring several interviewers, the investigator is immediately struck by the ease with which some experienced interviewers handle a questionnaire. These interviewers extract data from respondents sometimes in spite of awkward wording and chaotic organization of questions. Using short phrases, voice intonations, pauses, brief comments, and other techniques of creating transitions and smoothing over absurdities, the experienced interviewer can make the difference between a study with definitive results and one with mediocre findings. The training of interviewers seems of crucial importance to the success of the study.

When I was preparing interviewers for my studies of kinship and families with retarded children, I found it helpful to organize the training in several phases. These phases can probably be built into interviewer training more readily in a family study than in investigations dealing with deviance or large-scale organization. The first phase is the mastery of technical aspect of the study. The interviewer in a kinship study who cannot prepare a rudimentary genealogical chart is at a loss in the discussion of ways in which kin are related to one another. He must also be aware of basic concepts related to the study in order to master the mechanics of the interview. Accordingly, in studies of kinship the interviewers should be encouraged to prepare their own genealogies and those of their friends. They can then ask questions about these genealogies and thus learn the rudiments of the study of kinship.

The second phase concerns the use of interview forms and guides. The novice interviewer is requested to review the forms and the guides pertaining to special instructions. These instructions may point out the significance of some questions and may clarify those that can be interpreted in several ways. The interviewers are then encouraged (and paid) to interview close friends and their families. If the interviewer can try out the forms with people who will not be a threat to him, he can experiment in a number of ways. He does not need to fear making mistakes. Usually a half dozen of these interviews are sufficient.

In the next phase, the several interviewers are brought together to ask questions and to interview one another. Tape recorders are used in this phase, so that the interviewers can obtain feedback on their performances. As a final examination in this phase, the interviewers are asked to interview the supervisor, who takes the role of a reluctant and often hostile interviewee who tries to control the situation. Interviewers will seldom encounter such a difficult respondent in the field.

Following the intramural practice in interviewing, the novice interviewers are then assigned respondents with whom they are not familiar. Unknown to them, these respondents are paid to take part in the interviewer training. In order to be consistent, the respondents generally answer questions truthfully and report the quality of the performance to the supervisor. At this point, the novices who have been having difficulty in using the questionnaire or in functioning in an interview situation are weeded out. The criticisms of the training respondents are used to correct specific problems. Tape recorders are used whenever possible.

This training procedure generally takes about two or three weeks and is an expensive procedure. It is usually worth the cost, however, for the quality of the information obtained by interviewers who have undergone this training is generally high. In addition, the interviewers themselves have undergone a series of dramatic episodes that define interviewing to them as a craft rather than as an unskilled task.

SUPERVISION

The supervisor of fieldwork performs a number of duties. First, he is responsible for the completion of interviews. This responsibility requires him to maintain a file of persons in the sampling frame and a detailed account, completed by the interviewers, of their attempts at obtaining interviews. Generally three to five visits are made by the interviewers before a case may be classified as unobtainable. In the Illinois study of lower-class kinship, interviewers made as many as ten or fifteen visits to become acquainted with the respondents and to describe the purpose of the study casually. In some instances these efforts resulted in the respondents' participation; in others, sufficient information was gathered to characterize the nonrespondents. In a sense, some of the nonrespondents actually took part in the study.

A second duty of the field director is to make certain that all of the interviewers are maintaining their rate of work. Without some urging, a small proportion of interviewers may delay going into the field. This delay not only may impede the progress of the research, but may cause the interviewers to forget some of the special instructions and techniques required in the particular study.

The supervisor can maintain quality control in the interviews by several means. One procedure is to use either a tape recorder or a second interviewer to determine what went on in the interview itself. The information from this independent source can be compared with the interviewer's reports. A second procedure is to review the interviewer's reports to determine how complete and internally consistent they are. For instance, in the Illinois kinship study some of the interviewers consistently omitted large portions of the respondents' reports of their relatives' work histories. The interviewers were then required to return to the respondents to fill in the missing information. A third method of maintaining quality control is to have a follow-up interview by the supervisor. The follow-up can be used to ascertain whether the respondents were actually interviewed and whether certain portions of their interviews were recorded accurately. Still another procedure is to have the interviewers keep logs and to report their impressions about each family. These logs and impressions can contain special information that might be helpful in the interpretation. The interviewers can also assess the quality of the information obtained in the interview.

Finally, the supervision of the interviewers might entail closing-out interviews. In these interviews, the investigator himself interviews the members of his staff. Here he gains insight into the private hunches of the interviewers, the particular biases they hold, their perception of the interpretation made by the respondents, and their frank evalutaion of the quality of the data. The criticisms made by the interviewers may be helpful in divising procedures for analysis of data. The limitations seen by the interviewers, as well as their own private conceptions of the study, provide a basis for evaluating the quality of the supervision itself.

The limited perspective of each interviewer should not be interpreted as a realistic evaluation of the total project. Only the investigator himself has this general perspective. Yet the logs kept during the fieldwork and the closing-out interviews afterward, by reinforcing the conception of interviewing as a craft, can help both the interviewers and the project director in the collection and interpretation of significant data.

Studying a College

This paper assumes a rather rare person in research on education — someone so aware of the need for independence, so alert to the possibility of bias that he chooses to study a college campus where he does not teach or study. He is a stranger to the college, without obligations; if his research is to be financed by funds other than his own, they will be secured from federal or foundation sources.

His approach is holistic in the sense that he wants to discover and report as much of the students' college experience as he can, not some part of it.[1] Having read the sociological literature on colleges and a good many novels and journalistic accounts as well, he has quite a few notions about what college is like, but regards these as hypotheses that will guide, but not limit, his efforts. He gathers data on both students and nonstudents — faculty, administrators, anyone connected with the school who may affect students' lives. He also collects documents, including university records and publications, student newspapers, yearbooks, and posters. He uses questionnaires when they are appropriate (usually at the end of the study), but participant observation and interviewing are his primary means of gathering data.

His study will focus on students, not as administrators or professors see them, but as nearly as possible as they see themselves. As a sociologist, our researcher has his own vision, and his report will be a sociologist's view of what college students know.[2] But during the fieldwork he

1. For a discussion on this point, see Robert S. Weiss, "Alternative Approaches in the Study of Complex Situations," *Human Organization,* 25 (Fall 1966): 198–206, and "Issues in Holistic Research" in *Institutions and the Person,* ed. Howard S. Becker *et al.* (Chicago: Aldine, 1968), pp. 342–50.

2. Severyn Bruyn, *The Human Perspective in Sociology* (Englewood Cliffs, N.J.: Prentice-Hall, 1966).

will participate with students and see things, insofar as he can, through their eyes.

Ethically, this paper assumes a researcher whose primary goal is the publication of basic research, but who plans to keep his data and tentative findings to himself during his research in order to minimize observed-caused change. He feels obligated to conceal when he can the identity of individuals and of groups in his final report, and to deal with those he studies in a way that will enhance rather than damage his colleagues' efforts to conduct similar studies. In the pages that follow I rely chiefly on my experience in studying undergraduates at the University of Kansas.[3]

Access

Successful access to any organization or group involves foreknowledge of its structure and distribution of power. Colleges are hierarchically organized. A small group of administrators with broad powers sits at the top. A larger group, the faculty, has powers now largely confined to the academic sphere but nevertheless retains some interest in nonacademic matters. At the bottom of the hierarchy are the students. They may be a highly organized group with powerful leaders of their own, numerous organizations, and a communications system superior to that of all but the smallest faculty.

THE RESEARCH BARGAIN

During the *period of bargaining* in which the researcher seeks permission to make the study, it will pay to take a cynical view of the enmities possible in such a three-level organization. Formal permission to study the college must come from the administration, but the faculty should also be informed, especially members of social science departments, who might regard the study as an intrusion on their territory. Neglecting to make a research bargain with the students themselves may seriously jeopardize the study.

Successful approaches to each group combine authority with respect in a mixture suited to the status of the group in relation to the researcher's. When the research group has several members, it may find it useful to pretend to a hierarchical structure it may not possess and give the job of dealing with the administration to its senior member.

The researcher wants permission to go anywhere, talk to anyone, examine all documents, and publish his findings without interference. Securing such a free hand is not easy. It may take months for researcher

3. Howard S. Becker, Blanche Geer, and Everett C. Hughes, *Making the Grade* (New York: Wiley, 1968).

and administrator to develop sufficient trust in each other to conclude a bargain. The approach to the administration should be authoritative. It would be advisable to take along books or journal articles done by the method to be used; the researcher's own reprints can do no harm. The administrator should know that the researcher is not embarking on a fishing expedition, that a number of experienced social scientists have already made researches of this kind. It should be made clear that the researcher will not study only those things that concern or alarm the administration, and that he will feel free to publish materials that do not flatter the college or advance its interests. The fieldworker will be well advised to keep careful notes on the bargain as it progresses.

The way the results will be published should be specified. Researchers may promise to show completed manuscript to interested members of the administration, faculty, and students before publication, but will not permit access to materials that would identify individuals.

Although their power is presently threatened by student uprisings around the country, college administrators are yet powerful enough in their own sphere to make the research bargain difficult. Complacent ones who feel they understand students must be persuaded that perhaps they don't. Those who fear student riots may be easier to persuade, since the utility of such a study will seem apparent. The scientist-administrator may be prejudiced against qualitative research; he must be provided with examples of such work.

In colleges of high prestige, the researcher may be hampered in his negotiations because the administrators cannot imagine that anything harmful to the college could be discovered. In this case, it is up to the researcher to explain the kinds of things that often turn up — homosexuality, for example, or poor teaching. The administrator can sometimes be drawn into a scientific partnership. By treating him as a broad-minded and sophisticated academic, one gradually works him around to a realization that although the study may be threatening, he and his college are big enough to take it. It may seem unnecessary to prepare administrators for the worst in this fashion, but it prepares the ground for the shock they may get when they see the manuscript at the end of a study. Administrators may attempt to prevent publication or feel that the college has been exploited and similar research should not be authorized. However, the administrator who has committed himself to a generous research bargain is more likely to be proud of the results.

During the bargaining sessions the administrator may attempt to direct the researcher's attention to the sort of problem *he* wants solved. The researcher has to tread carefully here. His attention may be so directed to the administrator's problems that he loses the open mind with which he wished to approach a new study. This may be exacerbated by the fact that so much of the literature about colleges has been written by administrators or faculty who see the college and the students within the framework of their problems.

If he can maintain his open mind, the researcher will do himself a favor by making clear to the administration that the college may look radically different when studied from the standpoint of the students, and that problems students perceive will take precedence in the study. Many administrators, openly or secretly afraid of students, may welcome the researcher as a potential spy who will warn of unrest. It must be an explicit part of the bargain that the researcher will not inform the administration of anything he sees and will maintain silence during the study about the students' concerns and activities, no matter how disruptive they might be.[4]

We shock administrators when we say that we will not inform on students. They cannot believe that any right-thinking adult would not do so. They can also be concerned about failure to tell them about individual students in trouble—contemplating suicide, for instance.[5] The protective paternalism of those in authority seems to them a perspective the researcher must share. Occasionally, the administrator will give the researcher damaging inside information and expect an exchange. To counteract this, the researcher can openly interview the administrator himself so that he perceives that he and his administration are part of the study and not in the position of controlling sponsor.

While conversations go on with the administration, the researcher will want to pay courtesy calls on social scientists on the faculty, particularly those who have made studies of students. There may be quite a number of these. Some use the students in their classes as guinea pigs; others work on institutional self-studies. Such people will feel less threatened if the researcher points out that a study made by outsiders will necessarily differ from theirs and therefore will not compete with them.

A more touchy problem arises if social scientists on the faculty try to arrange an exchange of data with the researcher. The colleague relationship proffered suggests that each can trust the other not to use data in ways that may damage individuals or the study, but no matter how strongly a faculty researcher puts his case, to let him see raw data will violate the promise of individual anonymity that is part of the research bargain. Furthermore, the faculty will be under observation during the study, and exchange of data would violate a cardinal rule: Avoid feedback while research continues.

The researcher's relationship with the faculty will not take the same

4. Everett C. Hughes, "The Relation of the Individual to General Sociology," *Sociology and Social Research,* 41 (March–April 1957): 251–56.
5. Lewis Yablonsky, "On Crime, Violence, LSD, and Legal Immunity for Sociologists," *American Sociologist,* 3 (May 1968): 148–49.

form as his relationship with administrators. Individual faculty members will recognize that they do not have the authority to grant favors to the researcher. The researcher is not asking their permission to do the study; he has obtained permission from the administration. Those who understand holistic field studies realize that the faculty itself, although not the primary focus of the study, will be observed, and it may worry them. Structurally, they stand between two sources of power—the administration and the students. They know that if you say you are going to follow students around wherever they go, it means you will be attending classes. You could report derogatory information to colleagues or administrators.

Here the researcher's approach can be similar to that taken with the administration. You, the researcher, should treat the faculty member as an understanding human being and sophisticated scholar who will provide information and allow you to observe his teaching because he believes that such studies may prove informative if not helpful. The question of ethics has to be explored during this quasi bargaining with faculty members. They must be assured that their identity will be protected in final drafts and that the researcher will not be a talebearer. The best way to do this is to explain the poor results that follow from feedback. Education of faculty members by repeated conversations with them should be a part of the researcher's plan of work. In a sense, gaining access or making a research bargain is a continuing process that does not end until the study is published.

To complete the research bargain, the researcher must approach student leaders. Faculty members or administrators may lead the researcher astray at this point by suggesting that elected student leaders are not powerful or important on campus. But the observer must discover that for himself; common sense dictates that a bargain be made with them, if only to obtain the access necessary to estimate their importance. If, as is so often the case, student leaders feel themselves in opposition to the administration, sponsorship or initial introductions through the administration may be less than useful. The researcher should ask for an interview with the chief student leaders—the president of the student body and of any dissident groups.

Leaders should be accorded the same respect given administrators and faculty. They can, after all, make or break the study by opening or closing doors for the researcher. We found that the highest level of student leaders saw our study as potentially useful even though it might also be a threat. The leader may be in a difficult position, burdened by responsibilities that cannot be discussed with his fellow students or with members of the administration. He may find discussing his problems with a researcher helpful, but must assure himself of complete protection from exposure by taking steps to check the researcher's reliability. For example, the student leader can discover from other students how the researcher spends his time. He can check with the administration and faculty to discover what sort of bargain was made with them. If he is a strong leader, there is no doubt that he will engage in such activities. If the researcher survives each check, a good relationship may develop.

It must be made clear to student leaders from the outset that the researcher is not interested only in the activities of the best-known students. A leader may know so much about the college and how it works that he sees himself as the only informant the researcher will need. As with administrators, tact must come into play. Continuing education by the researcher must emphasize that a good study can result only from a wide variety of informants.

The virtues of continuing education of authorities was well understood by one of the student leaders in our study, who did what he called "touching base" as frequently as possible. He went from one administrator to another for an informal chat to keep them informed and interested in student problems. A good research bargain entails touching base on the part of the researcher. His list of bases might include the administrator who is most responsible for his access, interested faculty members, and a number of student leaders.

Campuses where some degree of power is shared with the administration by faculty and students or where students are in revolt must be approached differently from campuses where students neither have nor seek such power. My feeling now is that the first approach might be to radical student leaders. They can identify leaders of conservative groups, and also provide introductions to faculty leaders and administrators in a chain of quasi sponsors from bottom to top.

BEGINNING THE STUDY PROPER

Participant observation has been most used to study social process in relatively small face-to-face groups. When the observer first arrives on a large campus, he may not know how to begin. In our study, we knew that three full-time researchers could not observe all the students. Selection would be necessary, but how to select? The problem began to solve itself (as many do, I suspect) as we took a series of steps suggested by our methods, concepts, and certain practical features of a university and its sociological calendar.

A research method forces choices for the researcher in ways so obvious he is often unaware of them. The survey man must begin by amassing the kind of data he can quantify, the participant observer by finding people to participate with and observe.[6] Concept also guides

6. Blanche Geer, "First Days in the Field," in *Sociologists at Work,* ed. Phillip E. Hammond (New York: Basic Books, 1964), pp. 322–44.

initial action. As symbolic interactionists interested primarily in collective rather than individual action, we looked for people interacting in groups and groups interacting with each other.

Finding groups is superficially a matter of method — you go to places where they are — but concept enters even here. As interactionists, we had no hard-and-fast concept of groups. For us the term includes episodic gatherings and planned ones, voluntary and involuntary associations, fleeting aggregations or patterns that arise out of individual habit, chance meetings and organizations. Under this broad definition, finding a group usually begins with finding an individual; to accompany him is to participate in his encounters and learn of his affiliations.

We had met a number of entering freshmen during the summer orientation program and hoped to find them again in September. But we did not know where they lived on campus; the student directory would not be published until late October. Students are not workers who can be found in the same place daily; they scatter over the campus to classes and meetings on schedules unrepeated for a week or more. Very few students have their own telephones; phones in student housing are in almost constant use and message-taking is at best uncertain. Looking up all the freshmen we had met during orientation periods — a sensible first move — was impractical. We knew that freshman women were housed together and found some of our previous informants by checking dormitory lists. But the men had scattered over the campus in co-ops, scholarship halls, fraternities, and mixed-class dormitories. A few of our orientation acquaintances could lead us to others, but most freshman women were looking for people too. Abandoning the attempt to collect data on the initial days of college by reinterviewing preview acquaintances, we took note of an important feature of the university environment — its calendar.

The sociological calendar of an institution provides the researcher with certain imperatives. In a university, classes and meetings continue throughout the year and need not be seen on any particular day, but certain events — orientation week and fraternity rush, for example — take place at the beginning of school and will not be repeated for twelve months. We gave these priority.

Orientation-week events were easy to observe; we simply went to convocation and parking-lot dances. Rush was another matter. While dormitories are open to visitors, fraternities are not. The university administration does not give access to houses owned and run by students. Clearly, we needed sponsorship from fraternity leaders. During the summer previews, we had met the incoming student body president and explained the study to him. He had introduced us to several other leaders, including the president of the Interfraternity Council. Perhaps someone in the administration could tell us how to find him? One could and did. The IFC president, briefed on us by the student body president, suggested three fraternity men to call and provided phone numbers. One observer (male) chose a house described as important on campus; a second male observer chose a less important house; the third observer, female, did not attend rush, since fraternity officers felt her presence might prove a handicap in signing pledges, but received cordial invitations to come after rush.

Impressed by fraternity officers with the importance of living groups in directing freshmen into other campus organizations and orienting them to college life, we began to visit other types of housing. To some extent our strategy shifted at this point. We wanted to know if fraternities were as important as they thought, and how other living groups (co-ops, dormitories, scholarship halls, and rooming houses) differed from them. Throughout the study each observer returned to several living groups regularly. We visited students in their rooms, met their friends, invited ourselves to their classes, went along to meetings and out to beer joints, where we met more students. Soon the students were moving us about campus as easily as they moved themselves. We learned to approach still other groups in the ways students used themselves in making such approaches.

Members of most groups on campus solved the problem of finding each other during the day by having a hangout near their classrooms. We learned that business students had a snack bar in their classroom building; drama students had a lounge off the theater; many students living off campus in rooming houses maintained communications by eating in the Student Union cafeteria. These places became additional observing posts for us, so that our research design as developed in the field included a combination of strategies. We followed some individuals and some organizations over time; we became habitués of certain gathering places, and participants in the successive events of the college calendar.

Questions

We can distinguish three kinds of questions — orienting, participating, and testing. *Orienting questions* are most used at the beginning of a study. They are similar to the questions any newcomer asks in order to learn the rules of his new environment. *Participating questions* are appropriate when the observer has become an insider; he has been around long enough to be trusted and people are aware he knows what is going on. The observer uses *testing questions* when he has a hypothesis or partly formed model to check.[7] At any stage of the study all three

7. On models, see Howard S. Becker and Blanche Geer, "Participant Observation: The Analysis of Qualitative Field Data," in *Human Organization Research,* ed. Richard Adams and Jack J. Preiss (Homewood, Ill.: Dorsey Press, 1960), pp. 267–89.

types of questioning may be going on at once as the observer orients himself to one group, participates as an insider in another, and tests hypotheses about a third. Orienting questions nevertheless cluster at the beginning of a study, participating questions in the middle, and testing ones at the end.

During the process of making the research bargain and obtaining access, many sorts of orienting questions fit naturally into the observer's role as a stranger on campus. Getting an answer to such a simple question as "Where is the Administration Building?" and acting on the information serve to draw in his mind a topographical map of the campus which he can transfer to paper in his field notes. Initial meetings with student leaders may take place in the Student Union or some other leisure-time gathering place. Questions about the sorts of students to be found there and the uses of the building make it possible to draw a sociological map of the campus. Questions about when to meet provide natural opportunities to ask for information on students' patterns of communication and daily schedules.

It was by this means that we first learned to go to the basement of the Administration Building when we wanted to find a student leader enrolled in the College of Liberal Arts. The corridor was convenient to the college classroom. It had a post office and a snack bar, with tables for eating and studying. Leaders customarily met at one of the entrances when they wanted to see each other during the day, and suggested we do the same. Practically all the information we obtained from our initial questioning made finding students easier; conceptually, it enabled us to begin to map the campus communications system.

On first meetings with students, further orienting questions — "Where are you from?" — opened the way to brief biographies, yet remained within the bounds of American custom regarding initial encounters. If the self-orienting questions proper to a stranger on campus gave us much information, both practical and sociological, it also established us in comfortable information-seeking roles that could continue as the study proceeded.

As in everyday life, a time comes when the observer can no longer pretend to be a stranger, and his style of questioning must change. He wants to know how things work and what they mean. How is a campus organization run, for example, elections managed, or classes taught? He learns about these processes by being present as they occur and asking students to explain to him what happens or to check his interpretations.

One of our observers attended Student Council meetings over a period of two years, interviewed leaders of both parties, received official minutes, and followed stories on politics in the campus paper. Before the end of this period of observation, she had become an insider who sometimes knew more about what was happening or would happen at a meeting than some of the student politicians themselves, since they were sure only of the plans of their own party. At this stage participating questions may take the form of an extended interpretive discussion of events with students trying to control them. Personal goals, political strategies, and evaluations of others and self flow easily when the observer has been present at meetings and the leader knows he is well informed.

As an insider the observer may ask very few questions in the strict sense of the word. An innocuous statement — "Your party seems to be doing pretty well in the election," for example — will often set off a one-sided "discussion" of several hours. The observer participates largely by encouraging grunts, a raised eyebrow of doubt, or the laughter of agreement. Responses of this kind keep a person talking but do not redirect him. They are the tools of the interviewer's trade, but the observer's participant status makes them easy and appropriate to use.[8]

Testing questions take many forms, each calculated to confirm or negate some relatively well-developed hypothesis. One example comes immediately to mind: Several student leaders had described to us a prestige hierarchy among fraternities, but we argued among ourselves as to how widespread the notion was on campus. Did only student leaders or members of prestige houses share it? Did everyone assign houses the same ranks? To test the hypothesis that prompted these questions, each of the three observers undertook to ask each student he encountered to rank the houses as he saw their prestige and as he thought others saw it.[9] The answers revealed a complex situation, as we shall see in a moment.

Events

The fieldworker on a college campus is usually in luck with regard to the sociological calendar. He can obtain copies of the schedule of yearly events. The college newspaper will alert him to many of the meetings to be held by student organizations as well as those of the entire community. Many campus organizations have a number of students who make posters and put them up in strategic places around the campus announcing coming events.

The observer soon finds that periods of intense preparation occur before the major events in both academic and nonacademic spheres. He schedules his observing to make the best use he can of such periods.

8. Howard S. Becker and Blanche Geer, "Participant Observation and Interviewing: A Comparison," *Human Organization,* 16 (Fall 1957): 28–33.
9. Becker, Geer, and Hughes, *Making the Grade,* p.53.

The printed calendar of the college year tells when midterm and final examinations occur. Students are less easy to talk to during these periods, but groups of students can often be found in beer joints and other hangouts who will talk about how they are preparing for their exams and how difficult they will be. He can at this time discover when grades will be given out—another time when he will want to emphasize the collection of data on academic matters.

Before major events involving large numbers of students and alumni, the observer will find that students form numerous committees. A visit to the officers of the organizations involved will provide the names of committee chairmen and the places and times at which their groups will meet. These meetings can provide excellent information on many aspects of student interaction. Large organizations announce job interviews for candidates. Sitting in on these sessions can be particularly revealing of the criteria students use to evaluate each other. Some organizations, of course, meet regularly throughout the year; others have secretaries who will mail minutes of the meetings.

Several times during the academic year heavy schedules in a campus organization coincide with peak academic activity. Political elections, for instance, may overlap term-paper time. Being on campus and talking to students caught in such conflicts may be particularly revealing. I remember especially a student who told me about turning in a poor term paper to a professor he particularly respected. The student was an officer of a new political party, anxious to get many people to the polls in an upcoming election. He felt that his only mature course of action was to fulfill his obligation to the party and take a poor grade in the course. The decision might have gone the other way had his other grades that semester been low.

Students not only feel forced to make choices between academic and political responsibilities, but also find their time so taken up with one or both of them that personal relationships (they may be pinned, engaged, or married, for example) are threatened. As they decide what has priority, their definitions of the situation—what college means to them— emerge, and the observer in on the decision obtains invaluable data.

Subgroupings

Like many others, the student body we studied was divided into two subgroups—Greeks and independents. There was some enmity between the two, and if we had acquired a reputation of favoring one over the other, our fate on campus might have been different. There were attempts by leaders of both groups to co-opt us, especially at election time. We solved this problem by assigning one observer to one political party and a second to the other. Each researcher could then observe secret party conferences and make a separate report of political rallies.

The enmity between Greeks and independents may be real or it may be largely a pretense for election purposes; we learned of an underground secret organization that included student leaders of both groups. As leaders perceived that we were gaining more and more understanding of what was going on on campus, they felt it necessary to explain the organization to us and to point out evidence of its peace-keeping success. We obtained a membership list and reports of some of its meetings, but kept our knowledge secret.[10]

Mistrust between campus factions may be real in social matters even when it is politically negligible. Greeks usually have a highly organized system of social functions, which include attractive independent girls but exclude independent men—an expected pattern when the sex ratio favors women. Girls who were not considered attractive had a meager time and were isolated from campus social life.

Fraternities and sororities were much involved in the manipulation of a campus prestige system. This was most characteristic of those with the highest prestige or best reputation. These groups were in constant combat to attract the "best" pledges—students with high academic abilities, social skills, and organizational capacities. The most prestigious groups for both sexes were the older houses on campus and those with the highest scholastic achievement records. Just below these came houses more recently established on campus, with ambitious leadership and a membership that wished to improve its rank on campus. This group engaged in politics, whereas the old-line houses were more apt to participate in organizations of a philanthropic or social nature. Below these two groups was a larger group of Greek houses of the middle range. Each year some of these houses made efforts to raise themselves in prestige only to slump back the next year as the pledges they wanted chose other houses. Still lower in the prestige system were houses that were little more than boardinghouses, where each student might be so engaged in trying to make his grades that social or organizational activity on the part of the group as a whole was impossible. Students living in such houses often exhibited a certain degree of shame or shyness about admitting their membership. Other students rapidly identified themselves as belonging to a certain house and exhibited pride in this. Since it was one of the handicaps of the independents that they belonged to less easily identifiable groups, residents of some dormitories or floors of dormitories engaged in a variety of activities to publicize their houses or

10. Blanche Geer, "Student Government, the Fraternity System, and the University Administration," *Journal of the Association of Deans and Administrators of Student Affairs,* 3 (July 1965): 17–28.

dormitory floors. Those who lived off campus, of course, had not even this opportunity for self-identification.[11]

These subgroupings were seldom sufficiently divided to cause the observer trouble. If he took his initial steps carefully and did not offend by using in-group language injudiciously or pretending familiarity not yet earned, he would not find himself blocked from observation of any campus group. In talking to student leaders from other campuses, however, we realized that the open situation of the campus we studied was in some ways unique. On many large state university campuses the dislike of independents for Greeks is very great.

With the exception of access to students' rooms, observation of men's houses by a woman fieldworker or women's by a man presented no problems. Living rooms and dining rooms were not segregated, and we often found that an observer of the opposite sex could maintain a role of naïve stranger longer, thus obtaining useful data. In dating situations when there was more than one couple, we went along. We felt no hesitation in joining students we knew at snack bars or beer joints around the campus. Dances, receptions, sings, and parties can be observed easily with sponsorship from the students organizing them.

In student housing and campus organizations and classes, men and women play similar roles. We studied them in much the same way.

Related Groups

As already indicated, the three chief college subgroupings are administrators, faculty, and students. The first of these is nominally a very small group, but we found it useful in some types of analysis to include in the administrative category those graduate students or seniors who acted as dormitory counselors, since they often act as the eyes and ears of the administration among the students. Certain other students had the reputation on campus of acting for the administration while holding elective office in some sort of student government organization. Thus, while there may appear to be only a handful of administrators — president, deans, and their assistants — those who *act* as administrators may be more numerous.

Our original intention included a study of the faculty. We discovered, however, that most of the faculty were uninvolved in student life. Occasionally student protests or picketing brought a particular group on campus to the attention of faculty members who might become concerned over specific civil rights issues. We found little evidence that the faculty affected student life outside the classroom.

Faculty members were potential models for students only in the case

11. Becker, Geer, and Hughes, *Making the Grade*, pp. 24–25.

of those students who wished to become college professors—a very small group. Some students, usually in this category, wished greater contact of a personal nature with faculty members and valued invitations to faculty homes.

The faculty is often more involved with colleagues on the national research scene than with the immediate concerns of its own campus. There were, of course, exceptions who acted as advisers to student groups, but in a university of 10,000 students there were very few of this stripe—not enough to warrant extensive study.

Individual faculty members, of course, affect students in classes. We studied classes by attending with a student we had met elsewhere. Going to class with him, sitting beside him, and leaving with him provided opportunities for discussions of the class. Having the student introduce us to his professor and explain our study reduced role problems— professors seldom tried to treat us as colleagues. We also went to student meetings where invited faculty met students, and dinners in student housing which they attended. Most of these contacts were characterized by uneasy shyness on both sides.

Members of the administrative staff often served as models to campus leaders. A student may admire the way a man handles a meeting or a particular issue. Because their interests so often conflicted with those of the administration, student leaders became adept at figuring out administrators' beliefs and what they were likely to do. Administrators know students who get into trouble; they are much less familiar with the vast majority of students who just make it through college. Deans of students and their assistants know what is going on in most student groups with the possible exception of those in protest groups (more faculty-oriented). Our activities with students rapidly became known to members of the Dean of Students' office, and student leaders rapidly became aware of our contacts with the administration. Since the two groups were in a situation of enforced negotiation, open contact with both groups was not considered suspect by either. That is, we felt free to be seen walking down the street with a dean and were not embarrassed if we happened to run into one when in the company of students. In addition to our contacts with faculty and administration as they interacted with students, we interviewed many of them after we had become familiar enough with the campus to ask insider questions.

Occasionally parents and alumni appeared on campus. They are important to administrators but not, we feel, to students as a group. The students were absorbed in a life on campus which they felt few outsiders, including their parents, could understand. Protest groups were an exception. Several of these had close contacts with townspeople and with one or two faculty members. We interviewed these people as occasions arose.

Documents

OFFICIAL RECORDS

Most colleges keep many records. The files of academic deans, student deans, the alumni office, and the registrar may be useful, as well as the findings of self-studies. Allen Barton's excellent report on the sources and uses of such data makes further comment unnecessary.[12] We found the university cooperative in providing IBM runs that included grades and successive campus residence.

Certain cautions are nevertheless in order. We found that the registrar's figures on each class in college showed a thousand more seniors than one might expect from the number of juniors. On investigation the thousand turned out to be sociologically irrelevant to a study of the campus, since they were people who had left campus with one or two requirements unmet. Lists of graduating seniors are also inaccurate from the standpoint of sociological relevance. Although we compared the registrar's figures with official lists of graduating seniors and with the student directory, we never established a satisfactory total for the senior class. In using official statistics, the researcher will do well to inquire closely into the methods of compilation and intended use, as these may explain discrepancies.

Comparisons of data obtained from one college with those from another will be subject to large errors if the process of compilation is not checked. There is no standardization. Particularly in urban settings, quite a large population of "students" may be present on campus, some of them closely involved in its affairs, who do not appear on college books at all. Many of these are temporary dropouts who will register again. They may be between degrees if there is a graduate school, or they may enjoy participating in college social and organizational life without attending classes.

In fact, the researcher may find it necessary to reject the administrator's division of students into freshmen, sophomores, juniors, and seniors based on their credit hours. Students with low cumulative grade point averages may be academically freshmen but socially sophomores. There may be fifth- and sixth-year seniors. Part-time students or dropouts pulling up their averages at smaller colleges nearby may be so active in campus politics that undergraduate life cannot be understood without them. Students define college as a time of life in which one matures socially; administrators, as four years of courses and credits toward graduation. Since our focus was on students, we found their definition more appropriate.

12. Allen H. Barton, *Organizational Measurement and Its Bearing on the Study of College Environments* (New York: College Entrance Examination Board, 1961). For an example of the imaginative use of such records, see Burton R. Clark, *The Open Door College* (New York: McGraw-Hill, 1960).

STUDENT RECORDS

The student newspaper can be a useful record of campus events, particularly after the researcher has had time to learn about its editorial policies at firsthand. College officials seldom permit complete freedom of the student press. What appears to be a lack of interest in national or international affairs in a student paper, for example, may reflect the administration's fear of the conservatism of state legislators, alumni, or parents.

We found the student paper useful in other ways. At the beginning of our study, while we had some superficial understanding of most of its news, articles, and ads, the story behind the news was not clear. Later in the study, we measured our increasing knowledge by our ability to interpret the news because we had been present at the event described and knew the students involved.

Other sources of data include the publications and records of student organizations. Fraternities and sororities put out recruiting booklets and also keep formal histories. Large campus organizations keep budgets, files for incoming officers, public relations materials, and minutes. The yearbook documents the activities of many campus organizations and provides data on student organizational careers. We found all these sources useful, particularly after we had familiarized ourselves with the ways records were kept and could estimate what they might omit.

Most useful of all for the observer's daily activities was the campus directory. It furnished us not only with students' addresses, but also with data on their careers on campus. By consulting successive issues, one can trace a student's moves from one type of housing to another, find out if he married, and take note of office in major organizations. Of all campus publications our copies of the directory are the most thumbed.

Participation

Like most observers, no matter how experienced, we worried about our acceptance by students before entering the field. Very different from them in style of interaction, we were all over thirty, and one had gray hair. At least one observer was prejudiced against the kind of brainless middle-class kids people told us we would find on campus. How could we avoid being typed as the adults, academic style, that we were?

We decided to play it by ear, modifying dress and speech so as not to stick out in a group as nonstudents and following standard observer practices of entering and leaving rooms with students, asking them to introduce us, avoiding evaluative statements—above all, listening well. It worked. I can remember no serious problems, although no doubt there were many minor ones solved along the way. One member was pressed to become an honorary member of one fraternity he studied; another was disturbed when a number of students admired his shoes and bought some too. As a woman, my biggest problem was bobby socks. Most women students wore them, but they were too much for me – I brazened it out.

Illegal activities, with the exception of underage drinking, were rare. We followed a blend of our own taken-for-granted rules and the students' rules, I suspect. Drinking was so prevalent, accepted by students and ignored by the administration, that it presented no risks. Homosexual groups, unless otherwise notorious, usually had the same status as underage drinkers.

Using drugs may well be in this category on many campuses today. It can be a bad problem if there are police spies around, and I think an observer would do well to have a lawyer picked out in advance. Groups using drugs would have to be studied, but the ability of the researcher to protect them if he were subpoenaed remains at this writing unsettled.

One observer, who felt her uncritical listening might be seen as encouragement by freshmen girls experiencing their first heavy drinking and sex, explained her feelings to the girls, who assured her they were not trying to prove themselves sophisticated for the sake of the study.

Awareness of how students perceive you, and willingness to change to a more neutral role are probably the observer's best methods of preventing undue influence.

Language

Needless to say, the orientation of the researcher to the campus must include picking up the students' language and learning to speak it. His initial efforts to locate places, people, and groups provide many opportunities for learning local terms, nicknames, and slang. Some of the terms are known to all students. We found, for instance, that easy courses were universally called "pud courses," and difficult professors who were judged to be severe graders were "bears." Other words may be peculiar to certain groups or not used with full understanding by everyone.

Most students used the term "brownie points," for example, but among freshman girls it had no physical reference. Checking on differential meanings provides the observer with indicators of social distance between groups. The time it takes freshmen to learn the layers of meaning of some terms can be a rough measure of socialization.

Still other words are so central to a group's culture that students find them hard to define although they use them frequently. They may be opprobrious or ambiguously complimentary. The observer's questions as to meaning may elicit surprise or even shock at his ignorance, followed by vague replies and helpless gestures. For alert observers such words ring a bell. He recognizes them as possible key words—ones that once understood will provide the key to a concept so basic or so taken for granted by the group that it cannot be articulated. We found several of these terms in our study of undergraduates; "Mickey Mouse" and "gung-ho," for example. When we could not elicit clear meanings, we collected many usages over a period of time, finally checking our understanding by using the words ourselves to describe an action we had witnessed.[13]

Students usually take inquiries into the meaning of their jargon as proper for an observer. But *using* the words peculiar to a group or its particular gestures or patterns of touch may be presumptuous at first. Talk sprinkled with jargon, relaxed posture, and unself-conscious touch in a group when the observer is present are signs of his acceptance. The observer who comes to the last stage of his study without having himself received such signs knows he has failed.

Tactics and Strategies

Studying a large group of people necessitates certain modifications of field practice. A campus of 10,000 students requires more than one fieldworker if the work is to be done in a reasonably short time. In our study, although each observer had his own groups repeatedly visited, we sometimes checked on each other by going with another's students. This was most helpful when an observer felt himself going native[14] or when arguments arose among us about concepts.

We made use of informants to shorten the work and checked on them later by participating briefly with the group described. We chose students who seemed typical of groups and followed them all day. But mostly we did what students did. There were innumerable meetings, visits to classes, hours and hours in students' rooms.

We probably collected too many data, but when we came to write, things were missing and we wished too late we could go back to the field. Model building, begun in the field, became complicated when the observers scattered to other jobs. Inevitably, our concepts changed with subsequent experience, and some of the freshness of the data was lost. If I were to work on another large study, I would plan to complete it before taking on new work. In other respects our general strategies worked well.

13. See Becker and Geer, "Participant Observation and Interviewing."
14. See S. M. Miller, "The Participant Observer and 'Over-Rapport' " *American Sociological Review*, 18 (February 1953): 97–99.

Occupational Uptake:
Professionalizing

THE PROFESSIONAL MAN... values education as the key to progress... recognizes the importance of new ideas and improved techniques developed and taught in today's schools of mortuary science. The professional embalmer welcomes fresh knowledge from the newly educated and, in turn, shares his experience and skills with the beginner. Recent graduate... or mature practitioner, the professional embalmer continuously seeks to improve his skill... to increase his knowledge, in an effort to serve his clients better.

— Advertisement by L. H. Kellog Chemical Company

The study of professionalizing occupations provides a fascinating entrée into the basic processes of society. Particularly if you want to comprehend, perhaps even affect, the course of social change, the dynamics of occupational organization provides a logical focus for inquiry. The elements of such study are the social bonds created by workers self-consciously concerned about the status of their occupation. Fieldwork will be your research method *par excellence,* and pragmatically, by studying an occupation distinguishable by its efforts to advance toward professional recognition, you can be assured a meaningful and manageable subject area.[1]

1. The personification of occupation is deliberate but intended only for economy of expression. Properly, but inconveniently awkward, one would speak of "those in an occupation whose consensus is sufficient to represent that occupation for the most part," and so on.

Orientation to the Study of Professionalizing Occupations

Ever since Robert E. Park sent University of Chicago graduate students into downtown Chicago to study lowly and marginal occupations nearly four decades ago, researches in the sociology of work have tended to stress the differences in status and prospects in the kinds of work studied. Everett C. Hughes has spoken of "the humble and the proud," repeating the need for sociological study and analysis at both ends of the occupational spectrum.[2] However, the professionalizing occupations represent crucial cases, for they provide access to junctures and turning points for occupations seeking new status, and thus reveal social processes that for the study of the established professions have been determined for the most part after the fact.

The virus of professionalism attacks widely, almost indiscriminately, and the infection usually persists. It might be stretching matters to say, as Lee Taylor does, that "professionalism . . . becomes a model for occupational aspirations for most workers in commercial and industrial jobs."[3] But one must agree that "professionalism far exceeds professions."[4] Whether or not the occupational environment of the professions is as felicitous as those who seek it would believe, there is no doubting the glister of its symbol, whether solid gold or only plated.[5] In any event, we can easily distinguish at least some professionalizing occupations, for they are almost constantly in the public eye, their claims, strategies, and accomplishments chronicled regularly in the news media. Nurses, social workers, and public school teachers no doubt lead the list, but dozens of other service, scientific, technical, and administrative occupations make up an additional and rather imposing procession of claimants to professional status.

There is no need to try to set priorities for occupations most deserving study. The less heralded deserve attention because of the variation in data they provide and because through their study and accumulation valuable cross comparisons can be made and general principles validated.[6] But the well studied also need the sociologist's attention. Nurses,

2. Everett C. Hughes, "The Humble and the Proud," *Sociological Quarterly,* 2 (Spring 1970). See also Herbert Blumer's Preface to *Professionalization,* Howard M. Vollmer and Donald L. Mills (Englewood Cliffs, N.J.: Prentice-Hall, 1966), p. v.

3. Lee Taylor, *Occupational Sociology* (New York: Oxford University Press, 1968), p. 115.

4. *Ibid.*

5. The best discussion of profession as an evocative symbol is found in Howard S. Becker, "The Nature of a Profession," in *Education for the Professions,* ed. Nelson B. Henry (Chicago: National Society for the Study of Education, 1962), pp. 27–46. The concept of profession is questioned in Robert W. Habenstein, "A Critique of the Concept Profession," *Sociological Quarterly,* 4 (Fall 1963): 291–300.

6. The impediments to professionalization have in a very general fashion been identified, but their separate and/or combined importance in specific professionalizing occupations, at this stage of the field of sociology of work, can best be determined by empirically oriented case studies.

social workers, and schoolteachers do constitute some of the more vital of all our human service occupations and deserve continued study, for their role and function remain too important ever to be taken for granted, or worse, ignored.

Preparation for the Moment of Research

Despite the attention given to the study of occupations and professions at Chicago by Park and Hughes,[7] at Columbia by Merton and Goode,[8] and at Harvard by Parsons,[9] the literature of the field is not so voluminous that it defies assimilation. Whether you lean toward social process, structure-function, or general systematic theory, you will find that it is feasible to wade into the writings of the experts without drowning and come out with a good catch of ideas. While your frame of reference is your own affair, I suggest that you avoid grand syntheses and try to develop a conceptual framework that you can keep working for you in the course of your research. At the same time, avoid such a rigid application of it that you become insensitive or blind to new patterns, relationships, and processes that you weren't looking for at the beginning.

CHOOSING A PROFESSIONALIZING OCCUPATION FOR STUDY

Assuming you wish to study a professionalizing occupation, how do you select a particular one? No comprehensive list of occupations-on-the-move is handy, although, as we have noted, the protestations of professionalism of a few are quite audible. But you probably know enough about others besides nurses, welfare workers, and teachers to include librarians, funeral directors, chiropractors, pharmacists, news reporters, musicians, realtors, medical and dental technicians, career members of the armed services, and the police. Anselm Strauss has called attention to the burgeoning number of career-minded white-collar

---

7. Everett C. Hughes, *Men and Their Work* (Glencoe, Ill.: Free Press, 1958). This book epitomizes the best work of the Chicago "social process" approach to the sociology of work.

8. Most of the immediate products of the William J. Goode, Robert K. Merton, and Mary Jane Huntington seminars on the professions at Columbia University in the mid-fifties were mimeographed rather than published, and now are difficult to acquire. For Goode, the best available representative effort might be "Encroachment, Charlatanism, and the Emerging Professions: Psychology, Sociology, and Medicine," *American Sociological Review,* 25 (December 1960): 902–14. For Merton, see "Some Preliminaries to a Sociology of Medical Education," in *The Student Physician,* ed. R. K. Merton, George Reader, and P. L. Kendall (Cambridge: Harvard University Press, 1957). For Huntington, see "The Development of a Professional Self-Image," in *The Student Physician,* pp. 179–87.

9. The best introduction to Talcott Parsons' approach to the professions is "The Professions and Social Structure," *Social Forces,* 17, No. 4 (May 1939): 457–67, reprinted in Parsons, *Essays in Sociological Theory,* rev. ed. (Glencoe, Ill.: Free Press, 1954).

and technician groups, in and out of government, that "are busily staking out their own claims to professional status—with associated careers rather than mere jobs."[10] These latter kinds of workers are nearly always found caught up inside work organizations, and consequently find the problem of gaining work autonomy an important contingency. How do you find some of these hundreds of unstudied, unheralded occupations that may well be on the road to professional status?

Government agencies and publications. For over a hundred years the Bureau of the Census has in part been concerned with producing occupational statistics. Of the more than 35,000 jobs the Bureau must now deal with, only a very small fraction can be listed and examined individually, and these are chosen on the basis of what is felt to be the social need for the data at the time the decennial census is taken. Major categories of types of work are selected by officials of the Bureau, and the decision to bring a specific occupation into the status-bearing category of "Professional and Technical," rather than the less prestigious "Clerical or Personal Service" grouping, is, for the occupation with professional aspirations, a matter of great importance. Those who make it to the "Professional" category have obviously a highly impressive claim to general recognition as professional, whether or not by other standards (these sometimes gratuitously set by sociologists)[11] they fail to measure up to the mark. Twenty-three occupations have been included in the Census Bureau's list of professions: accountants and auditors, architects, authors, chiropractors, clergymen, college presidents and teachers, dentists, dietitians and nutritionists, editors and reporters, engineers (technical), farm and home management advisers, foresters and conservationists, lawyers and judges, librarians, musicians and music teachers, nurses (professional), optometrists, osteopaths, pharmacists, physicians and surgeons, social workers (except group), teachers, veterinarians.[12] The problems of justifying a list that changes a bit from decade to decade are real, and the Census Bureau admits receiving many requests from "groups desiring professional recognition for such

10. Anselm L. Strauss, Foreword to Barney G. Glaser, *Organizational Scientists: Their Professional Careers* (Indianapolis: Bobbs-Merrill, 1964), p. viii. Glaser's study reflects perhaps the best that can be done, and it is substantial, with secondary data based on questionnaires.

11. William J. Goode is probably the foremost sociological arbiter of professional status. For a recent example, see "The Theoretical Limits of Professionalization," in *The Semi-Professions and Their Organization,* Amitai Etzioni (New York: Free Press, Macmillan, 1969), pp. 266–313.

12. Listed and discussed intelligently by Lloyd E. Blauch in "The Professions in the United States," a chapter in *Education for the Professions* (Washington, D.C.: U.S. Department of Health, Education, and Welfare, Office of Education, 1955), pp. 1–8; derived from U.S. Bureau of the Census, *Summary of Detailed Characteristics,* Bulletin P-C, no. 1 (Washington, D.C.: U.S. Government Printing Office, 1950), Table 124, p. 261.

purposes as the enhancement of prestige, the securing of funds, or the granting of military commissions."[13] While the Bureau ventured its own definition of profession in 1940, it now prefers to rely upon the decennial *Census Classified Index of Occupations and Industries.*[14]

The major reason to review this official peerage of occupations is not to settle any argument about who is a "true professional," but to provide you with one list from which perhaps half or better of those selected, despite their inclusion by the Census Bureau, may yet be carrying on an uphill fight for professional recognition, to be achieved through a broad consensus of the public, and through their acceptance by other established professions. In searching for an occupation to study, then, you might first look over this group.

Another governmental publication that may help you is the *Dictionary of Occupational Titles.* The 1949 edition describes in brief detail over 20,000 more or less distinct occupations. You will not be concerned with these raw data, but you will be interested in the 1949 edition's abortive attempt to create a "semi-professional" major work category and a list of over 400 "semi-professional" occupations.[15] From this rather large group you can select a dozen or so likely candiates for study, look for other criteria indicative of professionalization, and end with a hand-picked, possibly never studied, professionalizing occupation of your own. Only take care to find out if it's really on the move. (Some help will be given in the next section.) The 1949 *D.O.T.* didn't guarantee mobility and professional aspirations for the semi-professions it lists. If anything, the *D.O.T.* implies that these groups are where they belong.

The subsequent 1965 edition dropped the effort to designate semi-professionals; yet under its first, most prestigious broad category, which now includes "Professional, Technical, and Managerial Occupations," most of the old semi-pros are included. It is up to you to sort them out for inspection by looking through the rather large section "Occupational Group Arrangement of Titles and Codes."[16] Importantly, note also how in the interim the new technical and scientific jobs have sprung up like crocuses.

Alternatively, you can look through the first third of the *Occupational Outlook Handbook,*[17] a substantial Department of Labor publication intended for use by vocational guidance counselors. Here you will find

13. Samuel A. Kramer, "The Professions in the U.S. Census," an appendix to *Education for the Professions,* p. 296.

14. *Ibid.*

15. *Dictionary of Occupational Titles,* 2 Vols., 2nd ed. (Washington, D.C.: U.S. Department of Labor, 1949), vol. 2, *Occupational Classification and Industry Index,* p. 13.

16. *Ibid.,* 3rd ed. (1965).

17. *Occupational Outlook Handbook* (Washington, D.C.: U.S. Department of Labor, revised every 2 years).

rather detailed descriptions, with occasional photographs, of occupations that might have some career appeal to the young. The work is described, along with statistics of employment in the occupation, salaries, prospects, and other useful and often revealing information. Since the earlier part deals with the professional, technical, managerial, administrative, and service jobs, by inspection and a little cogitation you can use this reference to isolate some likely candidates for your study.

Once you have chosen a professionalizing occupation for study, look for other statistics that government agencies may have generated about it.[18] Census Bureau publications will give you data on the size of the occupation, its regional distribution, rate of growth, and composition by age, sex, and color. Size is almost universally a variable of some importance in any social collectivity. Increasing size and rapid rate of growth portend internal changes, and, as occupations grow very large, opportunities for cleavages, fissions, and even social movements within them grow, with professionalism becoming one of the primary rallying points for the change-minded segments.[19]

Indices of professionalization. Although many sociologists believe that one or two basic characteristics can be isolated which *really* distinguish professions, you will find yourself looking for a holy grail rather than a body of useful data if you succumb to the game of trying to determine which are the "real" professions. Traditionally, the notion of independent skilled practitioners giving esoteric service to the trusting client in the context of face-to-face relations probably came close to filling the bill. But the face-to-face relationship with the independent practitioner comprises increasingly less of the professing done these days, while the growth of the professions, as revealed by census and other manpower reports, increases rapidly.[20] Much of the expansion in professions consists of a proliferation of technicians in governmental, industrial, scientific, academic, and other institutional research settings; also, public acceptance of the claims of professionalizing occupations seems somewhat easier to achieve today, particularly when the public relations mills drench the media with their daily persuasions. The avenues of strategy for the professionalizers—i.e., people trying to have their work accepted as professional—are numerous, and since the technological and organizational forces point in one direction, it is difficult to

18. Finding governmental publications in a large library can be a time-consuming and frustrating job. Best to find out if a specialist in such materials is available, and in any event don't tackle the shelves without talking to a reference librarian.

19. See Rue Bucher and Anselm L. Strauss, "Professions in Process," *American Journal of Sociology*, 66 (January 1961): 325–34.

20. See, for example, Max Rutzick and Sol Swerdloff, "The Occupational Structure of U.S. Employment: 1940–1960," *Monthly Labor Review*, 85 (November 1962): 1209–13. See also Lee Taylor, *Occupational Sociology*, pp. 118–32.

foresee any reversal of the trend toward proliferation of professionalizing occupations.

As convenient as it would be to have a few basic criteria of professionalism, and even more convenient to be able to scale these so that the weighted conjunction of certain characteristics would give you a foolproof criterion for deciding how successful specific occupations were in their quest for professionalization, the work world and its environing society can't be dealt with so neatly. What you can do is array the significant collective endeavors that characterize the *professionalization process,* and use these to decide, at least preliminarily, if the occupation of your choice is in the running. Harold Wilensky indicates the endeavors central to the professionalization process as:

1. Full-time activity in the performance of a bundle of necessary tasks.
2. Establishment of a training school.
3. Formation of a national professional association.
4. Redefinition of the core task, giving dirty work over to subordinates.
5. Conflict between the home guard and the profession-oriented newcomers.
6. Hard competition with neighboring occupations, especially at the later stages of professionalization.
7. Political agitation in order to win support of law for protection of the job territory and its prerogatives.
8. Rules and ideals embodied in a formal code of ethics.[21]

With the exception of the first characteristic in the list, all have plus and minus valences. That is, spokesmen for the professionalizing segments will point with pride to the accomplishments by which the valued goals are being achieved, while other countervailing groups will view these same activities with alarm. The professionalizing forces push for higher educational standards and longer training periods with more theoretically oriented coursework, try to bend the associational structure more toward the professional model and away from the trade and union models, lobby for license legislation so new profession-modeled laws can be passed in the states, set up accreditation procedures for training programs, and refine codes of ethics until the promised professional decorum will fall only slightly short of the saintly. But, also internally, resistance can always be found, running the gamut from simple demurral to outright conflict over the legitimate task functions, values, and prospects of the occupation. The situation becomes triadic when each group turns to the public and to policy-makers, politicians, lawmakers, law

21. Harold Wilensky, "The Professionalization of Everyone?," *American Journal of Sociology,* 70 (September 1964): 142–46. The sequence is typical but not invariant, *contra* Goode in his "The Theoretical Limits of Professionalization," pp. 274–75. Another progression of steps toward professionalization is given by Theodore Caplow, in his *The Sociology of Work* (New York: McGraw-Hill, 1954), pp. 139–40.

interpreters, and even other professions for credence and support. It should be clear that internal and external conflicts associated with professionalizing activities qualify as some of your most important data. You must not become a party to these struggles—at least not while you are in the data-gathering stage of your research.

Wilensky's indices are meant not only to help you decide whether or not the occupation you choose for study qualifies at the outset as a professionalizing occupation, but to give you some useful preliminary categories for gathering data as you proceed with your research. The patterning and combinations of strategies, transactions, campaigns undertaken rationally and deliberately, or nonrationally and almost blindly, including the tendency toward what Theodore Caplow calls the "sacralization" of the occupation, in some measure will remain specific to the occupation you may be studying. Thus your research task is in part to determine which behaviors have to be reported and dealt with as unique or specific to that occupation, and which can be brought under more general principles or concepts. Don't start out deductively in an attempt to decide what an occupation needs or must do in order to become a profession, or set yourself up as an amateur arbiter of professionalism. *Find out how the collective endeavors of workers, at various levels of organization, result in distinctive forms and patterns of behavior that can be described objectively and conceptualized sociologically.*

The Problem of Access

Professionalizing occupations take on some of the characteristics of a social movement.[22] The zeal engendered within them suggests one mode of entry for you as an uncommitted outsider who nevertheless might eventually become a convert. You will find at least three types of zealots: (1) those in the ranks, who often act as self-designated spokesmen, (2) the formal leaders who have come up through the ranks, and (3) the association staff, consisting of paid officers and functionaries whose role is to display enthusiasm and take continuing responsibility for promoting the cause of professionalism. The latter two types are found in or can be reached through the official headquarters of the association or associations that inevitably emerge in the professionalization process. Presidents, chairmen, other elected officers, whether out of zeal or pragmatism, will feel an obligation to respond to either a written query or a request for a personal interview. An executive secretary, of course, is obligated to respond, and sometimes an elected officer will pass on your original request to him.

Nothing guarantees full cooperation from any of these persons, but

22. See Bucher and Strauss, "Professions in Process."

professionalizing occupations do not present the structural impediments one finds, for instance, in the welfare agency with its concern for confidentiality, and the likelihood of two, three, or a half-dozen special-interest groups attempting to affect the agency's operation. While occupational associations also suffer from external and internal pressures, their major problem is not protecting or restricting the flow of information, but getting enough of the right sort of information to strategic outsiders and target publics.

Thus they will first respond to your request for help with a batch of persuasive literature, and often an invitation to write again or come and talk "if you have other questions." But they may also be wary, the wariness varying with their assessment of the harm you might do with your data, and also with the level of sophistication the leaders and staff officers have developed about the utility of and necessity for your kind of research. Universally, professions deal with matters of moment and not with trivialities. Matters of moment by definition contain aspects of danger and, if the professional service is poor or wrong, the results may be harmful, perhaps irreparably so.[23] Any occupation purveying a critical service must deal with client ambivalence,[24] and all professions have skeletons in their closets. Sensationalist writers, if they work at it, can have a field day with the professions, and public opinion, properly whipped up, can knock even a Supreme Court justice off the bench.

Anyone who sets about deliberately to find something shocking about any agency, institution, or association that has any sort of history can usually find enough truths or half truths to make a "story." Consequently, however anxious an executive secretary might be to give you the fullest cooperation, he must be concerned about the way you will slant your research report, dissertation, monograph, or book—particularly since a totally unslanted work is hard for him to imagine. Opportunities to bargain, trading a sympathetic treatment for cooperation, may suggest themselves, but you will be better off in the long run if you stick with the role of neutral social scientist in search of all the facts, and if necessary train the leaders to accept it. And, on balance, association leaders and staff officers *will* help you get the facts; they would rather you got too much material than a smattering, and (you should remember) they undoubtedly will want to interpret the facts for you as they make them available. But, as Bob Dylan says, the times they are a-changin', and you can expect that as value-free social science is replaced by value-full social science, those occupations social scientists

23. See Everett C. Hughes, "Mistakes at Work," in *Men and Their Work*, pp. 88–101.
24. An almost classical example is provided by the funeral directors in their relations with the bereaved. See Robert W. Habenstein, *The American Funeral Director* (unpublished Ph.D. dissertation, Department of Sociology, University of Chicago, 1954).

have found wanting will reject the neutral role you propose and ask for some guarantee that they won't be helping you dig their own graves.

What you should try to do ultimately, in the matter of access, is to build a body of strategic contacts with representatives of all segments and points of view in the occupation. Deepen these contacts by repeated visits, by follow-up letters, and by your presence at open meetings, rallies, and demonstrations. Your exchanges and questions will show increased comprehension of the complexities of the internal and external relations of the occupation you are studying. While an interviewing specialist such as Donald Roy can elicit forty-odd pages of information by calmly looking a "strategic" in the eye and missing the point repeatedly, you would do better to show that you are catching on. Problems always look simpler on the outside; when you begin to indicate you are aware of the picture from the inside, your informants and strategics will take you farther backstage.

Rank-and-file zealots may be harder to locate, but they live and work somewhere. Find out where. Leaders will sometimes identify some of them for you; others can be found at meetings and conventions, and still others can be identified by their contributions to the literature of the occupation, even the lowly "letter to the editor." When a crisis faces an occupation, particularly from the outside, stalwarts from all levels rise to the defense. Anyone who writes a letter to a newspaper defending some aspect of his occupation will in all likelihood answer your letter asking for an elaboration of details; if he is geographically accessible—another way of saying if you are research-funded for travel—he will probably see you.

In brief, nearly anybody in a professionalizing occupation will probably make an initial effort to be helpful to you, for he will anticipate your responses as helpful to his occupational cause. But getting to the leadership, particularly executive officers, is crucial, for they develop and execute the strategies, and the rank and file frequently occupy much the same place in their calculations as the public. Don't expect to get the full story from them, for there is no full story to be set before you by informants. In the last analysis, you as sociologist must construct your own, bit by bit, until after several months or more of working at it you finally succeed in putting together the sociological jigsaw puzzle.

Associations

Associations not only will give you help and information, but also are in their own right objects of study. Special-interest groups organized for limited purposes, they express and help achieve the goals of the occupations they represent, and also generate values and goals and feed these back into the lifestream of the occupations. They thus represent a sort of occupational demiurge. An association may in fact develop such power and autonomy as to become a tyrant over those who created it.

First you have to locate the associations. There is no better source than the *Encyclopedia of Associations*,[25] an enormous multivolumed registry of American associations, with supplemental lists that come out periodically. Typically, sixteen items of information, from name and acronym on through to frequency and location of national meetings, are included for each reporting association. By digging through an eighteen-section division, plus a master index, you can find almost any association of consequence in the country. By further browsing through the *New Associations* supplements you can identify from the fledgling associations (1) new professionalizing efforts of developing occupations, such as the Cowboys Protective Association (for rodeo performers) and the Federal Professional Association (for personnel employed in the federal government in all professional fields and disciplines); (2) segmentation of established professional or semi-professional occupations, such as the American Council of Women Chiropractors"; and (3) specially created qualifying associations[26] to function for a large professional association, such as the Academy of Certified Social Workers, established as an instrumentality for "certifying to the public that its members are both educationally prepared and experienced social workers in accordance with standards of admission established by the Academy."

Requests for cooperation on any continuing scale will probably have to be cleared through an executive board of officers of the association, and members of such a board usually take their cues from their executive secretary. He will want some kind of dossier or curriculum vitae, letters of sponsorship or other information you have available, along with written explanation in some detail, minus jargon, of what you are about to do, to put before the officers. To repeat: A simple request for help and a willingness to expend considerable physical effort to see, talk to, and see again the officers, spokesmen, and staff people remain the best bet for access.

Finally, sponsorship pays off heavily. You may begin as near as your university, for university personnel have many contacts outside academia. Some may be involved in an ancillary way in the affairs of the occupation you wish to study. This is particularly true for faculty in labor problems and labor economics, and there may be administrators

25. *Encyclopedia of Associations,* Detroit: Gale Research Co., 1964–1966), vol. 1, *National Associations of the United States.*

26. These examples are found in *Encyclopedia of Associations,* vol. 3, *New Associations.* Qualifying associations play a more specific and important role in the professionalization of British occupations. See Geoffrey Millerson, *The Qualifying Associations: A Study in Professionalization* (London: Routledge & Kegan Paul, 1964).

who can produce some kind of sponsorship also. One of my graduate students decided to study retail florists and was pleased to find and got immeasurable help from a nationally known floriculturalist teaching in another part of the campus. Also, university people are drawn into and often direct manpower studies. Through these persons you may get leads to the strategics, as manpower surveys often are conducted in cooperation with persons in trade and professional associations. One type of sponsorship you should be wary about is that of politicians. The cost of the access may be your misidentification with the politics of the politician sponsor; your best rationale for inquiry into professionalizing occupations, during the inquiry stage, remains scientific interest rather than political convictions.

Questions to Ask

Everett Hughes has observed that the most universally applicable first question to ask, and one sure to produce results is: "What were things like before they got to be the way they are now?" Since you have chosen a mobile occupation, its changes are likely to be rapid and significant enough to be felt and responded to by most of its members. Begin with "What's happened?" questions: "Can you briefly sketch the history of this establishment (your job)?" or "How does it happen that your establishment was located in this part of town?" or "When did cryogenics become recognized as an occupation in its own right?"

The "What's happening?" questions come next: "What led you to give up ambulance service?" "Is the new association on the right track?" "What's this I hear about a special gown for pathologists?" "Is information retrieval the big thing for you librarians?"

Next, and more revealing, since they get at interpretations and personal constructions of reality, are the "How come?" questions: "Why does your state association oppose more education for mortuary students?" "Why did you decide to start newspaper advertising?" "Do you think it was wise for your association president to debate Ralph Nader?"

After you have established yourself as a person knowledgeable about the complexities of the occupation, you can ask the more challenging "So what?" questions: "Did it make any difference to change the requirements for a license?" "Why didn't your leaders back the F.T.C. ruling?" "What good did the liaison committee actually do?"

While it is nice to have your subjects sociologize about their work relationships—you never know where you might turn up a good concept—the buck cannot be passed. Whatever the data and the indigenous interpretations, you have the personal responsibility for ordering and relating them in accordance with your frame of reference and your own sociological sensibilities.

Skills in interviewing are acquired only through practice and experience, but to start out you should have already formulated your major questions in your own frame of reference. Probing questions are as invaluable as they are impossible to preformulate. As a start, you might make Wilensky's professional process variables central to the formulation of your field questions and also to the questions you will be asking of the occupational data found in records, proceedings, journal and newspaper articles, and other media-related literature and information.[27]

The rhetoric of a professionalizing occupation tends to be optimistic and will be expansionist, progress-minded, exhortative, and even a little breathless. Service to humanity looms in the rhetorical foreground, obscuring crass subjects such as present remuneration or anticipated scale of pay and privilege. The problem here, if one arises at all, will be to develop a working knowledge of special terms, particularly if the occupation is lodged in the technical-scientific sector of the work force. All occupations to some extent develop idiomatic, helper languages. Glossaries may aid with the scientific and technical terms, but the everyday idioms are best picked up in direct experience with the people who do the work. Idiomatic lists quickly become dated, particularly in the case of professional jazz musicians and other categories in the performing arts.

One of the more common terms used by social scientists is "problem." For the research sociologist it carries little or no onus. People outside academia may think differently. For many the term "problem" may be associated with trouble, failures, or inability to cope. People in the South and Southwest do not take kindly to Northerners who want to discuss southerners' "problems," and people who lead or run the affairs of an occupation or association may also react negatively to the term. Stick with "developments," "happenings," "situations," and other neutral expressions, and wait for your informants to use the term "problem" first.

Events

If the occupation you are studying is attempting to forge a professional identity within the context of a larger occupational or organizational complex, you can expect to find schismatic and separatist groups.[28]

27. Everett C. Hughes some years ago mimeographed an "Outline for the Study of an Occupation." I have prepared a substantial elaboration of this, which can be obtained by writing to me at the Department of Sociology, University of Missouri, Columbia, Mo., 65201.

28. The process is neatly summed up by Bernard Barber in "Some Problems in the

These groups are most likely to be composed of the younger, better educated, best known, and perhaps most technically trained members of the occupation. Although the earlier stirrings may be informal, inchoate, or loosely organized, you can look for the tendency toward formal association as a prime instrumentality of those seeking change.

Whatever the cleavages and regroupings, those groups that have organized formally will always meet to transact business. Social activities may accompany these meetings, and to the outsider it may appear that providing the occasion for having a good time is their primary function, particularly at national conventions. You will find out differently when you — and you should — attend these meetings. At conventions, register as a visitor or guest, and, following prearrangement with one or more of the officers or paid staff, be introduced around, meeting perhaps for the first time the complete official family and other notables, past leaders, and what your hosts consider good contacts. These will be busy times for the staff and officers, so do not presume too much on their time. However, once you have been identified, registered, and given a badge, make every effort to talk to as wide a variety of conventioneers as you can. This is no time for formal questionnaires, schedules of prewritten questions, or any other obvious instruments of research. Meetings are rational, indeed, but they are also social affairs. There is always present some excitement, tension, and heightened feeling. Spontaneous demonstrations, unexpected floor speeches, nonscheduled caucuses and meetings all serve as clues to what is happening in the occupation.

You can locate opposition groups through casual inquiry. Try to penetrate them, but in the early stages of the game not obviously, at the cost of losing your cooperation and rapport with those who have been helping you all along. Special-interest groups, perhaps ancillary to the occupation, will be on hand. Find out about them, if you can; some interviewing with the marginals can be very revealing.

Go carefully through the exhibits, if there are any. A simple evaluation of the amount of sales merchandise and material exhibited, in contrast to that which is specifically for professional use, can give you some judgment of the "sell" versus the "serve" functions of the occupation — of whether it is one (like pharmacy) in which sales of goods are part and parcel of the presumably professional service. An impinging technology may also be revealed in convention exhibits. For example, marriage counselors may meet to find that the computer people are present to give them technical assistance.

Any and all persons attending a national convention are fair game for interview. Since persons from all parts of the country will be attending,

Sociology of the Professions," *Daedalus* (Fall 1963): 676–78. This issue is devoted in its entirety to the professions.

by merely looking not too obtrusively at badges you can develop an ad hoc national sample of the active membership. Introduce yourself, and start asking what's happening in cyrogenics out in Idaho, or down in South Carolina.

Subgroupings

It would be a unique occupation that was organized so cohesively as to be free from internal segments and divisive elements. When we speak of the dynamics of an occupation we are concerned in part with technological and other external pressures (right now the external pressures on schoolteachers not to strike are intense). But we are also concerned in good measure with the tensions that develop as members of an occupation shift allegiances, change values, and develop or accept new goals. Moreover, you should be concerned with the internal disjunctions and misalignments of purposive efforts to achieve desired ends, as well as the inevitable ambiguities that affect organization within a professionalizing occupation.

As already noted, formal organizational gatherings are likely sites for both cohesion-producing and divisive activities, and in the excitement of large gatherings there will be opportunities for new ideas to get caught up or imprinted in the minds of people who might ordinarily ignore them. But, apart from such gatherings, there will also develop less transient groups that reflect an expanding division of labor and which will emerge in the context of increased specialization, or appear in the more or less forced reorganizations that follow introduction of new technologies or work rationalizations.

Whatever the opportunities and imperatives for division and regrouping, two perspectives always seem to cut across and mobilize the sentiments and energies of those in professionalizing occupations. These are the traditional and conservative versus the progressive and change-oriented. Acceptance of the first perspective produces zealous guardians of the conventional and time-tested procedures and tasks that traditionally make up the work of the occupation. In the newly professionalizing occupations, such traditionalizers will for some time remain the majority, and constitute one sort of public within the occupation. In actual situations of work organization, such as a hospital setting with its complement of registered nurses, where power accrues and is exercised, the tradition-oriented gather into home guards, groups dedicated to the perpetuation of things as they have always been, resisting innovations and innovators, outsiders, visiting firemen, and the activities of any other change-minded newcomers. Edwin Christ and I unearthed more than one new hospital administrator who found himself completely stymied by a home guard of venerable registered nurses, determined "for the good of the hospital" not to let standard procedures of organization and practice be changed.[29]

The moral is that you should constantly be on the lookout for countervailing groups. Traditionalizers confront professionalizers in nursing; schoolteachers divide over whether to push for further professional status or settle for the power of union organization; social workers split over the way they should relate to clients; librarians disagree with one another over emphasizing service to the reader directly or the development of technological virtuosity in information storage and retrieval; and guidance counselors differ on whether they should ally themselves with administrative bureaucracy, dispense occupational information, or give psychological counseling to student clients. Among funeral directors the National Funeral Directors Association from its inception in 1872 has held out as its eventual goal full professional status, with the practitioner-client model as the most appropriate in the exercise of the funeral director's work. The countervailing group in this instance has been the National Selected Morticians, which since its inception in the late teens has allied funeral service with business enterprise pure and simple, and which has for many years conducted summer courses in funeral merchandising. A correlative split in mortuary education philosophy has seen the university and college-associated schools favoring higher educational standards, including college work as a prerequisite to mortuary school, while the generally older trade schools not only favor a simple high school prerequisite but are collectively seeking court action to prevent any agencies other than state embalming boards from setting college prerequisites.[30]

Finally, every occupation has its out-of-the-mainstream task specialties that provide work niches — a dead end for one but perhaps a shelter for another. Look for these and the people in them. Their perspectives may be illuminating. You should, of course, be aware of the presence of less desirable and less prestigious aspects of some of the tasks that make up the occupational bundle. Often these tasks are hidden from view and not ordinarily publicized. They will comprise the dirty work of the occupation, and in the course of professionalization they will be dropped, avoided, or if possible foisted on a lesser occupation. Or a segment of the occupation will be assigned such tasks as a specialty, and

29. Robert W. Habenstein and Edwin Christ, *Professionalizer, Traditionalizer, Utilizer,* 2nd ed. (Columbia: University of Missouri, Department of Sociology, 1963).

30. The trade school slant is reflected in a recent editorial, "The Monkey Is Off the Mortuary School's Back," in the August 1969 issue of *The Southern Funeral Director.* The monkey in this case is the American Board of Funeral Service Education, a multimortuary interest group serving as an accreditation agency for schools of mortuary science.

the specialty itself forced into a less prestigious status. The backstage of
the funeral home, where the embalming is done and the embalmer
physically situated, when contrasted with the front of the establishment,
where the embalmed, dressed, and cosmeticized dead are dramatically
displayed, made clear to me one of the persisting elements of strain
within an occupation where social front and backstage view are physically, visually, and in status value categorically separated.

Related Groups

Occupations today tend increasingly to exist within broadening work
environments or systems of delivery of needed goods and services. The
public image that is presented or has been achieved is always a matter of
concern to a professionalizing occupation. From the standpoint of the
researcher the public image may or may not accurately reflect what he
thinks is reality, but it is a *social reality,* and it is always taken into
account by a professionalizing occupation. The response of the public
not only provides a benchmark of success, but sometimes directly
affects the actions of public servants and politicians. Licensing legislation is always a crucial matter, and the chances to obtain passage of
state laws favoring and protecting a professionalizing occupation are
very much contingent upon having first created a climate of public
acceptance.

The best way to keep tabs on the occupation's public image is by
keeping up with the output of the communication media. Clipping services are expensive for the unsupported researcher, but if you have
some funding, by all means consider subscribing to one. Occupational
associations will probably subscribe, and you can ask for access to their
clippings. You may even be able to help by setting up a simple classification system and from time to time organizing their clippings. Don't
forget that the *New York Times* is indexed, and any reference library
will have several indexes to periodical technical and scientific literature.
These indexes list occupations by name, and the names of people associated with them. Occupations that take professionalizing seriously seldom let the news media operate without "help" from their public relations arm. Often the executive secretary of an occupational association
finds himself routinely spending a large amount of time interpreting and
feeding to the news media developments, strategies, and accomplishments, or just refuting charges. In this respect he is a well-paid
troubleshooter who must muster a variety of skills to keep the image of
his occupation viable.

There may be something finite about the amount of help, services,
stimulation, excitation, and social felicity-producing activities that a

society can assimilate, and perhaps some upper limit to the amount of prestige and status, if not power, that can be achieved by any one occupation in it.[31] In any event, most occupations have their competitors, and often the struggle for occupational status is carried out in an almost unending series of minor skirmishes along a wide front. Perhaps the most obvious example is an occupation with lesser status seeking to arrogate to itself the higher status tasks of another occupation whose higher prestige has been long established. This is the reciprocal of the effort of the higher occupation to slough off its dirty work to a lower one. Licensed practical nurses weren't always licensed, but now they have taken on many of the work and status characteristics of the professional nurses, who have for a long time been aspiring to some of the tasks of the physician, and have been quite willing to help the LPNs increase standards of training and performance of tasks so long as they don't encroach on the RNs' prerogatives.[32]

Sometimes occupations will compete as in a zero-sum game, with the success of one dependent on the failure of another. The surgeon uses the scalpel, the psychiatrist the word; chemotherapy conflicts with physical therapy; teaching machines replace live teachers, records musicians, and computers diagnosticians. Around your occupation you will find marginal groups. They are not only part of the picture, they are themselves a dynamic element in the broader occupational complex. Some characteristics of physicians stand out more clearly when one studies their relationships to chiropractors. But if one studied chiropractors as a professionalizing occupation, he would concern himself not only with physicians, but with osteopaths, bonesetters, faith healers, and physiotherapists as well. He couldn't study them deeply, obviously, but he would want to know how they responded, as occupations, to the professional protestations of the occupation he was studying, and what the interorganizational relationships were.

Social workers, concerned more with costs than with ceremony, often dislike funeral directors, probably because consumer economics rather than cultural anthropology figures in their training and ideological indoctrination. Physicians as a group are mostly ambivalent toward funeral directors, who must often deal with the end product of the physician's failure, but who are also of strategic value to medical research in helping secure autopsies and human material for study and utilization in transplants. But radical autopsies make the work of the embalmer much more difficult than it usually is, and a funeral director who turns unsympathetic to the needs of medical science can make things much tougher for those medical authorities whose job it is to find an adequate supply of

31. Goode, "The Theoretical Limits of Professionalization," pp. 269–70.
32. Habenstein and Christ, *Professionalizer, Traditionalizer, Utilizer.*

bodies and human tissue. I use the example to indicate that there will nearly always be necessary or potential reciprocities and accommodations among some of the related occupational groups, although these relationships may be undercut with ambivalence and sometimes destroyed in public conflict. Look for and ask about liaison committees between occupations; they lead you directly to interoccupational relations.

Though not technically a related group, former members who have left the occupation for some other work represent a strategic cateogy of persons to contact and interview. State licensing authorities, who are in many ways excellent sources of information (they are always part of the executive branch of the state government), will have lists and addresses of members who have let their licenses lapse. Associations also can be helpful here, as can persons still on the job. Lifelong dedication and service of its personnel are among the necessary conditions for an occupation's existence as a profession; thus you will want to check out the amount of worker turnover, and if possible the reasons for it. Statistics may be available in publications of the U.S. Department of Labor, in various manpower surveys, and in surveys conducted through the auspices of the occupation itself. What, for example, can be said about the professionalization aspirations of airline stewardesses, when in some airlines the turnover has been as great as 100 percent a year?

Records and Literature

Associations, nearly all other formal groups, and some informal groups keep records. Legally, records must be kept by all incorporated organizations; business activities or any activities involving financial transactions must be recorded, and a variety of forms and reports must be sent to governmental agencies. All modern organizations keep records and generate files, governmental requirements or not. They may not mean to, but almost all collectivities, as they organize formally and seek to accomplish diverse goals, eventually inundate themselves in paper. And you too will probably come to the point where the last thing you will want to see is another record, letter, form, or any other piece of paper. Nevertheless, some things written you should particularly try to obtain or to have access to, in particular the official proceedings of the meetings of the associations relevant to your study. They provide the best raw historical data, particularly when they have been stenographically transcribed and reproduced verbatim. An occupational association will always have some sort of library, files of records, correspondence, and other kinds of generated and collected literature, and on occasion it will have its own archives. Past leaders, their widows, self-appointed histo-

rians, and descendants of the pioneers of the movement will often have
trunks or attics full of materials that, if possible to locate, will give
you invaluable glances into the past and even present dynamics of the
occupation.[33]

Likewise, the journals of the field become a good source of data, and
journal editors can be extremely helpful, for not only do they have
information, but most of them will have found it almost impossible to be
uninvolved in the movements, shifts, and changes in the occupations
they service.[34] Often the rhetoric of professionalism is most professionally developed by trade journal editors, who, if the occupation they
served were completely to professionalize overnight, might find themselves out of trade. Journal editors are definitely strategic to you in your
research, and their journals are, next to associational proceedings, perhaps the best source of literature you can find. Only make sure you get
the editorial slant or ideology of all the journals or most of them; don't
settle for just one journal because it is the thickest, or thinnest.

How do you find out where and by whom journals are published? The
Encyclopedia of Associations lists the literature routinely produced by
the respective associations, and the journals of the associations are
usually listed by name. Reference librarians again should be consulted;
also try a letter to the Library of Congress, asking for lists of trade
journals, and to the Superintendent of Documents at the U.S. Government Printing Office, to see if there are any guides to associations or
associational literature published through governmental agencies. Look
through the dissertation abstracts kept in most libraries. There may
already have been two dissertations written about cryogenicists. Get
them on interlibrary loan and read them; perhaps your conceptual framework and the prosecution of your research can be improved through
taking advantage of previous work.

Archives have an intensely personal appeal for some, but for any
researcher a well-put-together archive pertaining to his subject of study
can be an absolute gold mine. My own master's thesis was based
completely on a special (the only) collection of cremation literature — that of the Cremation Association of America, which at the time
of my research reposed in the John Crerar reference library in downtown Chicago. Joseph Gusfield found the library and collection of the
Woman's Christian Temperance Union invaluable in his research on the
temperance movement, and several dissertations could be written from
the special library of funerary literature at the National Foundation for
Funeral Service.

33. Biographical and autobiographical materials should not be overlooked, and these are
more likely to have made their way into the public catalog. There are at least two dozen
biographical directories to be consulted, not the least of which is *Who's Who in America*.

34. The older journals are likely to have larger files of early issues, perhaps collections
of the literature of the competitors of the time.

Special libraries assembled by those in or representing an occupation may have thoughtfully omitted the work of detractors. But it is my experience that the better instincts of librarianship usually prevail, and that if it is published and if it has anything to do with an occupation, it will probably find its way into some association's collection. If you have the true historian's bent, you will not want to forget the libraries of the state historical societies. These often have an astonishing volume and variety of social history and data of the past. Look particularly for old city directories listing occupations, and newspaper advertisements as well. What you are looking for is both genesis and variation in the early forms your occupation took, decades, even centuries ago. In developing the occupational history of funeral directing I found the libraries of the Massachusetts and New York State Historical Associations excellent sources of both printed and photographic materials.

In your zeal for scholarship, don't forget the most obvious and mundane source of literature: the publications specifically designed to give you occupational information. Your library's card catalog will have a section with some such heading, but for a starter you probably couldn't go wrong with the excellent — for its purposes — *Occupational Information* by Robert Hoppock.[35]

The Role of the Investigator

Unless you have been trained in the occupation you are studying, your chances of participating as a member are likely to be slim. The observer role described in Chapter 12, by Donald Roy, probably comes closer to fitting your case. Sustained interaction with members of the subject group will undoubtedly make up part of your field activities, but often your contacts will be more transitory. In the latter case, your chances of missing or misunderstanding the information gathered in interviews and through casual observation are real enough to make you want to double-check what you are writing down or committing to memory.[36] On the other hand, as many researchers have noted, lengthy interaction with a few subjects almost inevitably produces sympathy with, perhaps adoption of, their values and goals. There is no easy answer to the problem of oversocialization of the researcher. However, by making an effort to get the perspectives of all the interest groups, particularly through personal contact with their principal spokesmen, leaders, and men of zeal, you may balance out or compensate for a natural tendency to absorb the sentiments of those with whom you interact most in-

35. Robert Hoppock, *Occupational Information* (New York: McGraw-Hill, 1957).
36. For a thoughtful and useful discussion of how to go about checking observations, see Howard Becker, Blanche Geer, Everett C. Hughes, and Anselm L. Strauss, *Boys in White* (Chicago: University of Chicago Press, 1961), pp. 33–45.

tensively. Moreover, some observation and a minimum of participation on the firing line with the foot soldiers is almost certainly indicated if you are to balance impressions gathered by your association with a leadership whose goals and strategies may not always be understood or, if they are made explicit, approved by the rank and file.

W. Richard Scott suggests some additional antidotes: "(1) . . . reviewing early field notes, taken in a period when some of the group's ways seemed strange and inexplicable, and (2) discussions of the research with outsiders who may be able to sensitize the researcher to blind spots in his analysis."[37] Certainly if you are working under someone's direction you will want to have frequent review sessions in which field notes and interviews and other varieties of information you have gathered are scrutinized and your tentative explanations or hunches about the anomalous or problematical aspects of your data discussed. When you move on to the stage of preparing working papers it is time to tap the resources of your colleagues; paper them heavily, while not forgetting an occasional flyer to an authority in the field.

Perhaps your most serious role problem will stem from the vagueness in your subjects' comprehension of what you are attempting to do. The natural tendency will be to place you within a limited repertoire of stereotypes, none of which will suit, or worse, to assign you one of a number of crippling roles,[38] which, although they get you placed, may well keep you excluded from the areas and subjects you most keenly want to study. Scott has listed some of these roles as they are applied to the researcher in organizational settings: management consultant (or spy), inspector, clinical psychologist, efficiency engineer, visiting expert, and student amateur.[39] For the professionalizing occupations the crippling roles applied to sociological researchers might include social reformer, "consumerist," muckraker, detractor, student amateur, sensationalist writer, liberal-tinted-red, and socialist. There are still some persons who confuse sociologists with socialists, and many more who label all sociologists as social reformers. The problem of establishing your preferred identity is difficult and takes time. Your first line of defense lies in developing in clear terms, with unambiguous referents, a truthful statement of who you are, your research interests, your base of operations, your sponsorship, and the kind of assistance or cooperation you are

---

37. W. Richard Scott, "Field Methods in the Study of Organizations," in *A Sociological Reader in Complex Organizations,* ed. Amitai Etzioni (New York: Holt, Rinehart & Winston, 1969), p. 569. Scott's chapter is well worth careful study even though he is dealing primarily with the study of established organizations.

38. *Ibid.,* p. 565. The term "crippling roles" comes from Rosalie H. Wax. "Twelve Years Later: An Analysis of Field Experience," *American Journal of Sociology,* 63 (1957): 133–42.

39. Scott, "Field Methods in the Study of Organizations," p. 565.

specifically seeking. All this you should have rehearsed until it comes out easily, naturally. And once you have put together such a package of identity, don't allow yourself the luxury of becoming bored with it and for the sake of variation start making changes.

Finally you will have to face up to the matter of reciprocity. Having associated yourself with a collective movement and in a sense made demands upon it, having presumed upon many people's time, gotten underfoot, and probably interfered to some extent with the purposive activities of the workers for the cause, what, reciprocally, are *your* obligations? The question has both pragmatic and moral dimensions. At any moment in your research you may be asked for help, and by giving it you may immediately find cooperation and acceptance enhanced. Subject to the limitations of time, small-scale reciprocities would seem to be in order, particularly when you will not be risking public identification with the subject group. Certainly you can offer suggestions that will lead to greater sociological sophistication on the part of the occupational activists without becoming known as "their" sociologist. It is when you are presented with the opportunity to become a part of the movement that the problem of negative identification arises, and it is then that you will have to bite the bullet and make a moral decision. I hesitate to legislate morality for the new researcher, but I can categorically say that should you become a paid researcher or spokesman for an occupation, your collegial status will be jeopardized and your writings and utterances severely discounted. Unless you are a lot smarter than the people you have been studying—an unlikely eventuality—your new-found expertise may not be so effective in the strategies of professionalization as you think it will be, and you will find you are unable to deliver the goods, either to the professionalizers or to your profession.

Strategies for the Sociological Study of Criminal Correctional Systems

I believe prison and parole are two institutions of formal social control best studied as interrelated subsystems of a wider governmental system. That wider system — let us refer to it as criminal justice and law enforcement — is an organization of the resources of the state for the definition, identification, prosecution, defense, and disposition of violators of the criminal laws of the state. The exercise of the capacities of this system is inseparable from the most fundamental political question: Under what circumstances may the state intervene punitively in the lives of citizens?[1] In Europe and America, the pivotal institution for the disposition of a convicted offender is the jail or prison; increasingly the custodial authoity of the state has been extended to cover not only the term of confinement but an indeterminate period after release.

Prison and parole are reciprocal parts of a law-enforcement and corrections loop. Prison inmates are regularly or upon petition seen by a

---

1. That the ideological rationale of the intervention may be rehabilitation and client welfare does not alter the effect of compulsory custody and treatment. Even though the ideology of treatment has seemingly displaced the objectives of punishment, control, and deterrence, in fact they remain in the language of the popular mandates as well as in the foreground of operating organizational concerns. From the point of view of the prisoner or parolee, the involuntary nature of his clienthood is almost always experienced as punishment. Moreover, "Experience has demonstrated," writes Francis Allen, "that in practice there is a strong tendency for the rehabilitative ideal to serve purposes that are essentially incapacitative rather than therapeutic in character" (*The Borderland of Criminal Justice* [Chicago: University of Chicago Press, 1965], p. 34).

122

governmental board and are eventually released to parole. Parole violators are returned to prison. Part of the prisoner's record is added to the parole record and vice versa. Staff decisions in one agency may be influenced by previous actions in the other. Often prison and parole are under the same administration. In jurisdictions employing the indeterminate sentence, both the length of prison term and date and length of parole are decisions of the same board.

In addition to prison (including work camps and mobile crews) and parole as conventionally understood, a number of related programs invite inclusion in any sociological consideration. I have in mind work or home-visit furloughs from prison, the halfway house or conditional release center, the outpatient clinic and other community programs. In addition, important patterned linkages of police, jails (usually under the county sheriff's office), lawyers, welfare agencies, and private organizations such as the Salvation Army, the John Howard Society, and Synanon fall into the area of interest. For convenience, we may use the term "criminal correctional system" to refer to this array of official and nonofficial punitive organizations (and their transactions with inmate welfare and aid organizations).

The work of studying an institution such as prison or parole may be conveniently divided into three broad categories:

1. Clarifying the basis of the study by making explicit the reasons for doing the research.
2. Obtaining the information relevant to that problem.
3. Analyzing this information and reflecting on the entire enterprise in such a way as to produce warranted conclusions relevant to the problem.

Since I believe all inquiry stems from a working problem, it is necessary to discuss briefly the clarification of the basis of the inquiry.

Clarifying the Reasons for Doing the Study

The research may be undertaken for any of several reasons. While it is typically said that research proceeds from a theoretical question or a need for answers to an administrative problem, it is surprising how unclear these original motivating questions are when actual projects are scrutinized. Nonetheless, projects appear to have grown from beginnings such as the following:

A study might be said to stem directly from a *theoretical problem* if a theory exists from which certain influences or deductions have led to a hypothesis to be tested. Or it may have led to two or more tenable or likely conclusions, and data would help determine which or under what conditions each is correct. The theory may or may not deal primarily with prisons or criminal justice, but it should motivate the inquiry by posing a logically derived question that the research will endeavor to answer.

Since little rigorous theory exists on coercive social control, it is perhaps not surprising that no correctional research has been undertaken to test deductions from a theory. A number of studies have used prisons as the setting in which to investigate questions arising from a general theory or view of social control. Richard McCleery justifies his interest in the dialectic between prison staff and inmate community by asserting that the prison is a microcosm of political processes in open communities.[2] Stanton Wheeler reasoned that if prison deprivations produced inmate subculture and inmate types, one should find similar prisons giving rise to similar inmate types regardless of outside culture differences, and he sought to test this by studying prisons in Scandinavia.[3]

Practical problems in the restricted sense are those whose solution or elucidation would have direct utility to an agency or would provide an informed basis for political criticism of that agency by outsiders. These may be framed because interest in the operation of an agency or organization, or in the behavior or fate of persons who come to be subject to agency supervision, creates a need for information, or calls into question a prevailing conception of the correctional system. Among the most important examples of this type is program evaluation, to be discussed later.

The inquiry may in fact not be initiated either by a theoretical problem or by a practical need for information; it may be considered because the *opportunity* to do a study is present. This may be extended in a number of forms. A granting agency or an individual may invite you to do a study, or the institution or agency itself may invite research.

Sometimes a study is set into motion by the arousal of individual curiosity, when the student is struck by the recognition that little is known about a certain practice or system. This seldom sustains an inquiry, however, and unless the student is extremely fortunate, he must explicitly relate his curiosity to some theoretical or practical problem, or at least locate an opportunity.

In the early 1960s David Ward and I were simply curious about the general nature of a prison for women (having seen a number of men's institutions) and particularly in whether communication and role patterns tended to resemble the informal structures described in studies of men's prisons. After initial visits and interviews at a prison for women,

2. Richard McCleery, "The Government Process and Informal Social Control" in *The Prison,* ed. Donald R. Cressey (New York: Holt, Rinehart & Winston, 1961), pp 149–188.
3. Stanton Wheeler, in personal conversation.

our interest shifted to the surprising prevalence of homosexual relationships among the inmates, which finally became the focus for an analysis of the inmate social system there.[4]

Note that definitions of theoretical questions tend to reflect prevailing consensus in the field of sociology, while practical questions are more often raised or recognized by administrators in the field of corrections. Opportunities may come from within sociology, from the corrections field, or from more remote sources, with or without reasons for their utilization.

The happiest occasions doubtless are those uniting theoretical relevance, extended opportunity, and the investigator's unabashed curiosity. Practical utility is so closely tied to sociopolitical climate that it may or may not coincide with the academic complex of motives. Surely it is naïve to assume that for every practical question of consequence there will be an appropriate theoretical problem at hand, and vice versa. It is also necessary to remain open to the possibility that preliminary inquiry may reveal an unrecognized functional need for information not currently available, or that inquiry or agency reaction to inquiry will result in new objectives for the agency, and consequently a new need for information.

The initiation of any actual study is likely to reflect more than one animus, but these will probably not be of equal strength, and it will be possible to establish the operating priorities fairly easily. It is my feeling that any study greatly benefits from self-conscious reflection on these priorities at the outset, if only to dispell illusions. But more important, prolonged contact with a governmental agency is almost certain to present numerous successive questions, offers, opportunities, and problems, branching further and further from the original course. If that original course were a tentative response to the research opportunity, following the most promising digression may be the best strategy. On the other hand, if the research began with hypotheses of an "if X, then Y" sort, each new venture must be evaluated by comparing the data or insights likely to be produced with the requirements of the original theoretical problem. Most delicate of all is the task of maintaining an experimental design over a period of time during which one or more other aspects of the system are undergoing change.

Collection of Data

Gaining access to many social situations or populations is an informal tactical exercise in social research; in the case of correctional systems, entrée usually involves securing formal approval, and the security proce-

4. David Ward and Gene Kassebaum, *Women's Prison* (Chicago: Aldine, 1965).

dures of the agency, as well as legal factors, may impose certain constraints on the conduct of the study. In any event, gaining access to the situation or people of interest in correctional systems is much more likely to require deliberate planning and consideration than is the same phase in many other settings.

One of the more distinctive structural features of correctional systems (particularly places of confinement) is the extent to which they exhibit in exaggerated form nonconsensual solidarity. That is, they are social systems not bound together by basic consensus but rather organized around a cleavage in values and interests, knit together at certain places by patterns of accommodation and collusion, and frequently marked by conflict. Thus many specific studies very quickly raise questions concerning patterned evasion of norms and particularized implementation of ostensibly universalistic prevailing norms — problems concerning which the prison administration can be assumed to be sensitive. The tactical question then of how such studies can be introduced must be regarded as a major factor in their feasibility.

A department of corrections may have a research division, which usually serves both to conduct research within the department and to monitor — at least to some degree — any research from outside the department. Typical routes to approval of a study are (1) via the director to the research division, and (2) via the research division. In the latter case, approval of firm study plans must come from the director of the department. Seldom would the superintendent of an institution grant access without referring the matter up through departmental channels. This means that the sociologist should have some initial understanding of the structure of the department in order to approach the appropriate offices for information and approval most intelligently. Much time will be saved if the student makes contact first with the director of the department for approval to see the research division or the statistics and records division; at those offices he should identify himself professionally and obtain information available to the public on the organization of the department, annual reports, and any special reports and publications on its operations. It is important that reports even indirectly relevant to the study interests, and in particular the general outline of the records regularly kept by the agency, be known to the sociologist in advance of again meeting the department director's staff and formally proposing the study. The problem may be more clearly outlined if the information already in departmental record files is known. To propose a study on the assumption that certain information is not available when in fact it is creates an impression of naïveté which does nothing to advance the proposal.

At the same time, it is also important to question the sources and reliability of the data available in routine files. Conversations with record-keeping staffs may reveal that informal practices or discontinued procedures or changing procedures result in unreliable or incomplete information. It may be prudent to collect certain information from original sources even if it is already collected or summarized in files. For example, in a study of a prison counseling program we originally planned to obtain from the summary attendance figures maintained in the files a measure of exposure of inmates to the program. However, we discovered that informal practices among prison inmate record clerks introduced a considerable degree of error, and we were obliged to compile our own attendance data. It would have been easier if we had planned on this from the beginning. Having even a rough picture of the organization of the department, the available information, and something of the actual operations that produce the information most directly relevant to your interests does much to increase the value of the discussions that aim at gaining approval for a study.

Any study involving extensive cooperation of the staff, alterations in assignment or programming, or extra record-keeping or evaluation of programs must be discussed fully with the department's research professionals as well as with the executive staff of any prison or parole divison that will be the study setting. The most careful presentation of research requests at this point will stimulate objections or suggestions from the department sooner rather than later, and the experience of discussing or even jointly developing some of the research procedure will have the additional function of eliciting more support from the department. This may not seem so important in the beginning as it will later, when inevitable disenchantment and operational fatigue set in. For it is not unlikely that the early phase of the study will be one of extreme cordiality, with numerous statements affirming the value of the research, the desire of the department to cooperate with the study, and its willingness to open any doors to the inquiry. When at a later time some of the glow has faded, or when the inquiry begins to move into areas not clearly envisioned by the department in the beginning, the study will need some support more solid than mere good feelings. The experience of having talked the project over in some detail and having committed some staff time and energy to the planning conferences may carry the study through a bad phase later.

I believe the initial phase of any study of prison or parole should be devoted to familiarizing all the researchers with the recurrent patterns of conduct that make up the work of the staff and the activities of the inmates and parolees. There is no substitute for spending some time with the parole agent in his office and in the street, or for acquainting oneself with the hour-to-hour activities of prisoners and staff in the prison. This should precede inauguration of more focused fieldwork or study designs, and should include even research staff who may have little further to do with direct collection of data.

STAYING CLEAR

The initial period is not only an orientation phase but also the time when the researcher will be tested by inmates and possibly staff. To test whether interviews are in fact confidential, an inmate may provide a piece of fictitious news about an impending action posing threat of serious danger or injury to someone. If the naïve researcher informs the staff of this impending event, and extra surveillance, an investigation, or some other change in prison routine suddenly takes place, inmates have a perception of the extent to which statements to the research team are in fact confidential. Doing an illegal favor for an inmate such as posting a letter, calling someone outside to say hello, or carrying an innocuous verbal message may cause the researcher problems by making him vulnerable to inmate pressure later. Staff members may test the investigator's loquaciousness, or attempt to establish informal constraints on certain of his interests or actions. Both inmates and staff will be quick to spot slang and argot as a ridiculous affectation of the academic researcher unless he is quite comfortable in its use. Since both inmates and staff are experienced in sizing up newcomers and in the techniques and tactics of influence, the unwary researcher may find himself quickly backed into a corner. Since the sociologist may have had most of his sparring experience with students and secretaries, whose techniques are no match for the skills of prison inmates and staffs, he may be cut up very badly before he realizes it. There is much to recommend an extremely careful and prudent demeanor when commencing the inquiry.

If a homily is tolerable at this point, it may be said that while rapport is essential, the student has to stay clear of entanglements, no matter how benign or uncalculated they may seem. Becoming compromised at the outset, and actually or potentially vulnerable to pressure from either staff or inmates, will pose serious difficulties.

OBSERVATION

Let us assume that the researcher has succeeeded in gaining working access, and is adroit enough to stay clear while remaining where things are happening. He has the repertory of data-collection techniques of sociology to use, and must consider their suitability within the setting of prison and parole. A project may combine a number of methods. Daniel Glaser, for example, used prisoner and parolee interviews, prison record files, and postrelease follow-up in nine separate research enterprises in his study of the federal system, including an analysis of statistical relationships between crime, age, and employment, an analysis of recidivism from prison record data on released offenders, a comparison of returned parole violators with "successful" releases, a longitudinal panel study of parolees, a nationwide survey of financial aid to released prisoners, a panel questionnaire survey in federal and state prisons, a time-and-activity study in prison, and a survey of federal probation (parole) officers.[5]

By *observation* I mean the act of obtaining data by looking at or listening to social conduct, or by examining objects or physical traces. Thus merely having contact, even interpersonal contact, with some people does not constitute observation. Rather the role of the observer includes *(a)* being self-conscious of the selective attention to experience, the active mode of observing, and *(b)* specifying the level of abstraction on which observation is made (for example, one may be interested in overt behavior, in the consequences of the behavior for others, in influences about disguised intentions, or in inferences about the unconscious, but not in all of them indiscriminately). The role of the observer also entails *(c)* selection, sharpening and making more explicit what is happening; *(d)* rumination on the observer's own experience; and *(e)* sensitivity to the impact of the observer on the situation observed. Finally *(f)* the observer must make provision to have access to the experience subsequently (make some kind of recording).

The social position of the person observing is nowhere more critically important than in studies in criminal correctional systems. Is the observer known to be an academic person, or is he thought to be one of the prisoners, subject to the same milieu as they? Cross-cutting this question is the tactic of overt observation versus covert observation (that is, observation that is identified as such versus a surreptitious or disguised

Activity of observer

		Participant in action	Outsider (visitor)
Identity of observer or recording device	Overt	A	C
	Covert	B	D

5. Daniel Glaser, *Effectiveness of a Prison and Parole System* (Indianapolis: Bobbs-Merrill, 1964).

coign of vantage). There are examples of the effective employment of each of the resulting four types of observer roles in the general literature of sociology.

Laud Humphreys' recent work on homosexual pickups in public lavatories was conducted by masquerading as a homosexual onlooker[6] (hence in our diagram, type A). Howard Becker's early account of marihuana use among musicians was obtained while he was a musician but known to be a graduate student in sociology at Chicago[7] (thus a type A observer). In studying social organization in a machine shop, Donald Roy became a regular employee and did not reveal his academic role[8] (hence type B). Many studies of small-group behavior in the laboratory[9] have been made by observers outside the group but known to be observing (type C). For type D we have Strodtbeck's use of concealed recording devices to study jury deliberations.[10] Jerome Skolnick was an observer among policemen who knew his identity, but because of his presence with the police and active assistance to them, citizens thought he was a detective.[11]

There are formidable practical problems in each of these situations. The overt observer's risk of intruding too forcibly on the situation and stimulating deliberate falsification of behavior and feelings is balanced by the difficulty and dangers of secrecy. The outsider has a barrier to empathy; the participant often suffers restriction of mobility or information. Covert participant roles in prison I frankly believe to be beyond the dramatic abilities of any sociologist I know; the few sociologists who have written from their own experience as prisoners were genuinely prisoners at the time of writing, which is rather a different thing.[12] Even to recruit an inmate as a secret employee seems to be inadvisable because of the virtual certainty of eventual exposure. Indeed, in studies of criminal correctional systems I believe one is well advised to put aside the temptation to be too clever and to avoid the use of concealed data-collection devices or procedures. They are seldom necessary and are always potentially disastrous in a situation of initial suspicion and continual surveillance. The tolerance of an ongoing sys-

6. R. A. Laud Humphreys, *The Tearoom Trade: Impersonal Sex in Public Places* (Chicago: Aldine, 1970).

7. Howard S. Becker, "On Becoming a Marihuana User," *American Journal of Sociology,* 59 (November 1953).

8. Donald Roy, "Efficiency and the Fix," *American Journal of Sociology,* 60 (November 1954): 255–66.

9. For a classic example, see Robert F. Bales, *Interaction Process Analysis* (Cambridge: Addison Wesley, 1961).

10. Fred L. Strodtbeck, "Social Status in Jury Deliberations," *American Sociological Review,* 22 (December 1957): 713–19.

11. Jerome Skolnick, *Justice Without Trial* (New York: Wiley, 1966).

12. See Ned Polsky, "Research Method, Morality, and Criminology," in *Hustlers, Beats, and Others* (Chicago: Aldine, 1966).

tem to clearly known observers is powerfully demonstrated in the documentary film *Titicut Follies*. With sufficient time to get used to the presence of observers, even observers with sound movie cameras, staff and inmates can apparently carry out even incredibly incriminating actions. The use of covert recording or observing devices would be very difficult to conceal over any length of time, and the slight advantage gained by such secrecy would be more than lost by the consequences of exposure. I might say that I am not categorically opposed to unannounced or even deceptive observation in some social research, but in many situations (such as prison and parole) I find practical as well as ethical objections to it.

The use of participant observers (that is, prisoners and parolees) who are known to be employees of a research project seem to me to offer most of the advantages and virtually none of the risks of imposture; it does, of course, depend on the approval of the authorities, and success rests heavily on the qualities of the particular persons employed and the nature of the tasks assigned them, in view of their lack of formal training.

The observer has a two-phase job. He must get to where the action is *and* he must obtain information that can be taken away with him. It is surprising how often the first phase is successful only to be followed by failure in the second. A project may have a field observer who becomes personally well acquainted with many aspects of the prison community, but is able only to tell anecdotes, not to provide information, formulate hypotheses, or draw conclusions.

The observer learns to seek strategic situations, where time is well spent (that is, productive of relevant information). One of the best rules is to place observers in problematic situations, where decisions are made, trouble arises, control is exerted, and so on. This may be difficult. In our study of the treatment program at a medium-security prison, we placed an observer at the regular meetings of the prison disciplinary committee. He took notes initially on a roughly coded sheet, but after a few sessions the prison administration called me in and inquired why we were watching the disciplinary committee when we were supposed to be interested in group counseling. After explaining that we were interested in seeing how staff and inmates confronted one another over rule violations as well as in group sessions, we were allowed to continue, but staff members continued to show concern, and notes were made after the committee meeting rather than during the session.

The tactics of observation vary with the primary task. The researcher will not use the same tactics to gain general orientation to what is going on as he will when he is concerned with describing effectively the patterns of relationships or testing some hypothesis. In the latter cases the observer is more likely to use a structured procedure for noting and counting critical instances of some pertinent activity (such as who initiates behavior to whom, whether prisoners walking to meals or other events walk in racially mixed or homogeneous pairs and groupings, what topics are discussed in group counselings, how many prisoners speak to an officer, and so on).

For the observer, the principal difference between a correctional system and other settings lies in the reality of surveillance in the daily life of the prison. There is no innocuous bystander to a prisoner. He is under surveillance by his captors, and he knows it. Information is gathered to keep the staff informed about him for custodial purposes, and he knows it. Any study must conduct its observations in such a way that inmates or parolees are not under greater surveillance than they would ordinarily experience; the observer must be understood to be benign both in his intention *and in his impact,* and able to avoid further complicating the lives of those he is studying. With only slightly less force the researcher has the same obligation to the staff. Correctional staff members are likely to be concerned with maintaining a posture of authority in the presence of inmates, and will distrust a sociologist who appears unaware of the realities of his situation.

INTERVIEWING

The interview is a focused exchange between interviewer and respondent which may be more or less structured, but which must always remain to some extent asymmetrical in the sense that initiative remains in the hands of the interviewer. The respondent may raise topics, take various lines of conversation, determine pace, but if there is to be a distinction between conversation and interview, it is this: The interviewer retains the initiative concerning the questions covered, and makes some recording of what transpires. The interview is distinguished from simple observation by greater contact with an individual respondent and the active eliciting of responses to questions.

Interviews in correctional systems must be planned so that rapport is achieved with the respondent without the surrender of objectivity. A successful interview strategy must correctly assess the way the prisoner, parolee, or officer perceives the interview. Why does (or should) the respondent cooperate with the interviewer? Is an inducement consciously or unconsciously extended? Does the respondent think the interviewer will actively help him, possibly injure him, or probably make no discernible difference in his life? Prisoners are particularly vulnerable to surveillance and may have good reason to be reluctant to express themselves on even seemingly innocuous questions. Only the demonstrated honesty and capacity of the interviewer to safeguard the privacy of the respondent and not to compromise his interests will suffice to enlist the cooperation of wary inmates. Under some conditions, however, the interview may provide an occasion for the respondent to discuss something with someone who is not another inmate, a keeper, or a therapist. Among inmates in a women's prison, for example, David Ward found an unusual readiness to talk about homosexual behavior in the prison because of a combination of factors: his professional status, outside affiliation, and absence of therapeutic intervention (i.e., there was no question of attempting to discourage or "treat" the homosexual behavior discussed). Specifically, cooperation with interviewees on sensitive topics will be aided by:

1. Making it clear that the interviewer has no connection with any legal, welfare, police, or correctional agency.

2. Identifying the interviewer as a university researcher. The respondents are likely to accept the legitimacy of a general sociological investigation of the experience of imprisonment by a researcher affiliated with a university, because they accept the role of the university in doing such research and because they feel that the results may reach a wider audience through publication. Implicit here is the distinction between university research, which may be directed to "nonpractical" topics, and research conducted by prison staff members and the department of correction. These latter efforts are viewed by inmates as being limited in scope to the solution of some "problem" and the results distributed only among department personnel.

3. Identifying the researcher as a sociologist. Most of our interviewees stated explicitly at one time or another that they felt that other persons (principally non-clinical prison staff) could not understand some kinds of behavior (notably deviant behavior) because they were not sociologists, phychologists, or psychiatrists. They also remarked that persons from these latter groups would not be shocked or personally distrubed by what respondents told them.

4. Using the label of "Doctor." By legitimizing questions through formal title use, and thus helping to establish an atmosphere of professional understanding, the respondent was made to feel more at ease in talking about taboo topics.[13]

THE QUESTIONNAIRE SURVEY

Observation, costly in time and effort, is often necessary for the intelligent preparation of systematic interview schedules, and for the collection of data on behavior that may not be easily or truthfully verbalized. The interview may produce more data comparable from respondent to respondent (where standardized schedules are used) while encouraging rapport and permitting probes of areas that appear especially promising. The advantage of a *survey* is largely derived from sampling

13. Ward and Kassebaum, *Women's Prison*, p. 244.

considerations (getting enough cases for analysis, and reducing bias due to unrepresentative cases), but typically depends on the feasibility of the self-administered questionnaire. It is only realistic to bear two things in mind: Prisoners and parolees are in most cases men with little education, and functional illiteracy is not at all uncommon; and prisoners may be more likely than respondents in free society to appear to comply with the survey when in fact they do not understand the question. Some screening or at least careful scrutiny of item wording and item responses is required if survey questionnaires are to be used. Sometimes inmate advisers or critics are useful in getting proper wording or in eliminating poorly phrased items.[14]

The survey may generate a large number of written questionnaires, and great care must be taken to ensure that neither casual nor deliberate reading of any of the forms is possible by persons not on the research team. Both staff and inmates should be assured that the responses will be confidential. This impression is *not* sustained if question-naires are stacked on an unwatched table, carried out of the prison by staff, or coded by an inmate clerk. On our study of men's and women's prisons, Ward and I made it a point to decline offers of assistance in carrying boxes of completed questionnaires and inmate record abstracts to our car, even when this meant making extra trips through a large area of the prison. This fact was noted and commented on favorably by inmates later. Field notes, tape recordings, etc. should not be left over-night even in locked offices; experienced men on prison staffs and inmates as well assert that unauthorized keys exist for nearly all locks. Everything confidential should go back to the office or hotel room every night, even when no apparent ground for suspicion may exist. We know, for example, of a project director whose field notes were obtained by the custody staff and used in a dispute over a project. (Not, in-cidentally, any of our projects.)

RECORDS

Since correctional systems are bureaucratic organizations, and are more-over in an important sense political agencies, records in these studies provide the student with some of the more important data. The use of formal records as a source of data, however, must not be confused with the actual content and statements that constitute the record information itself. The record may not have use as data as it stands; demonstrated inaccuracy of official records in some instances may itself be an impor-tant datum to the research. In addition to the manifest content of records, the manner in which records are created, accumulated, updated, distributed and used provide important information about the operation

14. *Ibid.,* "Methodological Appendix."

of the system. What are the sources of given items in a record? Who makes the entry? Is it updated or cross-checked against other sources? Does the same information appear elsewhere in a collection of records?

Records may be conveniently divided into summary information about the activities of specified correctional or law-enforcement agencies, facts on the operation of an institution or office, and information kept on individual inmates or parolees, and in some cases former prisoners or parolees. Each of these types is somewhat different from the others.

Records of state or federal agencies are typically collected annually, and issued for the year previous. Characteristics of persons in prisons, both state and federal, are published. Recent establishment of the *Uniform Parole Reports*[15] permits compilation of parole data for all fifty states, something that was not possible before.

The various states publish annual reports, typically for the entire department of corrections, division of paroles, and youth authority. It may be difficult to obtain records for each prison separately. There is apparently enormous variability from state to state in the manner in which annual reports are compiled.

When we speak of a man's "criminal record," we are of course using a metaphor. There is no single record, even for a person who has come to the attention of only one state correctional system. Some information collected by the police or by a court may not be in the prison record. Juvenile and adult records on the same individual may not be in the same file. Misdemeanor and felony records may be in different places. All the material in the prison file is not always transferred to the parole file. While the present trend toward computer-based, integrated, statewide police and judicial record systems may result in the ready availability of a complete file of information on a given individual, at present the safest initial assumption is that information on any person is probably stored in more than one place. For the sociologist, the primary questions related to such files are: (1) How is the information obtained and organized? and (2) What is done with it—particularly, how does it affect the career or life situation of the subject of the file? Aaron Cicourel has contributed significantly to the thinking on this question, and so have Edwin Lemert, Erving Goffman, Marvin E. Wolfgang, and Thorsten Sellin.[16] In my experience, some of the most valuable information about the pitfalls, intricacies, and complexities that are to be

15. Coordinated by the Research Center, National Council on Crime and Delinquency, Davis, California.

16. Aaron Cicourel, *Social Organization of Juvenile Justice* (New York:Wiley, 1967); Erving Goffman *Asylums* (New York: Anchor Books 1962); Edwin Lemert, *Human Deviance, Social Problems & Social Control* (New Jersey: Prentice Hall, 1967); Thorsten Sellin and Marvin E. Wolfgang *The Measurement of Delinquency* (NY:John Wiley, 1964).

encountered in the interpretation of official correctional records was provided by the head of the records and statistics division of a state department of corrections. Such persons are often extremely sophisticated about this area and are willing to instruct when approached in a reasonable manner. The sociological research project is often (indeed, should be) in a position to cross-validate certain conventional information in the records, to determine the manner in which the information is obtained and coded, and to raise questions concerning the interpretations of this record information. One of the more serious mistakes a research project could make would be to relegate record-room coding to a casually instructed project clerk or assistant. On the contrary, an analysis of the *meaning* of the inmate or parolee records is among the more demanding and sophisticated research problems confronting the student.

A Note About Evaluation Studies

One of the more important functions of sociologists employed in correctional systems is the evaluation of program effectiveness.[17] Indeed, the world at large, and particularly the legislatures and the executive branches of government that approve budgets, demand evaulation of the correctional system as of all government bureaucracies. The evaluation is seldom if ever attempted with the hope of proving a program to be of no value; on the contrary, evaluations are often in the nature of disguised demonstrations of an innovation's payoff. However, it is not undue cynicism to expect the most likely outcome of an evaluation of a new program's effectiveness to be something less than a demonstration of its potency. This is particularly so if the criterion of a program's effectiveness is the reduction of postrelease criminality, which in turn is measured by the rate of returns to prison. A review of studies in the immediate past will not reveal many that show differences in postrelease performance clearly in favor of the treatment group.

The more interesting aspects of such studies, however, may lie in the investigation of the manner in which policy and discretionary decisions influence the rate of return to prison from parole. The sociologist who seeks to account for variation in postrelease returns to prison should examine the nature of the decision-making at the time the prisoner is considered for parole. In particular, how is the prehearing summary of the inmate's record prepared? What, if any, are the risk level and other release criteria used by the parole board in reaching its decision? (And

17. The question of evaluation is discussed at length in Gene Kassebaum, David Ward, and Daniel Wilner, *Prison Treatment and Parole Survival: An Empirical Assessment* (New York: Wiley, forthcoming).

what are the characteristics of the prisoners not released compared with those who do secure parole?) What are the general policy considerations with respect to given offenses or offenders? For example, is the public demanding greater protection from persons with histories of violence? Is the state or municipal government conducting a drive on certain kinds of offenses in connection with an election or other political event? Similarly, how are revocations of parole handled and where is relevant policy effectively determined? And who constitutes the parole board? What is the pattern of relationships between police and parole officers? What are the procedures actually followed in revoking paroles? Finally, what happens to the person whose parole is revoked and who is returned to prison (particularly, does he drop from the sample at that point, or is he retained in the follow-up in some way)? Without a fairly detailed consideration of organizational factors in the administration of parole, the postrelease survival rate of former inmates may be interpreted in a truncated manner (as a funtion of parole behavior solely) and the subtle complexities of the organization of the total correctional system may be missed. This requires not only primary data collection (observation, interviews, etc.) with actors in various positions (inmates, staff, parolee, parole board, parole officer, significant others in the parolee scene) but also some overall model of the functioning of a system of criminal justice.

A Closing Call to the Fray

In the course of thinking about writing this short chapter, I reviewed published and some unpublished research reports and theoretical treatises on institutional populations. This literature, both in sociology and in psychology, reveals few formal examinations of problems associated with methods and techniques of data gathering. Yet chief among sociology's woes is the general problem of eliciting information from persons who have little to gain and much to lose from revealing something. This is nowhere more clearly encountered than in military and police interrogation, and in social science research in prison, reformatory, mental hospital, and criminal populations, where there are traditions of inmate distrust of contacts with both staff and free persons. (The same may be said of secondary education. *Tom Brown's School Days* is in fact an essay on the convict code.) All this poses *par excellence* the problem of rapport. No less a question is the formal illegality of much of the behavior about which information is likely to be sought (posing the problem of respondent veracity) or the high degree of social visibility, rapid transmission of rumor, and closeness of sustained interpersonal contact that are characteristic of prisons, hospitals, and other closed communities (raising the problem of confidentiality). Thus small-scale studies devoted explicitly to methodological development are necessary to the larger operations aimed at increase of substantive knowledge. There is normally little opportunity in any large-scale inquiry to study the effects of various forms of interviewing and survey techniques, or to try out different methods of achieving rapport. When done at all, these operations are restricted to the pretest or pilot stage of the research. Yet a methodological inquiry could devote itself (or at least a major portion of its time) to testing alternative ways of obtaining rapport, or to determining differential probabilities of rapport associated with various types of inmates, staff, topics, and situations.

It may thus be a wise expenditure of time if the research begins with a period of assessing the best strategy for the kind of information needed and for maximizing the likelihood that the data obtained are, in the end, useful to the resolution of the problem.

Suggestions for a Study of Your Hometown

This presentation is written as if you were visiting Hometown for the first time, and as if your organization had instructed you to arrive as quickly as possible at a comprehensive knowledge of Hometown so that you might effectively represent it there. Toward the end of the presentation I shall have something to say about the advantages you, with your long experience in the community, would have over a newcomer in your *own* Hometown.

To do this job of community analysis there are certain tools you will obviously need. A map of Hometown is your first tool, for a brief glance at it will provide the trained eye with more facts than could be secured from any other source. (This of course depends upon the map; most street maps are featureless, without an accompanying street directory.)

Prior to 1890, American street directories were even more useful than they are today, but they are still an indispensable part of any such investigation as this. There are three principal divisions of the average directory; (1) the alphabetical name section for individuals and business firms, organizations, etc.; (2) the street directory, listing each house or building, and usually each separate family or business occupant of such buildings; (3) the classified advertising section. Most, if not all, such directories also contain an introductory section in narrative style, containing facts about the town statistically arranged from the census and other sources; there is usually also a section devoted to the city government, giving the principal officeholders and often a great deal of detail about the personnel of the various city services.

Reprinted by permission from *Human Organization*, 11, no. 2 (1952): 29–32.

For the fastest orientation, it is ideal if you can find a series of older maps of the city (usually accessible at the public library) so that you can trace the characteristics of the city's growth.

Before you have gone much further with your investigation, it will be advisable to learn more about the earlier inhabitants. For this purpose you will need another tool: one or more volumes of local history, usually to be found in the form of county-wide accounts of the history and biographies of the area, with sections devoted to the towns and cities in each county.

Other tools will be suggested later, but we shall start with those mentioned and see whether after a week in town we could arrive at any understanding of its social structure.

Let us start first with the county history. Here we shall assign fictitious names to typical characters. Sooner or later in the county history we will come across the name of Jedediah Early, who was connected with the Early Trust Company; perhaps we shall also be able to establish that William A. Newcomer married one of the Early girls. If we can also connect the Early and Newcomer families with the foundation of the Hometown Manufacturing Company, we have a good running start on a reconstruction of the way people have earned their living in Hometown for many years. This is, of course, a roundabout way of approaching the matter. There are probably in the county history many names of families who have moved away, and others whose names have died out, at least in the direct line, although they may survive as middle and even first names.

The quickest way to find out where the major economic decisions are made in Hometown is to go to the public library and ask to see a copy of Rand McNally's *Banker's Register* (if the library does not have it, go to one of the local banks). There you will find the names of all the Hometown banks as of the year of publication; however, because of the mortality of banks after 1929 there are great advantages in looking up two volumes: the current one and one prior to 1929. Take this list of banks and look up another publication, Moody's *Banks*. Here you will find the names of the directors of your Hometown banks, together with the history of the mergers which have taken place and which have contributed to the present condition of these banks. In this book there will also be found a current bank statement of assets and liabilities and probably the dividend record.

Another set of tools becomes necessary: a card file. Some people prefer three-by-five-inch cards because they are handy to carry; others use five-by-eight-inch cards because they provide more space for notations. Use one card for each bank and record the names of the directors on the ruled side and the history of the bank on the reverse, unruled side. Then make a separate card for each bank director, with his name (last name first) in the upper left-hand corner. Put his address, if it is available, on the top right, and his directorships (with his principal connection on top) in the middle. On the reverse side of the card record his personal history, data of birth and parentage at the top, marriage, children, education, etc. These cards should be alphabetically filed in the boxes in which the cards were bought, thus dispensing with the added expense of buying special files.

Card files become your most important source of information, and you will find that it is necessary to cross-reference them constantly. They constitute the basic difference between our approach and that of the census-taker: we are primarily interested in individuals and their patterns of relationship, while he is interested in the overall statistical aggregates.

With the list of bank directors in hand, turn now to another tool volume: Poor's *Register of Directors*. Here are listed all the most important corporate directors in the United States. These men do not always record their directorships, but the listing is as complete as the editors are able to make it on the basis of their investigations. From Poor's *Register* you can find the *other* corporate directorates held by Hometown bank directors. This will lead you at once to the names of all important Hometown businesses, for banks tend to accumulate to themselves the leading financial and business talent in town. This method of analysis will be successful provided Hometown's bank is not part of a chain of banks which merely maintains a manager in your town. But, unless your town is very small, it did once have a bank, and not so very long ago, so that a study of earlier editions of the volumes cited above will reveal the names of Hometown's bank directors.

Such volumes as these may not be available in many cities and towns, but if there is a university in the neighborhood its library may carry them; they should also be found in large city public libraries. In many cities there are often business libraries attached to the chamber of commerce or elsewhere, and usually your Hometown banks subscribe to some or all of these publications. If among its successful sons who have moved away your town numbers a broker in some big city or a metropolitan banker, a letter to him may bring your library a copy of one or more of these volumes, which, although perhaps a few years out of date, will still be useful for your general purposes. The names of the directors of your banks for the current year can be ascertained by asking the local bank for a copy of its annual statement, which is usually published in a small folder on the back cover of which is a list of the directors. Business connections which are not corporate, such as partnerships or firms, will usually be found in your street directory.

Turn now to the Hometown Manufacturing Company in your directory, where the names of its officers and chief supervisory employees will probably appear. This will enable you to plot on the map the residences of superintendents or foremen and operating management. You will find that while only the top men live on High Street or in Hills and Dales, the others often tend to live as close to these neighborhoods as they can afford, the older men nearer High Street, the younger nearer Hills and Dales.

A number of directories also designate the place of employment of those who work in the Hometown Manufacturing Company by some such mark as "Hometown Mfg.," for example. This will enable you to plot on the map the residences of those employed at the factory. When the craft or special skill of the worker is also indicated, as it is in most directories, you can find out where the several grades of workers live. (It should be understood that the word "grades," as used here, has a purely technical usage, such as machinist" or foreman," and is a means of distinguishing the probable wage received, since this tends to determine what rent workers can pay and other economic facts we are trying to establish.)

Once you have begun to accumulate cards for individual residents in different parts of the city and have marked their cards according to their occupations, you are on the way to the preparation of a residential map of the city. It will be advisable to devise a system of symbols to designate the different income grades and occupational groups, and attach them to individual residents on the map in order to show the approximate location of their homes on the streets of the city.

Incidentally, if you are enterprising, one map bought from the local bookseller who handles the Hometown street directories will enable you to trace any number of copies on transparent paper. Once you have plotted on your maps the location of your bank directors, corporation directors, superintendents, foremen, and workers in the factory, you are ready to branch out into a neighborhood-by-neighborhood investigation of Hometown; this will include its churches, neighborhood and nationality clubs, formal and informal social groups, political and business groups, etc.

Such an investigation will lead you back in the direction of your census materials, which are also to be found in the public library. But the model for the investigation is not to be found in the census, but in the publications of social workers. For information about census tracts it will be necessary to approach someone connected with a public or private charity, or a governmental office dealing with welfare or relief. In many cities (and their number is increasing), students have made area studies of the different neighborhoods, showing the number of cases of one sort or another falling in a given area; types of sickness, law violations, social maladjustments, such as juvenile delinquency, have been indicated area by area on city-wide maps. This is one of the most fruitful parts of any study you may make of Hometown. However, these findings must be considered very carefully and you should avoid arriving at a hasty conclusion on the basis of any one type of case as it appears on the map.

From this wealth of material, a comprehensive pattern of neighborhood distribution of these various groups will emerge. By turning to the street section of your Hometown directory you may be able to discover whether or not the resident is a homeowner and sometimes whether he has a telephone. This information will help to confirm your guesses about income status. By working back and forth between the street section and the alphabetical section of your volume, you will be able to verify your sampling on a street-by-street basis. In this way you will soon know a great deal about the distribution of Hometown population, group by group, and income, class by class. If your organization were interested, for example, in a door-to-door selling campaign, this information would be of considerable help.

For some purposes it may be necessary for your organization to know the national origins of different groups in the community. In past times many of these groups tended to live in their own separate neighborhoods and to develop separate national institutions, such as churches, parochial schools, clubs, and organizations of one kind or another. Increasingly these distinctions arising from national origin are breaking down in this country. The younger generation is tending to move out to newer suburban developments, where they mingle with people of other national origins. This is part of the melting pot of which the Americans are so properly proud. A study of your Hometown map as prepared by the method described above will reveal, however, that the melting process is far from complete in many communities.

Any study of local politics will reveal that politicians are highly aware of group differences of all kinds, including those just described, and that they are a factor in the political, social, and economic life of the community. By turning to the first section of your Hometown directory, where information about City Hall and other city services is listed, you can make a card file on the political structure of Hometown. A study of this file will show that it reflects some of the divisions within the community, as already indicated in the foregoing.

The life of most communities is still dominated to a large extent by the oldest inhabitants and their descendants. Usually they exercise the chief influence on the boards of local banks, and insofar as businesses are locally owned they tend to retain a controlling interest. But today this is by no means a universal pattern, since the influence of out-of-town corporations has become more and more important in all but the leading cities of the country. As a first approximation we can say that the social system of a community (with its various organizations, such as the community chest, Red Cross, etc.) leans heavily upon the families of those long established in the community; the economic leadership is drawn from the ranks of newer individuals and groups; and the political leadership is even more frequently in the hands of the representatives of newer groups.

To understand the social system of the community insofar as it can be distinguished from the political and economic systems, it is usually necessary to begin with the churches as the oldest local social institutions. These are in turn distributed throughout the community, and a map showing their location will be very instructive and assist in pointing up some of your other findings. Since most churches are not only religious but neighborhood social organizations, incorporating many nonreligious activities, a study of the leadership of these subgroups within the church will also contribute to your understanding of the community.

Any young businessman coming to the city for the first time and expecting to establish residence there will want to know about the other social and charitable organizations, their functions, and their representation of various groups. Some of these can be called "total community" organizations, for instance the community chest or, within the business community, the chamber of commerce. Others are representative of special groups in the community. One of the most significant keys to the social grading system is to be found in the structure of the more exclusive clubs. There is usually a club to which only the older inhabitants are admitted, and their method of choosing even among this older group displays their attitude as to the necessary qualifications for membership in the inner circle of their group. If you can secure a list of their membership and compare it with other parts of the social structure, such as leadership in total community organizations, churches, charities, and clubs, you will have a useful key to the relationship between the older and the newer groups in town.

In this type of study it is easy to lose sight of the fact that getting a living is the backbone of community life and that the jobs held by men and women are bound to be the ruling factors in their lives. The increase of absentee ownership of factories and stores, and even of newspapers and banks in towns and cities of the United States, makes it more and more difficult to understand the patterns of organization of individual communities. To find out what is happening to these plants and businesses, you need new tool volumes. For industries, consult Moody's (or

Poor's) *Industrials*. One or the other of these will give you a picture of the extent to which your local factory is still locally controlled, or to what extent control has passed to out-of-town groups. While these sources are adequate for our present purposes, if a really extensive study of these matters were being made, it would be necessary to consult the records of the Securities and Exchange Commission in Washington. If the language used is unfamiliar, some acquaintance who has experience with reading such source material should be called upon for help. Here you may find that the local company (though still locally owned) has perhaps undergone a series of mergers prior to arriving at its present size; if you are interested in the historical aspects of the community, it will be worthwhile to study the companies that merged to form the existing one. The story of your local industries is paralleled by what has happened to your local, privately owned electric light, gas, water, and street-transportation system or systems. A similar tool volume is available for investigation of these companies in Moody's (or Poor's) *Public Utilities*. All of these facts should be recorded on file cards and properly catalogued.

In a short space of time you will now have gathered a very comprehensive picture of the life of Hometown. (The size of the community will of course determine the length of time this job will take, although much will depend upon your previous experience in making such studies.) Nevertheless, there are many things you cannot find out by these mechanical methods. The most important facts which tend to elude this approach are of a personal order. It is essential to live long years in a community in order to be aware of some of the most important of these facts. As an outside observer, or even one who has had a short residence in the community, you cannot hope to find a completely adequate substitute for this experience. However, as the representative of your organization, you are expected to find a short cut which will be the best possible substitute for such long residence.

The best substitute for your long residence is to gain access to certain of the oldest inhabitants. Experience will show that there are certain people in the community, not always members of the socially elect group but frequently drawn from among them, whose type of mind reproduces the patterns we have just described, without resort to our complicated methods. Frequently these individuals have recently retired from the most influential positions in the community and are still active in the local historical society. If you are properly introduced and they respect you as a scientific investigator and believe you have the best interests of the community at heart, they will often be of invaluable assistance in providing that type of information which can generally come only from a lifetime knowledge of their town or city. You will do well to try to find at least one such person (and if possible several) who is willing to assist you and who will talk to you freely. By working with more than one of these individuals, you will be able to triangulate your results and so avoid some of the inevitable effects of bias. Even the most objective of these persons is bound to see the life of his community from a slightly different vantage point than would any other such observer.

If you are a lifelong resident of Hometown, you will be able to supply the same sort of information as this oldest inhabitant and will want to correct your bias by the methods I have described. Nevertheless, a lifelong resident will have a great advantage over our supposed representative of an out-of-town organization. You will know, for example, who married whom, and what the grandparents and even the great-grandparents of many of your fellow residents contributed to the life of the community. Without having to make maps of the historical growth of the community, you will know at what point in time which suburbs developed, and just when different local businesses came under out-of-town control.

Without referring to the files of the local newspapers (which by the way are indispensable to a visitor-observer) or having to talk to the local newspaper editors, you will know just which events in the life of Hometown are of the greatest importance in the estimation of its citizens. You will know when crises arose in the life of the community and how they were solved. You will know what effect the depression and mass unemployment had on the town or city and what happened when labor tried to organize the local plants and businesses. Above all, you will know the personalities and dispositions of the human beings who make up Hometown, and you will realize what an important part such personal traits can play in the average community. In short, these mechanical methods I have recommended are bound to produce a dehumanized picture. It is essential for the observer to try to restore the characteristics of a living community, with its hopes and fears, its shared pleasures and sorrows.

One of the most elusive things you must try to understand is community spirit, and in this connection you must attempt to discover what individuals or groups in the community hold the symbols of community leadership at any given time.

In addition to the churches, there are two places to look for the symbols of community integration. One of these focal points is the cemetery, and the other is the patriotic organization. No community, modern or ancient, can be understood without reference to these two sets of facts. It has been said that "the most important people in Hometown are dead." Even to American society, with its gaze fixed upon expansionism and the future, ancestors are of great symbolic importance. If ancestors in general are important, those who participated in our military history are of great significance. Certain patriotic organizations in each community tend to be regarded by the rest of the community as safeguarding the symbols of patriotism. It is necessary to study the structure of these patriotic organizations as an important factor in the advancement of Hometown life, to be present on the day of their most symbolic activity, Memorial Day, and watch the course taken by the parade—from High Street down through the business section of the town and out to the oldest cemetery. This will usually contribute many useful facts about the nature of community spirit.

All this is bound to sound like an overwhelming job; for the largest cities, of course, it is much too great an undertaking for any single individual to carry out in a reasonable period of time, even as a first approximation. Nevertheless, if you will reread these proposals with care, you will find ways and means for short-cutting and sampling, depending upon the size of your community; after operating with this outline for only a few weeks, you will find the characteristics of your community taking on new significance even if you have lived there all your life.

Sociological Research in Big Business

Big business institutions comprise cultural phenomena both in their range and in their complexity. One of the more productive research methodologies for their study is that variant of ethnomethodology which essentially combines historiography or documentary research with field study and quantitative data gathering.[1] In face of the compelling, persuasive business mythology that pervades so much of Western thinking, particularly in America, and in view of the widespread lack in understanding of the converging economic, social, and political forces that gave rise to modern corporate enterprise, let us start our study with a brief and I hope not too sanguine historical sketch.

Emergent Corporate Enterprise

The development of big business institutions in Western culture has come about as the institutional counterpart of the later phases of the industrial revolution, going back approximately to the beginnings of the nineteenth century. This development is comprised of institutional modification, synthesis, and innovation paralleling the proliferation of machine industry and power technology. It involves the emergence of a new kind of corporate oligarchy and centralized political and social control, which currently is well along in the process of superseding earlier traditions of representative political government and social control, historically oriented in handicraft technology, with agriculture as the dominant industry.

Reprinted by permission from *Human Organization,* 11, no. 2 (1952): 29–32.

1. Jacques Barzun and Henry F. Graff, *The Modern Researcher* (New York: Harcourt, Brace & World, 1957).

148

Through the facility of the new technology, corporate institutions have extended into and permeated the fabrics of other cultures and societies in varying degrees in virtually all parts of the inhabited globe not barred to them by communist rivals or hostile local governments. Very few of the recently numerous primitive cultures are any longer completely isolated from their influences.

These developments have been rapid and profound. They have wrought massive change in the character of everyday living in countless subcultures at home and abroad, changes of catastrophic proportions in many areas. They have been continually characterized by pervasive conflict, ranging from varying degrees of subtle social disruption and maladjustment to innumerable uprisings, political overturns, and wars. Like traditional political oligarchies, corporations tend to be conflict organizations. As the primary organizational media of technological innovation, displacing older traditional institutions, they have shrouded their inner councils in secrecy. Their successful development and expansion of political and economic power have depended upon innovations in organization and an arrogation of economic and political control which, if open to the light of public scrutiny, would have been much more directly and vigorously opposed and subjected to traditional governmental control than they have been.

A striking fact about big business is the aura of mystery surrounding it.[2] The reasons for this are basically simple. In the first place, the suddenly accelerated development of corporate business institutions during the decades following the Civil War in the United States took place in an environment of severe industrial conflict over control of industrial resources, the new technology of production, and access to markets.[3] In the second place, the legal formula under which the American business corporation is organized has developed the principle of limited liability to the extent that those who exercise the final authority of decision-making and control commonly do so outside the formal legal corporate structure itself.[4] Moreover, the legal devices through which control is established and maintained enable those in control to shroud themselves in complete anonymity if they choose to do so. The political and social powers and influences of big business have grown so large as

2. Robert L. Heilbroner, *The Limits of American Capitalism* (New York: Harper & Row, 1965), p. 26.

3. Thomas C. Cochran and William Miller, *The Age of Enterprise: A Social History of Industrial America* (New York: Macmillan, 1943); James H. Bridge, *The Inside History of the Carnegie Steel Co.* (New York: Aldine, 1903), an extraordinarily informative contemporary account of the formation of the United States Steel Company; Frank Fetter, *The Masquerade of Monopoly* (New York: Harcourt, Brace & World, 1931).

4. Adolph A. Berle, Jr., and Gardiner C. Means, *The Modern Corporation and Private Property* (New York: Macmillan, 1932), pp. 233–46.

to rival traditional government.[5] Individual wielders of these new political powers and the actions they take, the policies they follow, and the influences they bring to bear on society are not, as in the case of elected and appointed officeholders in traditional government, subject to the normal controls of public opinion and governmental sanctions. Moreover, local community controls have broken down progressively as new, uninhibited innovators in technology and in business and industrial organization have displaced the older, more traditionally conservative family partnership businesses.[6] The new technology has made possible progressively rapid and massive scales of production within plants. It has made possible, by railroad and steamship transport, the marketing of products over regional, national, and international markets. It has made possible the rapid and massive dissemination of all sorts of news and information, including the establishment of private national and international communication networks, essential to broad geographic control of operations. It was in this milieu that the old chartered joint stock partnership, the family business institution, and the governmental corporation were synthesized into a new institutional complex, the corporate system of business government.[7]

By the late 1880s the waning effectiveness of state control of corporations created a massive public demand for the establishment of federal control, culminating in the passage of the Sherman Antitrust Act of 1890.[8] Though this act had some effect in checking the cruder manifestations of conflict in the building of interstate business empires, the incentive of big profits in big business induced experimentation with every kind of device of business operation and legal manipulation to make possible further expansion of business empires. A major breakthrough in this effort came about simultaneously with the movement for the enactment of the Sherman law. In 1888 an astute corporation lawyer, James B. Dill, succeeded in lobbying through the New Jersey legislature the first of a series of statutes that very effectively bypassed the whole corpus of common law underlying the state and federal controls over intercorporate empire building.[9] These empires had come to be known

5. Earl Latham, "The Body Politic of the Corporation," in *The Corporation in Modern Society,* ed. Edward S. Mason (Cambridge: Harvard University Press, 1960), pp. 218–36.

6. W. Lloyd Warner and J. O. Low, *The Social System of the Modern Factory* (New Haven: Yale University Press, 1947).

7. Berle and Means, *Modern Corporation and Private Property,* pp. 1, 356–57; Latham, "Body Politic of the Corporation," pp. 219–36.

8. Henry R. Seager and Charles A. Gulick, *Trust and Corporation Problems* (New York: Harper, 1929), pp. 339–85; Hans B. Thorelli, *The Federal Anti-Trust Policy: Organization of an American Tradition* (Baltimore: Johns Hopkins Press, 1955), pp. 108–63.

9. Fritz Machlup, *The Political Economy of Monopoly* (Baltimore: Johns Hopkins Press, 1952), pp. 240–44.

as trusts because of the use of the legal trust device for establishing complete proprietary control over numbers of legally independent and formerly competing corporations, most notably illustrated by the case of John D. Rockefeller and the Standard Oil Trust.[10]

The series of statutes Dill guided through the New Jersey legislature was to culminate in a general codification of the statutes of incorporation in 1896, carried out by Dill under commission by the governor and duly passed by the legislature.[11] Delaware followed suit by rewriting its constitution and corporation statutes from 1897 to 1899, installing substantially the same formula with Dill's able counsel.[12]

A principal purpose of these states in passing these revolutionary statutes was to attract incorporators from all over the country and abroad, who would then provide revenue from incorporation fees and annual taxes on capitalization. These fees and taxes, set on a sliding scale according to capitalization, were far lower than those of other states. Moreover, the powers granted in the certificates of incorporation served the purpose of bypassing virtually the whole corpus of state and federal regulation and control of the antitrust variety, so that they became highly attractive to business groups bent on collectivizing numbers of firms, an activity made technologically practical under power technology.[13]

10. Seager and Gulick, *Trust and Corporation Problems,* pp. 96–124; Thorelli, *Federal Anti-Trust Policy,* pp. 63–96.

11. Harold W. Stoke, "Economic Influence upon the Corporation Laws of New Jersey," *Journal of Political Economy,* 38 (1930: 551–79 (the only research found explaining the circumstances of the passage of holding company statutes); U.S. Industrial Commission, *Preliminary Report* (1900), vol. 1, p. 1077.

12. Russell C. Larcom, *The Delaware Corporation* (Baltimore: Johns Hopkins Press, 1937); *New Jersey Law Journal,* 33 (1910); 384.

13. According to Stoke, "Economic Influence," the provisions of the formula include:

A. Unlimited nominal capitalization, regardless of actual capital possessed by incorporators.

B. The issue of securities under this nominal capitalization to be sold to the public or to use in exchange for the purchase of any assets, including shares of stock in other corporations, with the power of exercising full property rights over assets acquired as though the corporations were natural persons. This power functions as the authority to print money. Theoretically and actually the market value of issued securities turns on the anticipated profits of business operation, just as money created by bank loans to businessmen depends for its value on the capacity of borrowers to repay out of their operations. The security arrangements are different but the function is basically identical.

C. Carry on any lawful business in any state or foreign country, and to do so in the name of the corporation without disclosing who the individuals might be that exercised the corporate powers behind the fronts of "dummy directors."

D. Dissolve and terminate the corporation without resort to the courts.

In brief, these provisions enabled the incorporator to create a paper corporation, capitalized at any figure decided upon, nominally representing money funds which might be large enough to buy up numerous corporations. He was then in position to go out and carry on negotiations for the purchase of other corporations, issuing shares to pay for them. This transaction consists of exchanging shares in the new corporation for controlling shares in the old firms.

A fundamental conflict of social goals that persists to the present time was involved in the situation. On the one hand, federal, state, and local governments were faced with continuing insistent demands for encouraging and facilitating the development of industry and commerce to meet the needs of the growing nation. On the other were demands for the imposition of sanctions and controls on business groups engaging in cutthroat competition, trade warfare, and innumerable conflict devices made technically possible under proliferating power technology and the flexibility of corporate organization.

The continuing efforts of the federal government to exercise some effective control over big business empires, principally through such regulating agencies as the Interstate Commerce Commission, the Federal Trade Commission, and the Securities and Exchange Commission, have served to mitigate some of the grosser forms of conflict. But the essential anonymity of persons exercising top proprietary control of the holding companies through which numbers of operating corporations are in turn controlled remains unchanged to this day.[14]

EXTRACORPORATE CONTROL GROUPS

The identities of some of the principal major family interest groups are known in a vague way because of their great wealth and the occasional revelations of antitrust and intercorporate litigation, congressional investigations, and the activities of regulating agencies. Examples are the Rockefeller group and the Standard Oil empire; the Du Pont family and E. I. Du Pont de Nemours, General Motors, United States Rubber, and other firms; the Mellon group and Alcoa, Gulf Oil, Texas Gulf Sulphur, and so on; the Gianinni group and the Bank of America and the Transamerica Corporation; the Morgan group and United States Steel, General Electric, numerous railroads, and numbers of other firms. But the specific identification of individual decision-makers, the precise mechanisms of control exercised, and the relationships between the complexes of extended family groups and the empires with which they are vaguely identified generally escape detection.[15] Some attention will be given to these matters below.

Another key to the understanding of the exercise of control in particular industries is the activity of trade associations. Access to markets—markets for products, for finances and securities, sources of supply, technical personnel, machinery and equipment, and strategic proper-

14. Machlup, *Political Economy of Monopoly*, pp. 239–40 *et passim;* Corwin Edwards, *Maintaining Competition: Requisites of a Governmental Policy* (New York: McGraw-Hill, 1949), p. 142; Heilbroner, *Limits of American Capitalism*, p. 26; Thorelli, *Federal Anti-Trust Policy*.

15. Ferdinand Lundberg, *The Big Rich and the Super-Rich* (New York: Lyle Stuart, 1968).

ties – is crucial to the success of any new enterprise. These are generally controlled through trade associations, directly and indirectly, much in the way that the American Medical Association and state and local medical associations control entry and access to medical practice. An enterprise possessed of potentially profitable new technical or organizational devices must gain access to all these markets. Although ostensibly confined by law to the functions of statistical fact-gathering and reporting on the common business problems of member firms, trade associations actually operate as information-gathering agencies through which groups controlling established firms are alerted to the activities of other firms in the industry, new and old, so that pressures can be brought to bear to regulate the trades represented. Since trade associations inevitably are dominated by the major firms, the latter are in the best position to apply pressures and to take advantage of opportunities to take over firms unable to survive the pressures.

As a consequence of the highly unstable organizational control situation in American firms, big and small, a variable but pervasive instability has characterized the economic subculture throughout the history of power technology.[16] Hence the rise and fall of business organizations comprise a continuing history of unique events the study of which is essential to the development of systematic analysis of the sociology of big business.

The Problem of Access

Big business organizations have become so complex and pervasive in Western culture within the past century and a half that even the most sophisticated members of control groups heading the major business empires probably are only approximately aware of the ramifications of intercorporate empires other than their own. Organizations never spring into being fully armed as from the brow of Zeus. Before approaching any particular firm in the field, a researcher should investigate it systematically by consulting standard business reporting sources: Poor's *Register of Corporations, Directors, and Executives,* an annual publication available in banks as well as libraries, and the Moody series, *Industrials, Banks and Insurance, and Railroads,* are invaluable. These give brief histories of corporations, list the names and titles of current top managements, indicate the principal lines of industry or commerce in which firms are engaged, principal subsidiaries, states of incorporation, and similar information. All of the major business firms have publications concerning them which can be obtained in any adequate city or university library. Often a major library will have a reference librarian who

16. Cochran and Miller, *Age of Enterprise.*

specializes in business publications. In the major university and public libraries materials exist in such profusion that one can devote his career to library research alone and virtually never run out of data.

At the minimum, prior to attempting field access to any firm directly, the researcher should investigate documentary materials sufficiently to build up a fairly clear outline history and extended organizational structure of the firm and the industry or branch of commerce in which it operates. In particular he should determine at least tentatively whether the firm in question is independent or part of a larger intercorporate complex. This is a matter of some moment. Lacking historical, organizational, and broader business area orientation, the researcher will in all probability fail to notice local policies and behavior that are significant to the larger organization and its objectives, and to the broader business milieu in which it operates; if he does notice them, he is not likely to understand them.

Alvin W. Gouldner's report of the use of students in the gathering of data demonstrates an access resource really indispensable to extended fieldwork.[17] Where the departmental program includes adequately designed, systematic fieldwork training, preferably beginning immediately following the introductory course, the amount of substantial high-grade fieldwork that students can accomplish by the time they are seniors will be incredible to academic researchers who have not participated in such a program. Moreover, fieldwork so motivates students in standard lecture courses, as well as in courses in statistics and other methodology, that departments that include such programs will find they have to pitch their offerings at levels considerably higher than are practical in traditional programs. As students discover through cumulative field research training the relevance of their own experiences to the theoretical abstractions of classroom and literature, they will draw on their work experiences, family contacts with firms, and similar resources to become important sources of information, contacts, and theoretical development for research teams.

Organizational Surveys

In general, firms should always be approached at the top of the accessible organizational structure, the top having been established by preliminary documentary investigation. All corporations are governed under the proprietary authoritarianism of the American corporate system. However, like the local variations of agricultural feudalism noted by medievalists, variations will manifest themselves in any survey involving

17. Alvin W. Gouldner, *Patterns of Industrial Bureaucracy* (Glencoe, Ill.: Free Press, 1954), pp. 247–69.

numbers of firms.[18] In relatively stable industrial situations involving long years of operation at the same sites with relatively small technological and market change, the patterns of bureaucracy will exhibit very different characteristics from those that engage in volatile technology and short-run operations. In general, there is relatively much greater stability of structure in the former. Gouldner's case[19] illustrates the stable type. It also illustrates nicely some of the characteristic variations of personality and primary group interaction characteristics associated with different occupations in the same organizations. Some of these factors in the internal organization, notably what he terms the "indulgency factor," which is central to authority and control characteristics, the technological factor, market forces, factors of personnel selectivity, and community setting, all show up more vividly under conditions of crisis and change.[20]

At another extreme, there are industries where operations are for short runs and involve rapid technological change in esoteric technology with an extreme range of personnel mix from common labor through teams of scientists. Examples are certain recent war industries, which meet the problems of extreme organizational instability in ways very different from those used in more normal operations. Some of these are: virtually no promotion, only movement of personnel into and out of the organization at all levels, either from other subsidiaries or by raiding competitors; production schedules and tie-in of operational runs with contracts and subcontracts involving a high frequency of minor and major crises associated with more or less complete reorganization and radical turnover of virtually whole groups of personnel; peculiar patterns of extreme indulgence and extreme control, rationalized and ritualized by reference to security and technological necessity; continually changing ritualization and symbolism of office, work place, secretaries and assistants, parking, and other appurtenances in relation to status, role, function, and authority.

Since the security controls in vogue in this type of firm frequently make them relatively inaccessible to outsiders, much of the data must come from informants who have worked there. As there is a great mobility of personnel, the accessibility of informants is relatively high in communities where such firms operate. The personnel problems in these firms are rather extreme and frustrating, and investigators who can obtain clearances can in many instances do well-paid participant observation work as consultants. However, there is no reason to expect the consultant's job to be any less crisis-prone or unstable than anyone

18. Joan Woodward, *Management and Technology* (London: H.M. Stationery Office, 1958).

19. Gouldner, *Patterns of Industrial Bureaucracy*.

20. Alvin W. Gouldner, *Wildcat Strike* (New York: Harper & Row, 1954).

else's. In any case, consulting should not be attempted until after extensive comparative survey experience in varieties of firms and extensive interviews with informants have been accumulated.

The organizational survey technique starts with compilation of lists of firms in particular categories for comparative purposes. An example might be some industry or commercial category: manufacturing firms, transportation firms, retail firms, financial firms, etc.; or geographic category: a sample of all the firms in a geographic area; or technological category: samples of firms using certain classes of technical processes and equipment, particularly interesting when major technological change is under way and comparisons between old and new technology can be made.[21] When students are used as interviewers, surveys dealing with employment opportunities provide excellent motivation for training purposes. By the time a resourceful and perceptive student has interviewed personnel in a dozen or fifteen firms, starting at the top in each case, he will have accumulated so much knowledge and sophistication about organizational characteristics and their recurring problems and employment potentials that he probably will never be a job hunter again!

Management personnel at higher levels are rather rigorously confined to their own firms and operational sites. Consequently they are extraordinarily ignorant of parallel operations, problems, and solutions in other firms. After a few studies a student becomes something of an expert, since he can describe comparable problems other firms have encountered and suggest similar solutions. Anyone in the student or academic role can pursue this procedure profitably. It has one serious drawback, however: Many of the best sociological interviewers turn up or create for themselves business offers and interesting positions they will find hard to refuse, especially since insistence on the researcher role is as attractive to prospective employers as the job-hunter role is repellent.

Because of the basic insecurity of all corporate business organizations, an approach to business research through the problems of individual respondents is a peculiarly effective avenue of access. There is no assured tenure in business organizations above the level of unionized workers. Technological innovation, organizational succession and change, proprietary succession and change, market change, and changes in government regulation, all have their differential incidences. Hence everybody has problems, and getting respondents to talk about them is relatively simple, once essential rapport has been established.

Orientation of Questions

EXTRACORPORATE CONTROL

The question of ultimate extracorporate control is essential to the under-

21. Woodward, *Management and Technology.*

standing of any big business organization. It cannot be answered without considerable systematic research. The problem is one of spelling out in specific terms the mechanisms through which control is exercised and by what individuals. As Berle and Means point out, control essentially falls outside the scope of formal, legal corporate entity,[22] and hence it is exercised through the corporation. This means that control lies in the hands of informally related individuals or groups; people whose power to exercise control can be identified only by the circumstantial evidences of each particular situation. For phenomena of this nature, the circumstances must be unique to the particular case in the same sense that the differences between the forms of power exercised in the governments of Britain, France, the United States, and other countries depend upon the uniqueness of historical circumstances.[23]

The question of control must not be assumed to relate only to obvious examples of big business firms such as American Telephone and Telegraph or General Motors. Dill's holding company formula enables corporations to be formed by virtually anyone. It further makes it possible for any firm to be sold to another holding company. Organization, operation, and sale of corporations can be carried out by individuals or groups in complete anonymity through agents or employees. The strategic advantages of maintaining anonymity are so great that it is commonly done as a matter of course, particularly by operators determined to build empires.

For these reasons it can never be assumed that any firm, large or small, is not controlled ultimately by a big business organization. "Dummy independents," subsidized by big business firms, have long been widely used to undercut prices in local markets for particular products or services in order to cause competing firms to sell out. This may be done when some individual or group has developed a potentially valuable technical device or productive system that threatens to displace older devices or systems on which big business depends. The instability of industrial technology and the unpredictability of its productivity in the hands of numbers of actual or potential producers have been the roots of economic and social instability virtually from the beginnings of the industrial revolution.[24] Following the introduction of the steam engine and its development to universal practicality by the 1830s, the proliferation of power technology has progressively increased the uncertainties and instabilities of society. The source of this instability is in the detail of technological organization, which, in the main, is the function of the corporation: the organization of industry.

It is imperative for survival, then, that big business engage system-

22. Berle and Means, *Modern Corporation and Private Property*, pp. 233-45.
23. Barzun and Graff, *Modern Researcher*.
24. Neil J. Smelser, *Social Change in the Industrial Revolution* (Chicago: University of Chicago Press, 1959).

atically in the suppression and control of small businesses. Big bureau-cracies are relatively inflexible despite the very substantial successes in decentralization of authority and control for essential functional flexibility, particularly in big business organization.[25] The development of large-scale industrial organization depends upon the "finalizing" or stabilizing of technical systems. The control of these phenomena is essential to the survival of big business. The further development of technology, however, virtually never stops. It goes on in tens of thousands of shops and laboratories and plants virtually everywhere, so that new and revolutionary breakthroughs are occurring continually, involving more or less serious potential threats to the capital establishment of big businesses committed to older technology. To control such development within their organizations, corporations almost universally require their employees as a condition of employment to assign any patent rights in technical developments to their employers. To keep abreast of external technological developments that may be relevant to their business interests, they commonly operate research and development divisions or subsidiaries. These organizations continually seek out new technology in order to acquire control over it, and if possible prevent the growth of new firms that might cut into their business interests.

ORGANIZATIONAL SUCCESSION

Since organizations are ultimately comprised of people, and people are subject to the biological cycles of aging, the phenomenon of organizational succession poses a continuing problem in the analysis of big business organization. In the matter of organizational control, succession turns on the character of the control groups as human groups, and on the sociological character of the business organization as a bureaucracy.

Prior to the establishment of Dill's legal formula, the corporation was substantially and legally first a public governmental agency, and later, as the principles of limited liability were evolved, a quasi-public organization.[26] Dill's formula was designed to complete the conversion of the corporation to an item of private property. In the public utility field this has produced the anomaly of the private public utility, such as the American Telephone and Telegraph Company. With control concentrated in the hands of anonymous individuals outside the formal organization, the question of the succession of control turns on the disposition of property.

25. Alfred S. Sloan, "Comments on Inertia in General Motors Bureaucracy," in *Relative Efficiency of Large, Medium, and Small Business,* T.N.E.C. monograph no. 13 (Washington, D.C.: U.S. Government Printing Office, 1941), p. 130.

26. James B. Dill, *Business Corporations, Their Formation and Advantages* (Jersey City: New Jersey Registration and Trust Co.; pamphlet).

When the corporation or the intercorporate empire under common control is built up by an individual or informal group of individuals, succession depends upon the disposition of control as property over the generations. In general, the succession of control follows two common patterns.

If the control group establishes a strong family organization determined to retain its role as proprietor over the generations, the typical big business family emerges as a consequence. The Du Ponts,[27] Rockefellers, Fords, and Mellons are well-known examples.[28] The establishment of inheritance taxes at increasingly high levels has made the problems of retaining control over the generations increasingly difficult, particularly when the older people lose their adaptability and vigilance and their firms suffer heavy financial losses. Taxes have to be paid in cash to exacting deadlines, and the weakening of firms typically involves shortages of cash. Hence there is a disposition to sell out in order to realize something on remaining equities, either before the holders of control die off or as an incident to the settlement of estates. The device that has come to be used widely to meet this contingency is the tax-exempt nonprofit foundation, a form of corporation established for public charitable purposes. The outstanding example of use of this device was the establishment of the Ford Foundation.[29] When estate planning is systematically worked out by lawyers and accountants, the advantages of dispersing proprietary holdings accrue approximately in proportion to the capacities of extended families to maintain their integrity, at least so far as the goal of retaining proprietary wealth and control over the generations is concerned.

A much more numerically common pattern is the business firm or empire built up during the lifetime of the individual businessman or partnership, whose descendants follow the tendencies more normal to the Anglo-American family system to disperse over the generations. The older family tradition of sons growing up in the father's business tended to weaken as the family business organization declined, and with it the educational functions of apprenticeship—displaced by power technology—and the emergence of public educational institutions. The influence of the frontier movement in American life and the individuating effects of population selection in the processes of immigration effectively prevented the establishment of proprietary entail in land, and undermined family authority between generations from the beginnings of colonial settlement. Hence the extended business family that

27. William C. Lawton, *The Du Ponts: A Case Study of Kinship in the Business Organization* (unpublished Ph.D. dissertation, University of Chicago, 1955).

28. Lundberg, *Big Rich and Super-Rich*, pp. 132–247 *et passim*.

29. Dwight MacDonald, *The Ford Foundation: The Men and Their Millions* (New York: Reynal, 1955).

persists over the generations with its accumulations of proprietary resources, which generally prevails in Europe and other older civilizations, has not been established, generally speaking, in the United States. This probably explains the early synthesis of the business corporation in the United States noted by Oscar and Mary Handlin.[30]

The holding company formula is peculiarly well suited to the dispersional tendencies of the American family over the generations. Whether a new holding company is formed to take over the properties, or acquisition is made by an established firm, the result, so far as the retiring family is concerned, is the same. The problems of family succession are notoriously difficult in societies where extended family systems prevail, typically buttressed by legal requirements of entail. The American corporate system, completely unencumbered by family tradition or entail, provides the universal solution to this problem.

Sources of Data on Big Business Phenomena

Fieldwork in business organizations, large and small, as the foregoing discussion indicates, inevitably will reveal data on big business, particularly when adequate sensitivity has been developed on the part of the investigators. As we have seen, the documentary sources are superabundant. For this reason, the essential scientific skills of historiography in pursuing data and in interpreting them with disinterested ethnological objectivity cannot be too strongly emphasized. It will become abundantly evident from the outset that the conflicts and controversies that have characterized the history of business institutions have colored the expositions of a very large proportion of commentators. There is a widespread tendency to regard the investigator of big business as bent on sensational revelation of chicanery, abuses of power, and invidious behavior generally. People favorably disposed to big business frequently interpret its investigation as a a species of spying on the private affairs of our most estimable citizens. There are good reasons for these suspicions. The dangers of partisan involvement are subtle, pervasive, and difficult to avoid. The uncritical acquisition of specific knowledge about big business phenomena inevitably tends to induce critical attitudes when such knowledge contrasts more or less sharply with attitudes generated from childhood by favorable business propaganda pervading the mass media.

The fact that much of the interest in big business has been generated by partisan stimuli must be kept continually in mind in assessing the

30. Oscar Handlin and Mary Handlin, "Origins of the American Business Corporation," *Journal of Economic History*, 5 (1945): 1–23; reprinted in *Enterprise and Secular Change*, ed. Frederick C. Lane and Jelle C. Riemersma (Homewood, Ill.: Irwin, 1953).

broad array of source data. In some cases the biases are clear enough in the titles: *The Rich and the Super-Rich; Giant Business, Threat to Democracy;*[31] *Management and Machiavelli*,[32] and the like. Yet the most biased sources may contain either abundant data or leads to data. The nature and existence of bias itself in relation to the context of its generation comprise data in social research. In any case, bias cannot be eliminated. It is simply amenable to relative degrees of control.

Finally, a rich source of information particularly pertinent to the conflict aspects of big business is to be found in trial records, generally available only in the courts of trial. Control groups are continuously involved in litigation. Antitrust litigation is central to the matter of control and its exercise. Such litigation is particularly rich in data because the building of government cases, oriented in the doctrine of conspiracy, requires extensive research on the historical background of corporate operations, the accumulation of masses of documents from company files and depositions of company officials, and, in larger cases, weeks of trial testimony. All of this material is open to the investigator as a matter of public record. With regard to technology, intercorporate litigation over patent and process rights, trademarks, and copyrights is highly instructive. Of particular interest is intrafamily litigation over control. For example, the take-over of the Du Pont company by Pierre Du Pont and the ousting of Alfred Du Pont and others from the control group in 1915 precipitated a series of *Du Pont v. Du Pont* actions.[33] The tendency of most economists and legal investigators is to confine research in litigation to the standard reporting of court decisions. But for sociological research, the trial records themselves are much richer in data, if the researcher can gain access to them.

Business and Theory

It is no accident that there is no social science directly oriented to the scientific study of business phenomena. New institutions invariably succeed by identifying their radical innovations with improved modifications of deeply rooted traditional institutions. Thus radical religious sects identify themselves as fundamentalists. The successes of the Morgans turned in large part on their successful identification as arch-conservatives; yet Morgan's principal legal adviser was our old friend James B. Dill, a radical innovator who was apparently so keenly con-

31. Theodore Quinn, *Giant Business, Threat to Democracy: The Autobiography of an Insider* (New York: Exposition Press, 1953).

32. Anthony Jay, *Management and Machiavelli: An Inquiry into the Politics of Corporate Life* (New York: Holt, Rinehard & Winston, 1967).

33. Marquis James, *Alfred I. Du Pont: The Family Rebel* (Indianapolis: Bobbs-Merrill, 1941).

scious of his radicalism that he seemed for many years to regard himself as a fraud open to exposure. And the elder Morgan sponsored Thomas A. Edison and had him wire his New York residence and business offices for electricity, the first to be so equipped — hardly the behavior of a conservative.

Economics, despite the protestations of economists, still is essentially a doctrinal system of moral philosophy confined in its methodology to deductive rationalism. It has no theory of institutions and no theory of technology capable of inspiring inductive research crucial to the understanding of changes from family to intercorporate business institutions and from handicraft to power industrial technology. This formidable task — the development of adequate research theory — has yet to be accomplished.

Field Research in Military Organization

Military organization provides a rich and convenient setting for field research. Research subjects are readily available during long periods of garrison life or captivity, or during quiet interludes in combat operations. They can be observed in a wide range of behavior. Comparative studies are facilitated by consistent organizational structure. Military operations generate salient issues in public policy. Yet this setting has been poorly exploited for field research. Before the survey work of S. A. Stouffer and others in *The American Soldier*[1] (which did include some data from fieldwork), few investigators had attempted to penetrate the boundaries of military organization to collect data for general hypotheses.

After World War II, however, many sociologists used their own military experiences as bases for field research or participant observation reports. The March 1946 issue of the *American Journal of Sociology* is exclusively devoted to such reports.[2] Elsewhere, similar reports introduce us to George Homans as the commander of a navel ship,[3]

1. S. A. Stouffer, *et al., The American Soldier,* 2 vols. (Princeton: Princeton University Press, 1949; New York: Wiley, 1965 [paperback]), vol. 1, *Adjustment to Army Life*; vol. 2, *Combat and Its Aftermath.*

2. *American Journal of Sociology,* 51 (March 1946). See Anonymous, "The Making of the Infantryman," pp. 376–79; Anonymous, "Informal Social Organization in the Army," pp. 365–70; P. L. Berkman, "Life Aboard an Armed Guard Ship," pp. 380–87; H. Brotz and E. Wilson, "Characteristics of Military Society," pp. 371–75; H. Elkin, "The Soldier's Language," pp. 414–22, and "Aggressive and Erotic Tendencies in Army Life," pp. 408–13; A. B. Hollingshead, "Adjustment to Army Life," pp. 439–47; M. R. McCallum, "The Study of the Delinquent in the Army," pp. 479–82; and Arnold Rose, "The Social Structure of the Army," pp. 361–64.

3. George C. Homans, "The Small Warship," *American Sociological Review,* 11 (June 1946): 294–300.

David Schneider as an Army clerk and basic trainee,[4] and John Useem as a military government officer.[5] More recent reports include those by Sanford Dronbusch as a cadet at the Coast Guard Academy,[6] L. A. Zurcher as a sailor,[7] Eugene Uyeki as a draftee,[8] C. E. Bidwell and W. J. McEwen as professionals serving as drafted enlisted men,[9] and David Olmsted as an enlisted man serving with a military government unit in Korea immediately after World War II.[10]

During the interval between World War II and the Korean conflict there was a large amount of research conducted by institutes affiliated with universities and supported by grants from or contracts with the armed forces. Investigators affiliated with such institutes had excellent opportunities for access to research sites. Unfortunately, most of their research was not reported in the sociological literature, but was published only as technical reports for the sponsoring services.[11] The major contributions were those of the Air Force Base Project, especially the work of Floyd Hunter, Ruth Lindquist, Raymond Mack, Richard L. Simpson, and James D. Thompson.[12] Leo Bogart has presented two reports of research on desegregation of the armed forces conducted during this period.[13] After the Korean conflict, studies were completed

4. David M. Schneider, "The Culture of the Army Clerk," *Psychiatry*, 9 (May 1946): 123-29, and "The Social Dynamics of Physical Disability in Army Basic Training," *Psychiatry*, 9 (August 1947): 323-33.

5. John Useem, "The American Pattern of Military Government in Micronesia," *American Journal of Sociology*, 51 (1946) : 93-102.

6. Sanford M. Dornbusch, "The Military Academy as an Assimilating Institution," *Social Forces*, 33, no. 4 (May 1955): 316-21 (reprinted extensively).

7. L. A. Zurcher, "The Sailor Aboard Ship," *Social Forces*, 43, no. 3 (March 1965): 389-400.

8. Eugene S. Uyeki, "Draftee Behavior in the Cold War Army," *Social Forces*, 38, no. 2 (Fall 1960): 151-58.

9. C. E. Bidwell, "The Young Professional in the Army: A Study of Occupational Identity," *American Sociological Review*, 26 (1961): 360-72; W. J. McEwen, "Position Conflict and Professional Orientation in a Research Organization," *Administrative Science Quarterly*, 1, no. 2 (September 1956): 208-24.

10. David Olmsted, "Two Korean Villages: Culture Contact at the 38th Parallel," *Human Organization*, 10, no. 3 (Fall 1956): 33-36.

11. For an extensive presentation of the diversified social research during this period, see Raymond V. Bowers, "The Military Establishment," in *The Uses of Sociology*, ed. P. F. Lazarsfeld, W. H. Sewell, and H. L. Wilensky (New York: Basic Books, 1967), pp. 234-74.

12. The following reports, originally issued by the Air Force Base Project at the University of North Carolina, Chapel Hill, from 1952 to 1954, are now available only from the Clearinghouse for Scientific and Technical Information, Springfield, Va.: Floyd Hunter, *Host Community and Air Force Base*, document no. AD 491 624; Ruth Lindquist, *The Family Life of Officers and Airmen in a Bomb Wing*, document no. AD 491 621; Raymond Mack, *Social Stratification on a U.S. Air Force Base*, document no. AD 491 620; Richard L. Simpson, *Friendship Cliques in United States Air Force Wings*, document no. AD 491 619; James D. Thompson, *The Organization of Executive Action: Authority, Power, and Wing Integration*, document no. AD 491 612.

13. Leo Bogart ed., *Social Research and Desegregation of the U.S. Army*, (Chicago: Markham, 1969).

independently by Oscar Grusky, Richard W. Seaton, and me, involving fieldwork in a variety of settings.[14] More recently, Charles C. Moskos has reported observations of an infantry platoon in Vietnam.[15]

Obstacles to Research

The meager product of this fertile field suggests some fundamental obstacles to field research in a military setting. Three can be identified:

The military stereotype. The public image of military organization is one of elaborate pageantry and ritual, esoteric rank and organizational designations, and a highly specialized and dangerous technology. Few members of the society have more than a brief experience with it, and even then, only in specialized and limited roles. History, literature, and the mass media have added to the mystique, rather than illuminated it.[16] On the other hand, the mass media have also fostered the development of caricatures of military institutions, especially of officer–enlisted man relationships, as limited in scope as those featured in other occupational dramas, such as the surgical resident and the trial lawyer. These stereotypes frequently make it difficult to identify common features of military institutions with other settings of human society.

The fraternity of arms. The initiation to military life, whether in basic training or in a service academy, is a socially and psychologically expensive process. Those who have successfully achieved membership are reluctant to accept others who have not endured a similar experience. Access to military organization is accorded in direct proportion to the extent that the investigator can display behavior or credentials that entitle him to the status of member. Consequently, the right to claim the status of ex-serviceman is exceptionally important to the researcher who seeks access to the military.

Operational secrecy. The prototype of all military organizational behavior is the combat event, in which disclosure of activities or plans is perceived as threatening the survival of its members and the success of the battle. Consequently, elaborate mechanisms of security have developed, and these impede scientific inquiry as well as enemy intelligence. Related to this guarded perspective is the normative implication of the term "investigation," which is interpreted as a process of determining

14. See Oscar Grusky, "The Effects of Succession: A Comparative Study of Military and Business Organization"; Richard W. Seaton, "Deterioration of Military Work Groups under Deprivation Stress"; and Roger W. Little, "Buddy Relations and Combat Performance," all in *The New Military*, ed. Morris Janowitz (New York: Russell Sage Foundation, 1965).

15. Charles C. Moskos, Jr., "Why Men Fight," *Transaction*, 7, no. 1 (November 1969): 13–23.

16. For excellent introductory descriptive materials that penetrate the mystique, see (for the Army), *The Non-com's Guide* (Harrisburg, Pa.: Stackpole Press, 1965). For the Navy, see *The Bluejacket's Manual* (Annapolis: U.S. Naval Institute, 1966).

responsibility for a misdeed or culpable action. So strong is the reaction to this term that it must be assiduously avoided in any research on military organization.

Diversification of Military Organization

Even more than prisons, hospitals, and other settings for field research, military organization is highly diversified. The research environment may be as flexible and congenial as the garrison or shore base, or as difficult to observe as the relationship between pilot and navigator in a cockpit built for two. At least three significant differentials may be identified.[17]

Status groups. All military organizations are rigidly stratified into two major status groups, officers and enlisted men, a ranking that pervades all aspects of their service, family, and community life and is proactive into postservice life. This distinction retains many of the symbols of its feudal origins, but is elaborated in a system of mutual expectations of suspicion, hostility, and relative competence.[18] The distinction is far more fundamental and extensive than that which prevails between such analagous status groups as managers and workers.

Echelons of risk. Military personnel are differently distributed in relation to the risks of combat, or in peacetime to the pleasures of the garrison or the shore. They constitute collectivities of differential deprivation, with a normative system that supports their relative positions in a system of values. Personnel management policies that manifestly distribute personnel according to their preservice education and measurable skills and aptitudes have the latent function of allocating them according to their social origins in the larger society. Consequently, the echelon takes on many of the features of the social class. Thus high-risk echelons have a residual population, little or no control over their destiny in the organization, poor elaboration of the environment, and a relative absence of ceremonial activities. Low-risk echelons have correspondingly more specialized and skilled populations, increasing control

17. Whenever practical through the remainder of this essay, for the sake of simplicity and brevity, Army terms will be used without reference to the synonymous Navy, Air Force, and Marine Corps terms. Unless you are actually serving at one, an Army base is the same as a naval station; the term "base" will be used here. When I mention the military police, let it not be thought that I mean to denigrate the air police and the shore patrol.

18. This differential is described and analyzed better in fiction than in the social science literature. For origins, see Mark Boatner, *Military Customs and Traditions* (New York: McKay, 1956). For implications in World War II, see *Report of the Secretary of War's Board on Officer-Enlisted Man Relationships* (Doolittle Board) (May 1946). Copies may be obtained by addressing a request to me at the Department of Sociology, University of Illinois at Chicago Circle, Chicago, Ill. 60680.

Table 1. Grade titles of enlisted personnel, U.S. armed forces

Pay Grade	Army NCOs	Army Specialists[a]	Navy[b]	Marine Corps	Air Force
E-9	Sergeant major		Master chief petty officer	Sergeant major; master gunnery sergeant	Chief master sergeant
E-8	Master sergeant; first sergeant		Senior chief petty officer	First sergeant; master sergeant	Senior master sergeant
E-7	Platoon sergeant; sergeant 1st class	Specialist 7	Chief petty officer	Gunnery sergeant	Master sergeant
E-6	Staff sergeant	Specialist 6	Petty officer 1st class	Staff sergeant	Technical sergeant
E-5	Sergeant	Specialist 5	Petty officer 2nd class	Sergeant	Staff sergeant
E-4	Corporal	Specialist 4	Petty officer 3rd class	Corporal	Sergeant
E-3	Private first class		Seaman[c]	Lance corporal	Airman first class
E-2	Private		Seaman apprentice[d]	Private first class	Airman
E-1	Private E-1		Seaman recruit[d]	private	Airman

[a] For rank and precedence within the Army, specialist grades fall between corporal and private first class. Among the services, however, rank and precedence are determined by pay grade.

[b] In general, titles for petty officers are according to "rating" (naval skill) such as boatswain, gunner's mate, yeoman, storekeeper, etc. Personnel in pay grades E-3, E-2, and E-1 are not considered as possessing ratings. The titles listed denote the "rate" or pay grade.

[c] E-3 pay grade also includes airman, construction man, dental man, fireman, hospital man, and stewardsman.

[d] E-1 and E-2 pay grades also include recruits and apprentices in 6 rates listed in footnote c.

SOURCE: *Selected Manpower Statistics* (Washington, D.C.: Directorate for Statistical Services, Department of Defense, 1969).

over their life chances, elaborate modification of the environment, and extensive forms of ceremonial behavior.[19]

Operational environment. Military organizations differ according to the environment in which they conventionally operate: land, sea, and air. Each environment requires distinctive solutions to the problems of adaptation and survival. Land forces operate in a familiar environment, highly plastic and modifiable, and in continuous contact with members of their own or another society. The environment of seamen is filled with the mysteries and superstitions of the sea. The sea cuts men off from physical contact with their society (and the enemy), denies them an opportunity to modify it in any way, and continually threatens their survival with storm and fire. The air is an equally unnatural and unfamiliar operational environment, but it is experienced only briefly and may thus be perceived as an exciting escape from reality, enabling the airman to view society as a panorama rather than a human entity. These distinctions, seldom noticed in descriptions of military organization, may have profound implications for the political ideologies that emerge from leaders of the various services.[20]

Access

At domestic bases, local commanders may grant access to researchers.[21] In preparation for the initial contact, letters supporting the research should be obtained from other investigators who have had contacts with military organization, or who are currently affiliated with research elements of the Department of Defense. If possible, letters may also be obtained from local chapters of such service support organizations as the Association of the U.S. Army, Navy League, and Air Force Association. All supporting evidence should indicate the potential value of the research to the service branch, the investigator's academic and (if possible) service experience, and a pledge of anonymity to respondents. If the research is supported by funds from a research agency of the De-

19. Little, "Buddy Relations and Combat Performance," pp. 195–223.

20. Irving Louis Horowitz, "The Organization and Ideology of Hemispheric Militarism" (unpublished paper presented to the Working Conference on Research Strategies in Studying Changing Military Roles, sponsored by the Special Operations Research Office, American University, May 26, 1965).

21. General procedures for applying to the Department of Defense for access to military information and research opportunities are routinely published in the *Federal Register*, which is available at most libraries and at all U.S. Department of Commerce field offices. More specific information is published in *Release of Information and Records from Army Files*, Army regulation no. 345-20 (Washington, D.C.: Department of the Army, 1967). Most bases of all services maintain adjutant generals' libraries where all unclassified regulations are available.

partment of Defense, initial access is assured.[22] However, the investigator shoud proceed at lower levels as if his request for access is initial, and use the funding approval as *support* rather than *license* for his activities.

At this point, the investigator will also have decided on a role definition. The role I have assumed is that of a conventional scientific investigator with a variety of research instruments. An alternative role, successfully used on several occasions by Moskos, is that of a university professor accredited as a journalist.[23] This method combines scholarly charisma with a familiar role in military organization. However, it may also define the kind of information that will be offered to the investigator because of the relative looseness of the ethical constraints by which he is assumed to be bound. Personnel and other individual and organizational records may not be so accessible to him. It is usually assumed that data gathered by journalists will be published much sooner than those obtained by scientists, and are more likely to be identified with the informants. The use of other methods such as questionnaires and projective tests are incompatible with the role. Thus the journalist role is probably most effective when the contact with the site is limited in duration and when brief interviews and observations are the only methods used.

The initial contact should be made with the base information officer, the staff officer responsible for external or public relations. Copies of all correspondence supporting the research should be available for his files. After several intermediate staff transactions, the investigator will usually be scheduled for an entry interview with the base commander or his deputy. It should be remembered that the commander is responsible for the implications of all data on persons or events within his command. He will be concerned with the methods to be employed, the extent to which research activities will interfere with military routines, and the use to be made of the collected data. Replies to questions such as these should be prepared in advance for *oral* presentation. No attempt should be made to present the commander with a dossier of written material at this time (although it would be proper to offer to leave such material with his adjutant when departing).

At this point and at each subsequent headquarters meeting, the problem of communicating information about the project to subordinate echelons should be anticipated. The investigator may suggest that the

22. The principal agencies of the Department of Defense that support sociological research and to which proposals should be directed are Army Research and Development Command, Department of the Army; Air Force Office of Scientific Research, Department of the Air Force; Office of Naval Research, Department of the Navy. All are located in Washington, D.C.

23. Moskos, "Why Men Fight."

project be discussed at a commander's staff meeting, and offer to come to answer any questions that might develop. Such an oral presentation at a staff meeting (or briefing) has the added value of endowing the project with the commander's implied approval. Written statements, outlines, etc. are of minimal value, are accorded relatively little recognition in military organization, and are usually subordinated to oral orders or comments.

The commander will also expect to be promised some information about the results of the research prior to your departure from the site (in the "exit interview"), and also upon publication. This commitment is rarely a problem because it is unlikely that any firm conclusions will have been reached at that point. It is usually possible to extract from the data some preliminary positive observations that can be communicated at the interview without establishing a commitment for corresponding final conclusions. If the data include comparisons with other commands, only parallel findings should be mentioned, never those that might affect the relative competitive standings of the commanders. It is also helpful to promise the commander a copy of any publication that might ensue from the study.

Since the entry and exit interviews may be the only opportunities to talk with the base commander (unless he is included in the research design), it often improves the relationship if an offer is made to report at weekly or monthly intervals to a staff officer whom the commander may designate. Such an offer implies the sincerity and candor of the investigator, and ensures that he does not get lost in the labyrinth of the organization. It may also prove a valuable resource opportunity if a recalcitrant subordinate commander is encountered.

Questions

The kinds of questions asked depend on the amount of military information the investigator has and the stage of the research. Initially, open-ended, provocative questions are most effective. The use of organizational idioms enhances the credibility of questions as well as the precision of the answers.

I have found the following kinds of questions most useful:

Questions about the tools of the organization. The unique technology of the organization is a major focus of identification and consequently of differentiation from other units. It is also the basis for most of the round of life of the organization. Much can be made of the rifle in the infantry company: as a reliable weapon (requiring meticulous procedures of care and inspection), as a security problem (entailing elaborate storage and accounting precautions), and as a ceremonial symbol (with an associated manual of arms for handling it). Similar analyses can be made of planes in fly-bys and ships on cruises.

Questions about the structure and content of relationships and activities. Asking for a description of the formal chain of command or table of organization and how it is filled out elicits a stream of related data, often with explicit statements of norms. What kinds of activities do you do together, such as belonging to the same squad, sharing tools on work details, going to the service or enlisted men's club or to town on pass? What do you talk about when you are in the barracks with your buddy?

Questions about the ideal structure and content of relationships and activities. With whom do you most *want* to do these things (in contrast to: With whom do you actually do these things)? What are the operational impediments to these aspirations? Usually these questions elicit material about the reward and control system.

Some questions, however posed, incur resentment. Topics that should be especially avoided in the construction of questions (although data will most certainly appear that bear on such topics) are the relations between officers and enlisted men, the technical competence of officers or other leaders, the relative standing of one organization and other specifically named ones, and political events or figures in the larger society.

Events

In the round of military life, the most important event is the meal or "chow." The exceptional importance of the event is indicated by the frequency with which food service is mentioned as a determinant of morale. Chowtime draws men out of their specialized roles in the organization and reinforces their common identity. A formation (or "parade in place") is usually held immediately prior to the beginning of service. Messes are subject to extraordinary surveillance, and the mess hall is often elaborately decorated. Usually there is free choice of companions at four-man or larger tables, providing an opportunity to validate sociometric data. Observation will enable you to answer questions such as these:

Do the officers and noncommissioned officers eat with the other members of the organization? In training centers they rarely do, and junior enlisted men are alone in the mess. In combat they usually do, although spatially segregated.

What is the quality of the relationship between food service staff (cooks and KPs) and members of the company? It may be tense and authoritarian, with minimal interaction (usually when there are many

Table 2. Grade titles of officers, U.S. armed forces

Army, Air Force, Marine Corps	Common titles	Navy
General of the Army		Fleet admiral
General		Admiral
Lieutenant general		Vice admiral Rear admiral
Majory general		Captain
Brigadier general		Commander
Colonel		Lieutenant commander
Lieutenant colonel		Lieutenant
Major		Lieutenant, junior grade
Captain		Ensign
1st lieutenant	Chief warrant officer, W-4	
2nd lieutenant	Chief warrant officer, W-3	
	Chief warrant officer, W-2	
	Warrant officer, W-1	

SOURCE: *Selected Manpower Statistics* (Washington, D.C.: Directorate for Statistical Services, Department of Defense, 1969).

complaints about the food), or congenial and generous, with the mess sergeant and cooks joining other members of the unit in the dining area when they all have been served.

Who eats early chow and late chow? Because some organizational roles must be continuously performed, one of the shifts must eat earlier or later than others. Usually night-shift personnel eat early chow. Often guard or watch details eat late chow. In either case they may be routinely absent from this collective event.

Another important event is the weekly or Saturday-morning inspection (SMI). Preparations for the inspection begin on the preceding night and continue until the inspecting officer appears at the door of the site. Conversations during the preparatory phase are especially descriptive of attitudes toward unit leadership. Observation here will yield information along the following lines:

Who participates in preparation for the SMI? Does the platoon sergeant or squad leader stay until the job is finished? What categories of members are excused from participation, such as headquarters clerks and food service personnel? Do informal leaders emerge who innovate devices for evading organizational requirements, or who attempt to become heroes by exceptional enthusiasm for the event?

What sanctions are promised and awarded as a result of the inspection? Passes (authorized absences from the base) may be granted or denied, the chances of promotion enhanced or destroyed, gigs (minor punishments or demerits) awarded; for a flagrant deviation, the offender may be demoted, or "lose his stripes."

How is the effectiveness of the inspection coopted, and by whom? The noncommissioned officers may encourage evasive practices, or fail to carry through on sanctions imposed by the commander, or increase the sanctions and demand more meticulous compliance with organizational routines than is necessary. If the inspection is conducted by an officer from a higher echelon, the immediate commander may also participate in a system of evasive techniques.

Work details constitute a third category of events. Such details (or ad hoc task groups) may consist of integral units, such as squads or sections, or (more commonly) be drawn from a duty roster by the first sergeant or other senior noncommissioned officer. The task to be performed has no relation to the routine duties of the members: digging a latrine or garbage pit in the bivouac, painting the mess hall in garrison, or pulling KP any place. Details provide special opportunities to establish new relationships and to demonstrate abilities not recognized by the assigned organizational role. Usually, however, they are considered dull, depressing, depriving events, only one step removed from punishment. By observing work details, the researcher may learn the importance of questions like these:

Who gets chosen regularly, and what categories are never chosen? Privileged characters are identified by exemptions, such as headquarters clerks, cooks, and officers' drivers.

When tools or tasks must be shared, who works with whom? The work situation, like the chow line, may be used to validate previous sociometric choices.

What does the leader do? The noncommissioned officer in charge of the detail may agree with the members on the ignominious nature of the task and join them in the work, or he may stand aloof (as cooks and mess sergeants do with KPs) and add further indignities by trivial demands and meticulous requirements.

Athletic contests may also be observed. Such events bring members of the company together in a context in which rank is theoretically irrelevant. Inferences may be drawn about identification with the unit, attitudes toward the commander, and clique formations within the organization. Such events may also be opportunities to observe a transition from competitive rivalry to overt conflict between units.

Finally, conversations in the common toilet facility—the latrine or head—should be observed. Since separate facilities are always provided for officers and enlisted men, interaction occurs without surveillance, The communal arrangement tends to promote intimate and expansive interaction and the exchange of viewpoints on a wide variety of topics. Its significance as a communications center is expressed by reference to the latrine rumor.

Subgroupings

The major subgroupings in military organization are, of course, officers and enlisted men. The distinction between combat and support (or rear echelon) personnel may also be a basis for division, but rarely for collective activity. Subgroups are nucleations from a core of undifferentiated regular duty members. The following are typical of those found to be significant.

Noncommissioned officers. The senior grades (sergeant major, master chief petty officer, chief master sergeant) are so remote and rare that they constitute a subgrouping only on a very high organizational level, if at all. The intermediate ranks with direct supervisory duties may be observed as a subgroup. They usually have a separate alcove in the mess hall, are exempt from details and mandatory instruction, tend to gather in small clusters before unit formations and join their elements only just before the parade or other activity begins. Equally significant, of course, are their status peers who identify more strongly with their men, work with them on details, and go on pass with them after duty, rather than with other noncommissioned officers.

Supply sergeants or petty officers. This is one of the few roles in military organization that requires frequent meetings and transactions with counterparts in other organizations. Consequently, supply personnel often exchange evaluations of other units. Collectively, they frequently operate an informal system of exchange, called "scrounging" in the Army and "cumsha" in the Navy, in which one supply sergeant makes up for a deficiency in his inventory by exchanging his surplus goods for those of another supply sergeant. Scrounging or cumsha is technically forbidden but is tolerated and tacitly encouraged by commanders because it keeps their supply accounts in good shape and avoids embarrassing surveys and inspections by higher level supply officers.[24]

The supply room is an important source of other kinds of information. When a unit is alerted to move into combat or to be relieved by another unit, the supply sergeant is one of the first to be told so that he can arrange for collection and loading. The supply room is also a critical stage for many individual events. When a man turns in his property — bedding and baggage — it means that he is enroute to the hospital or stockade, being transferred out or being discharged.

The kitchen staff. Despite the crucial service provided by the mess sergeant and his cooks and kitchen police, they tend to be isolated from the rest of the organization. The tasks they perform and the garments they wear are considered effeminate. Their work-sleep rhythms differ from those of other members. Although their work places (the kitchen and mess hall) are subject to rigid daily inspections, their sleeping area in the barracks is rarely inspected. The ability to provide food also implies the ability to withhold it, or to manipulate it as a means of influencing their positions in the organization.

Headquarters men. Men who are selected to work as office clerks usually have some superior social attributes. Since they usually work in the small office of a headquarters staff officer, they are in close and frequent contact with officers, with whom they develop more cordial (often first-name) relationships than prevail in the line elements. Since they are exposed to a wider range of officer behavior, the officers lose their ceremonial mystique and the headquarters men develop a cynical attitude toward military organization in general. They are also spectators in the officer and unit evaluation process and consequently are privy to most of the secrets of the headquarters. Their work place is also a refuge from the barracks, an alternative that men of the line do not have. From

24. Little, "Buddy Relations and Combat Performance."

the viewpoint of men of the line, they are privileged characters, exempt from work details and parades, serving out their time in the plush environment of the headquarters.[25]

Each of these subgroupings has its own ecological niche. There are others, such as the unit dayroom, a large-scale waiting room with old magazines and indoctrination materials, television, and pool and ping-pong tables. There are the clubs that attract men of all units and are roughly stratified: the service club, with a middle-class environment (writing materials and dances with "nice girls" from the town), and the enlisted men's club, with lower-class beer-drinking and pizza-eating facilities. There are also the clubs for the elites: the officers' club with a pretentious aristocratic aura, and the noncommissioned officers' club, which resembles the meeting place of a veterans' organization.

Related groups

There are groups and categories of people both on and off the base who have frequent contacts and relationships with members of the military, and although not actively affiliated with the organization, make significant observations in a variety of contexts.[26]

Civilians who work on the base but live in the surrounding community include barbers, schoolteachers, and waitresses. Moskos found local barbers in Germany to be good informants.[27] Schoolteachers are good observers of military family life. Waitresses hear discussions about unit activities and evaluations of commanders, and observe significant subgroupings. There are also military roles that are so marginal that their personnel maintain and express an external perspective: military police (strongly identified with the local civilian police), psychiatric clinic staffs (always involved in events of eccentric or spectacular behavior), and chaplains (who often define a respite from duty as an invitation to sin).

Off the base, especially in the fringe of shacks at the gates, there are numerous personal service roles, such as bartenders, barbers, tailors, laundrymen, waitresses, and prostitutes.[28] Collectively these establishments often comprise a boom-town community that is worth observing because of its parasitic relationship to the military base, and because of its easy access to personnel who are off duty for relatively brief periods. There are also (at a greater distance) voluntary associations such as the USO, which arranges social occasions between local girls

25. Little, "Headquarters Soldier," *Army*, 7, no. 4 (November 1956): 58–65. See also Schneider, "Culture of the Army Clerk."

26. Hunter, *Host Community and Air Force Base*.

27. Charles C. Moskos, Jr., *The American Enlisted Man* (New York: Russell Sage Foundation, forthcoming).

28. William Caudill, *American Soldiers in a Japanese Community* (unpublished paper, 1958).

and enlisted men, and the American Red Cross, which provides emergency financial assistance and investigates family conditions. There are civilian clergymen and church groups who augment the religious facilities of the base. Public officials — mayors, councilmen, public health officers and nurses, and especially policemen — observe the impact of the base on the local community. Realtors are good sources for ecological data. Finally, there are local chapters of the service support organizations, such as the Association of the U.S. Army, the Navy League, and the Air Force Association, which sponsor joint base-community programs.

Information About the Military

Very little information about the military base or its elements will be discovered at the base or in the local community. Civilian newspapers of the host community often contain accounts of base activities, and of relations between base personnel and the community. Significant events occurring on the base which are interpreted as reflecting adversely on the command, such as officer delinquency or riots, may never be mentioned in the official post newspaper but will be reported in the civilian paper. In overseas areas, the *Overseas Weekly* performs the same function as the local community press does at home bases. Published independently of military control, it provides intensive coverage of the military community, with some tendency toward sensationalism.

Public agencies frequently have data about military families living in the host community. Police have records on military off-base delinquency. Public health officers and nurses frequently have information about health problems created or aggravated by the presence of military personnel (communicable diseases). Public schools have information on the number of children from the base, and of transfers in and out of the community. Chambers of commerce may have data on the military payroll and how it is spent in the community.

RECORDS

Very few records about *organizations* are maintained at any level. At the company or squadron level the most important record is the morning report, a tabulation of the numbers and types of personnel present for duty, which is valuable as census data. The morning report also includes brief and cryptic comments about unit activities. The unit diary (at battalion and higher levels) contains accounts of messages received from lower levels and sent to higher levels about field operations. The diary is compiled with a view to history, however, and is not likely to be accurate. Negative events are often omitted or positively reconstructed.

There are many more records about individuals.[29] The Military Personnel Records Jacket contains social background data, intelligence and aptitude test scores, assignment and occupational experience, records of disciplinary action in the current term of service, and copies of all correspondence pertaining to the individual. (These records are maintained at a separate unit personnel section, apart from the unit itself.) The health record describes all transactions between the individual and military medical agencies from the time of entry into service. The basic item is the report of medical history (standard form 89), which includes social background data (family constellation, preservice occupation, bahavioral difficulties, etc.). The health record may also contain psychiatric or mental hygiene reports with a social-history summary. Access to medical records is through the medical officer in charge of the facility.

Some records are maintained about individuals involved in specific kinds of behavior or organizational events. The provost marshal (military police) keeps a blotter (log) and name file in which are recorded the names of all persons involved in fights, riots, family quarrels, or other forms of delinquency. The judge advocate keeps a file of court-martial orders, indicating the names, offenses, and punishments imposed within the command. The surgeon or hospital commander has a file (usually at the registrar's office) of men admitted (with diagnosis) and discharged from the hospital.

Finally, there are archival depositories. The old files and records of organizations and discharged personnel are maintained at various records depots of the General Services Administration, where they are accessible for research.[30]

LITERATURE FROM THE MILITARY

The most useful publication on a military post is its telephone directory. Such directories contain both organizational and person listings. The organizational listing contains the same information as a simplified organizational chart, indicating both major and subordinate units and their hierarchical relationships. Personnel listings contain names of all officers, senior noncommissioned officers (usually above pay grade E-5), and civilian employees in officer-counterpart positions. Both constitute useful bases for sample selection.

29. For a detailed description of records maintained on individuals, see my chapter "The Dossier in Military Organization," in *On Record: Files and Dossiers in American Life*, ed. Stanton Wheeler (New York: Russell Sage Foundation, 1970). For a general guide to personnel and unit records, see C. M. Virtue, *Company Administration and the Personnel Service Division* (Harrisburg, Pa.: Stackpoli Press, 1965).

30. For a complete listing of service files and archival depositories, see *Records: Records Management Files Systems and Standards*, Army regulation no. 345-210, reprint including changes 1 through 3 (Washington, D.C.: Department of the Army, October 1962).

Bulletin boards may also be viewed as a form of literature. All units are required to maintain one, on which is posted most prominently the daily bulletin. Frequently several echelons will publish such bulletins, each of which must be posted and presumed read. Usually such boards are divided into new and old sections, the first being changed frequently and the second rarely. Besides such authorized displays as official orders, announcements of approved court-martial sentences, political indoctrination materials, special duty rosters, and organizational events, there may also be posted expressive graffiti and underground materials.

Many units and all posts publish newspapers containing public relations materials. Such publications are retained by the post information officer for varying periods, but rarely for more than three years. The usual problems of validity of information from house organs apply. In overseas areas, *Stars and Stripes* is the authorized daily newspaper, but external items from the wire services dominate its pages. It is usually supplemented by organizational papers that cover unit activities more intensively. Broadcasts of the Armed Forces Radio Service may also be monitored from off base.

Service journals provide accurate interpretations of new regulations and departmental policies, news and ideas of the military community, and statements reflecting the ideological posture of the services. Such journals include the *Army, (Navy,* and *Air Force) Times* (separate journals by the same publisher with unique coverage for each service), *Journal of the Armed Forces, Army, Navy, Air Force,* and *Marine Corps Gazette.* The *Times* provides the best coverage of issues concerning enlisted men and junior officers. *Journal of the Armed Forces* is keyed to senior officers and civilian appointees of the services. The glossy professional magazines—*Army, Air Force, Navy,* and *Marine Corps Gazette*—are published by supporting civilian organizations, such as the Association of the U.S. Army, the Navy League, etc. Controversial and derogatory issues are usually avoided in all but the *Times* series.

Each of the services publishes a variety of official materials that enunciate policies, announce changes in equipment or formations, and describe the structure of organizations. Typical are *Airman* (Air Force), *Army Information Digest,* and *All Hands* (Navy), all available from the U.S. Government Printing Office on a monthly basis. All Army units in divisions are described in detail (grade structure, occupational specialties, and equipment) in *Infantry School Reference Data.*[31] Similar data for other services may be obtained from their service schools.[32]

31. *Infantry School Reference Data* (Fort Benning, Ga.: Infantry School Bookstore, 1969; published periodically).

32. For a complete listing of the names and addresses of service schools, see James C. Shelburne and Kenneth J. Groves, *Education in the Armed Forces* (New York: Center for Applied Research in Education, 1965).

There is an extensive literature of guidebooks for the orientation of persons in new roles. *The Non-com's Guide, The Petty Officer's Guide, The Airman's Guide,*[33] and The Bludjacket's Manual[34] apply to enlisted men. For officers there are *The Officer's Guide, The Air Officer's Guide,*[35] and *The Deck Officer's Guide.*[36] Customs of family and social life are described in other guidebooks.[37] There is even a *Guide to Army Posts* with details of post facilities and characteristics of adjacent civilian communities in the United States and overseas.[38]

INVESTIGATORY MATERIALS

Military bases, as federal installations, are never investigated by others, except for occasional congressional committee hearings and by the General Accounting Office. Reports of such investigations are available from the agencies, but they are usually not kept locally, and will probably not even be known of.

Reports of internal investigations of units are retained in the files of the investigatory agency and are rarely available for study. Proceedings of boards of officers may sometimes be obtained from the appropriate staff officer, although if a senior officer is the subject of the investigation the report will probably not be available. Reports of trials by court-martial may be studied at the office of the local judge advocate, if a case is recent, or at the service level (in Washington) if the case is more than a year old. Investigatory materials are more likely to be filed with the records of the affected individuals than with those pertaining to the organizations to which they belong.

UNOBTRUSIVE MEASURES

Major commands maintain composite records of "morale indicators," which, although of doubtful validity, may be used as unobtrusive measures. Factors assumed to be indicative of variations in morale are rates of sickness and hospitalization, unauthorized absences (AWOL), courts-martial, vehicular accidents, contributions to charity drives, chapel attendance, evaluations of proficiency in training test and inspections, and so on. Such data are usually readily available, but are highly dependent on the conditions under which they are generated or collected. F.

33. All published Harrisburg, Pa.: Stackpole Press, 1968.

34. Annapolis: U.S. Naval Institute, 1966.

35. Both published Harrisburg, Pa.: Stackpole Press, 1968.

36. Annapolis: U.S. Naval Institute, 1966.

37. See Mary Kay Murphy and C. B. Parker, Fitting In as a New Service Wife; Betty Kinzer and Marion Leach, *What Every Army Wife Should Know*; Esther Wier, *What Every Air Force Wife Should Know;* and *The Answer Book on Naval Social Customs* (all published Harrisburg, Pa.: Stackpole Press, 1966). See also occasional articles in *Army* by Katherine Elder.

38. Harrisburg, Pa.: Stackpole Press, 1966.

G. Harris and I found that a company with the highest number of company punishments in a period of five months had incurred them all on a single Saturday inspection from one officer.[39]

Other records are available that may serve as unobtrusive measures. The company pass register and sign-out book indicate the number and destinations of persons leaving the post after duty. The duty roster reflects the categories of persons available for work and other details. The morning report contains basic census data and indicates changes in the composition of the unit.

Participation

One of the major limiting factors in participation is the rigid adherence to an organized format in most activities. Consequently, an observer becomes conspicuous because he does not fit the format. Participation is thus easiest in those situations in which format is at best irrelevant: the mess line and period in bivouac, the smoke break on hikes or work details, or the group on pass together in town. Participation is difficult in barracks (the number of beds conforms to organizational format, with no extra spaces), at parades (except as a spectator), and in combat operations (observers must be cared for but make no contribution). Participation is facilitated by performing a useful organizational role.

The investigator must be prepared to ensure the immunity of all reports from surveillance by higher command levels. Thus he must develop a delicately balanced posture of identification with the values and mission of the organizaion, but of independence from their influence and control. Enlisted men are especially sensitive to evidence that the investigator has "joined the officers" by living with them, attending their club, or being present in situations in which the enlisted men's confidence might be broken. Officers are relatively less sensitive to investigators who reject their perquisites.

Participation may be hampered by an identification of the investigator as a VIP. The VIP usually comes equipped for a safari and his most conspicuous badge is a camera (leading to an informal definition of the VIP as "a bastard from the rear with a Leica"). The VIP imposes unusual ceremonial, economic, and spatial problems on members of the unit ("parades, parties, and pads"). A research investigator should bring a minimum of impedimenta. If photography is necessary, it is better to use a service photographer from the base information office. In participant observation, the observer should wear clothing like that he is

39. F. G. Harris and R. W. Little, "Military Organization and Social Psychiatry," in *Symposium on Preventive and Social Psychiatry*, ed. David McK. Rioch (Washington, D.C.: U.S. Government Printing Office, 1957), pp. 173–82.

observing, either fatigue (work) or dress. In other situations, conventional civilian clothing may be preferable, emphasizing the investigator's independence of military values.

Generally, the longer the period that members of the unit expect the research to last, the greater are the number of opportunities for participation. In periods of a month or more, defensive postures relax, spatial and organizational accommodations are made, and there are sufficient opportunities for members of the unit to test and observe the loyalty of the investigator. On the other hand, if the research is expected to be only a brief incursion, these adjustments are rarely made.

Linguistics

There are abundant opportunities for linguistic analysis in totemistic inscriptions on weapons (e.g., informal names of planes, tanks, and ships), references to power at higher or lower echelons (being screwed), evocative graffiti on protective gear (such as helmets and armored vests), the dialogue of deprivation from conventional satisfactions (genital and excretory references), and argots of functional roles (such as clerks, airborne personnel, etc.).

Strategies

Military organization has increasingly been penetrated by research efforts, so that most commanders have had varying kinds of experience with research methods. Access is obtained most easily if conventional, unthreatening methods are initially suggested and used, without reference to subsequent ones that may be contemplated. In a team study of an American regiment and a Japanese community by a psychiatrist (Harris), anthropologist (Caudill), and sociologist (Little), a survey questionnaire was initially designed and discussed with the post commander for suggested additional items. The questionnaire enabled us to gain the support of the senior commander, to explain the purpose of the research to the entire regiment, and to reinforce our assurances of anonymity. Subsequent stages of the research, although neither announced nor anticipated by the command, were not interfered with. From the data obtained from the questionnaire, Harris designed an interview schedule and Caudill a projective instrument for more intensive study of small samples of the total population (and their contacts in the local Japanese community).

The availability of a variety of research methods and flexibility in their use is essential. Methods must be compatible with an unpredictable sequence of organizational activities, ranging from intensive combat or field training to long and monotonous periods of garrison routines. Survey methods are ideally adapted to garrison conditions, when large numbers of persons can be gathered into mess halls or classrooms. Interviews and observational techniques are best employed in the field.

Participant observation can often be used, especially by persons who are on active service. Sullivan, Queen, and Patrick had one member of the research team fictitiously "enlisted" in the Air Force to study changing attitudes in basic training and a technical school. The observer selected a real enlisted man as a confederate coach and developed a cover story to conceal his professional identity.[40] Moskos identified himself as a university professor in his study of a combat platoon in Vietnam, but was given access to the research sites as an accredited journalist. In my own study of a combat platoon in Korea, I openly acknowledged my rank (captain) and performed the role of an enlisted man (company aidman).

Occasional removals from the field should be included in the total program. Continued immersion in the total institutional life of military organization is exceptionally oppressive, blocks insight, and contributes to early fatigue and intellectual despair. Some access to colleagues should be arranged to renew motivation and to discuss preliminary observations. Our experience confirms Harris' suggestion that research teams investigating military organization would do well to include a psychiatrist.[41]

Strategies in field research in military organization seem to range between two poles. At one pole is the investigator who proceeds with the assumption that he has a right to access because of his research grant or contract. Such an assumption ignores a basic principle of military authority: that the local commander has the ultimate responsibility for everything that happens within his command and the right to act accordingly. Thus the difficulties reported by Arlene Daniels in her study of military psychiatrists are partially due to an excessive reliance on the mandate of the granting office and her demands for supportive services.[42] In my study of the Korean conflict I encountered a company

40. Mortimer A. Sullivan, Jr., Stuart A. Queen, and Ralph C. Patrick, Jr., "Participant Observation as Employed in the Study of a Military Training Program," *American Sociological Review*, 23 (1958): 660–67.

41. F. G. Harris, R. W. Little, and C. O. Frake, *Explorations with a View Toward the Establishment of an Ecology of Adjustment Under Military Stress* (Washington, D.C.: Walter Reed Army Institute of Research, 1957).

42. Arlene Kaplan Daniels, "The Low-caste Stranger in Social Research," in *Ethics, Politics, and Social Research*, ed. Gideon Sjoberg (Boston: Schenkman, 1967), pp. 267–96. Daniels does not, for some unexplained reason, identify her informants as primarily military psychiatrists, or the setting of her research as a military mental hygiene clinic, but this should be clear to a descerning reader (e.g., references to "consultants" who are employed only on a local military base by the medical service, attendance of military officers at national professional meetings, which is extremely rare except for officers of the medical service, etc.). The attempt to generalize from her experiences with this marginal category of military officers exaggerates the difficulties of research in other military settings.

commander initially hostile to my research because I had been preceded by a team of psychologists who had required him to displace the occupants of a bunker and to set up a portable generator (for tape recording), which then drew enemy fire. The validity of data subsequently collected under such circumstances is questionable.

The other strategy is to assume the role of the avenging angel. Members of military organizations, like those of other total institutions, are continuously seeking resource persons who can transcend the boundaries of rank and organization to reach people who can do something about what they perceive as a miserable state of affairs. Because the role is so ineffectively performed by the inspector general, alternatives are sought. Often it is the chaplain, sometimes the medical officer, especially the psychiatrist—roles that are familiar in the civilian world. Thus also it may be that the civilian researcher is perceived as one who can invoke the power of higher levels. So gross are the conditions and so monstrous the misdeeds that the investigator often becomes excited with the spirit of reform. Gratified by the confidence placed in him by his respondents, and innocent of any grasp of the implications of their reports, he is often used in a way that destroys his technical relationship to the command. Not only is his own research setting thus spoiled, but so also is the setting for any further research long after he has disappeared with his incomplete data.

Studying the Hospital

The hospital is a tempting object of study. Its functionaries and its clients seem clearly delineated, its frontiers underscored by rituals of entry and departure, and its territory outlined by physical structures. The hospital, therefore, ought to attract any sociologist, not only those whose research specialty is the medical world *per se*. Problems of all shades of sociological interest, distinct from medical context, can be fruitfully studied here.

Issues of Entry

HOW TO LOOK AT THE HOSPITAL

The hospital has very different meanings to the various significant participants in its affairs. To the physician it frequently is a laboratory, an extension of his office and private practice. To the members of the governing boards the hospital is one of their civic and charitable activities, a view likely to flavor their perception of the institution. To the patient it may well approximate a total institution.[1] Among those who work in the hospital, nurses are likely to come closest to sharing the patient's point of view. Others vary in their view of the degree of totality that they ascribe to this institution.

To the sociologist *all* these views are data. He should beware of traditional views of reality, such as the generally accepted principle of the physical sciences that in any one unit of space at any given time

1. Erving Goffman, *Asylums: Essays on the Social Structure of Mental Patients and Other Inmates* (Garden City, N.Y.: Doubleday, 1961), chap. 1.

185

there can be only one object. This notion is so deeply ingrained in our perception that we tend to apply it unquestioningly to the social world. The notion that the hospital is a hospital is probably the very first trap the researcher needs to avoid when planning his strategies for a hospital study.[2] The degree to which all participants in an institutional drama are able to share their view of the institution depends on organizational unity, on common goals and definitions, as well as on the levels of communication and the degrees of common identity. Many of the groups that participate in the hospital business frequently participate only minimally with each other. Yet the hospital is not only a mosaic of many diverse human segments; it is also a formal organization harboring several (at least two) functional and structural systems. Some actors are members of only one of these systems, others of both, sometimes with a significantly different status assignment in each. Differences in identification with these systems affect the behavior, positions, and presentations of participants.[3]

The drama of the hospital's business will make it difficult to discern the complex web that forms the background of its manifest appearance. And so in contrast with the problems of those sociologists who study the fringes of social life and seek their objects of research in the shadows, the researcher who studies the hospital runs the risk of being blinded by the sharp chiaroscuro that is the result of high visibility, public concern, and the location of the hospital in center stage. Visibility can be just as misleading as darkness.

ACCESS TO THE INSTITUTION

The implication of the multiplicity of systems within the hospital is immediately apparent when the problem of obtaining cooperation in the conduct of the research is tackled. There is no one way of obtaining access to the hospital. The researcher needs to choose among the available routes the one that will lead him to the most appropriate vantage point for observation in accordance with the objectives of his study.

The two most commonly chosen approaches to the institution are through the medical staff and the administrative hierarchy of the hospital. The importance of this choice may vary according to the type of hospital and the actual relationship between power centers within the specific institution. In the general community hospital whose medical

2. I do not mean to imply that this observation is unique to the hospital. It is probably a generic issue in research in social systems, but it is particularly essential caveat in the case of research in the hospital. Likewise, other comments made in this chapter are not necessarily considered uniquely applicable to the hospital, but are selected because they are considered to be of special relevance to hospital research.

3. See Hans O. Mauksch, "The Organizational Context of Nursing Practice," in *The Nursing Profession,* ed. Fred Davis (New York: Wiley, 1966).

staff is typically composed of physicians in private practice, the problem of choosing between the sponsorship of physicians and hospital administrators is real and immediate. In government hospitals or in university medical centers with full-time medical staffs, the balance between these two power centers is not likely to be so delicate. In government institutions it is more likely that the administrative hierarchy is, in fact, the best road for entry, while the opposite might hold for the university medical center, which tends to be characterized by dominance of medical power. In any of these settings, the choice of entrance doors will determine the windows that are open to the observer and those that are closed. Stephen J. Miller, in his work on the intern, describes an occasion when the manifestation of suspicion and hostility on the part of a member of the administrative staff served as a gate-opening and legitimizing incident that ensured his acceptance by the house staff he was studying.[4]

If at all possible, it is desirable to initiate research in the hospital by simultaneously using several avenues of approach. Since all actors in the dramaturgy of the hospital are assigned labels that identify them either with departments or with the major power segments of the institution, the researcher has to cope with the question of sponsorship. There are several reasons why alignment with a medical staff appears most tempting to the sociologist. Of all groups in the hospital, they appear to be most attuned to research (an apparent but not always valid assumption). They seem to be the foremost agents of the activities that represent the main purpose of the hospital. They manifestly are the group in power, and thus their sponsorship is frequently the most logical one to obtain. But such sponsorship can lead easily to cooptation and loss of research neutrality. Julius Roth, a medical sociologist, has sharply criticized those researchers who adopt the concerns of medical management as their own research goals.[5]

Sharing the power, prestige, and charisma of the physician is one of the indirect benefits of alignment with medical sponsorship. While this appeals to some investigators, the personal satisfaction of other researchers might lie in helping the underdog. They might choose nursing as point of entry and nurses as the sponsoring group. There are, to be sure, legitimate reasons why this route is at times the best one. No one in the hospital can provide the observer with as close a view of the real, day-to-day business of patient care as the nurse. Regardless of which points of entry are chosen, these considerations should be accompanied by exploratory probing to discover, if possible, the relative costs and benefits of each mode of access.

4. Stephen J. Miller, *Prescription for Leadership* (Chicago: Aldine, 1970).
5. Julius A. Roth, "Management 'Bias' in Social Science Study of Medical Treatment," *Human Organization,* 21, no. 1 (Spring 1962).

ACCEPTANCE

Heroic literature is replete with tales in which the hero must pass a series of tests and questions before he is permitted to gain the prize. A similar experience, though less ritualized and unaccompanied by operatic music, awaits the sociologist in the hospital. The traditions of the world of patient care have identified research primarily with investigation of disease and disease control; thus research in the biological sciences or its "applied" extension into clinical research is recognized and legitimated. The affairs of human organization, on the other hand, are viewed as the traditional domain of administrative control and of personal involvement. The first step for the researcher is to cast his intentions in such terms that they can be clearly recognized as legitimate research. If he succeeds, he is likely to be confronted by the second hurdle, the question: "Is your work going to contribute to patient care?" The hospital is by mandate and tradition a normative institution. All activities are presumably justified by "doing good." The sociologist will be expected to justify his activities, and the imposition of his conditions for research on members of the hospital staff must be compatible with the dominant norms.

The sociologist passes the second hurdle successfully when he has satisfied the questioners without having compromised his research objectives. He should remember to utilize the hurdles themselves as data. He then is ready for the third test, which is more subtle and less clearly visible than the previous ones: "On whose side will you be in the chess game we play with each other in the hospital?" There are indeed few people in the hospital who can remain there for very long and protect their aura of nonalignment. Rose Laub Coser reports the expectations of social workers and of psychiatrists who saw in the sociological observer a potential ally.[6] The demonstration of the observer's actual neutrality was defined as simply lack of power. Particularly vis-à-vis physicians the matter of alignment can cause problems in relationships. The researcher, however, can establish a power base that is not perceived to involve the immediate process of hospital relationships. The most frequently used device for establishing such a power base is the securing of a project grant, which, although primarily a means of financial support, represents in fact an important importation of an externally legitimated power base, which implies appropriate cooperation on the part of the hospital community.

THE DECORATOR SYNDROME

In the early 1950s, when sociologists first began to conduct studies in hospitals and in other settings of the health care system, they were

6. Rose Laub Coser, *Life in the Ward* (East Lansing: Michigan State University Press, 1962), pp. xxiff.

rarely invited and even more rarely welcomed. There were exceptions, notably in the field of nursing, which embraced social science research during the late fifties and early sixties, partly because of conceptual affinity, partly because social science offered strategic advantages to nursing as an occupation and served as a change agent in its professionalization.[7]

Since the early sixties, however, a significant change has taken place. Medicine, hospital administration, even the supporting public are looking to sociology for help, indeed for leadership. Sociologists are being invited into the medical world. The shift is partly due to the pressure for improvement in the distribution and access of health care. Partly it stems from the call within the health professions themselves for increased attention to relationships, processes, delivery, and organization. Yet in all this effusion of welcome the success of the research will depend on the caution with which the sociologist responds to the red carpet.

In my own research experiences I have been reminded of the peculiar phenomenon that characterizes the advent of the decorator who will redecorate one's home. For nearly a year the lady of the house has probably been cajoling him to place her domicile on his schedule. He is sought after, he is wanted; his consent is, in fact, an achievement. This flavor of delight changes with the actual arrival of the decorator and his helpers. Their work is inevitably associated with major disaccommodation for the residents. Furniture is to be moved or discarded, dirt exposed, people's activities disrupted. Though the decorator was sought after, his real presence is experienced as an inconvenience, an interruption, and an imposition. Observations of decorators may yield clues for the behavior of sociologists in similar settings. Unlike the microbiologist or biochemist, the sociologist's laboratory is an open stage and he is underfoot. The very people who invited him are likely to be his objects of inquiry. The decorator syndrome probably applies to the business of sociology in many research sites. It is a particularly significant area of concern in a world in which a preexisting notion of what constitutes research is forced to undergo major changes if it is to accommodate sociological inquiry.

The Faces of the Hospital

PEOPLE AND PLACES

The identification of status and power holders in the hospital is a matter that has produced much discussion in the literature of medical sociolo-

7. See Everett C. Hughes, Helen MacGill Hughes, and Irwin Deutscher, *Twenty Thousand Nurses Tell Their Story* (Philadelphia: Lippincott, 1958).

gy.[8] In the typical hospital, the medical staff is composed of physicians in private practice who use the hospital as a place to which they can admit their patients when conditions of illness or the requirements of treatment make it necessary. To this extent the physicians are part of the hospital, but to a significant degree they also are external to it, relating to it on a client basis. This pattern is undergoing significant changes, particularly in the large urban hospital. The advent of the full-time employed head of a medical department foreshadows profound shifts in the role of the physician in the hospital. In other hospitals, particularly in those governed by universities and in federal institutions, most members of the medical staff may have the status of employees. Whatever his formal status, however, the individualistic, enterpreneurial tradition of medicine will influence the physician's behavior. The hospital thus not only serves the patient but, to an important degree, serves the physician. Interviewers of physicians should be sensitive to the fact that the physician has the choice of using "we" or "they" when referring to the hospital.

The hospital administrator represents the hospital's bureaucratic and formal organization. Still in the phase of demonstrating his professional identity and only recently recognized as someone requiring specific education, the hospital administrator exists in the typical hospital only at the top of the institution. Unlike other managerial systems, hospital administration has no managerial echelons diffused through the institution itself. The real running of the hospital is thus surrendered, *de facto,* to those who are continuously present at the institution's front lines, the nurses. In interviewing them, the sociologist should be aware, then, that the nurses are simultaneously the physician's deputies and the hospital administration's representatives.[9] They represent, furthermore, that group which in its own view really runs the hospital, and which thus has arrogated to itself the power of the permanent resident who considers himself more legitimate than transients.[10]

There are many others who make their appearance in the hospital. It is possible to suggest a superficial grouping that may be appropriate for initial orientation. One such group includes those who claim autonomous functions within the mosaic of patient care. The dietician, the social

8. Harvey L. Smith, "Two Lines of Authority Are One Too Many," *Modern Hospital,* 84, no. 3 (March 1955): 59–64; Richard T. Viguers, "Who's on Top? Who Knows?" *Modern Hospital,* 76, no. 6 (June 1956): 51–54; Charles Perrow, "Goals and Power Structures," in *The Hospital in Modern Society,* ed. Eliot Freidson (New York: Free Press, Macmillan, 1963).

9. Mauksch, "Organizational Context of Nursing Practice."

10. See the discussion of home guards in Robert W. Habenstein and Edwin A. Christ, *Professionalizer, Traditionalizer, Utilizer,* 2nd ed. (Columbia: University of Missouri, 1963), pp. 56–58.

worker, in special settings the psychologist, and the occupational or rehabilitation counselor fall into this category.

Other occupational categories continue to emerge from the growing specialization and development of special technical functions. Laboratory technicians, oxygen therapists, and X-ray technicians are only a few examples of the plethora of these continusouly increasing groups. Then there are those categories of people who serve the institution and support its processes without being directly involved with patient care. Personnel who staff the laundry, the kitchen, the maintenance and housekeeping departments are, to varying degrees, backstage actors. Nevertheless, many of them have occasional though very meaningful patient contact and can contribute invaluable insights to the sociologist. A series of observation periods at one hospital's switchboard provided me with some of my most productive periods of data-gathering. The switchboard operators knew more about the hospital's population than anyone else, with the possible exception of the janitors!

All of these people are part of the cast that participates in direct support of patient care. But other things besides patient care take place in the hospital. The sociologist will see, depending on the size and nature of the institution, a number of scientists and supporting staff engaged in research. Many of these are commonly not visible except when involved in the clinical components of their investigation.[11]

Most large hospitals participate in various forms of education. This might involve the utilization of the hospital for clinical experiences of medical students. To a degree the utilization of interns and residents involves an obligation to provide education to this group, the house staff.

The clinical education of physicians rarely involves special personnel exclusively devoting their time to education, with the possible exception of one physician who assumes primarily the role of educational coordinator. Among nurses, however, the sociologist may notice the distinction and division between those who are primarily involved in patient care and those whose primary commitment is to nursing education.[12] Many hospitals undertake programs of technical training for many categories of personnel. All these programs will tend to define certain situations and relationships and may offer clues to the meaning of observed behavior.

SIGNS AND SYMPTOMS

In approaching the hospital for research purposes, the sociologist has a

11. Renée C. Fox, *Experiment Perilous* (Glencoe, Ill.: Free Press, 1959).
12. *Roles and Relationships in Nursing Education: Viewpoints Expressed at the 1959 Regional Conference of Representatives of Nursing Service and Nursing Education* (New York: National League for Nursing, 1959), p. 11.

double task. With his desire to chart the unique characteristics of his objects of study and to observe and understand the unique features of the norms, customs, and behaviors of the investigated environment, he must also establish his own relationship to this world, come to terms with his own feelings and values, and do so in consideration of the success of his enterprise.

The work of the hospital is characterized by many modes of behavior that differ sharply from those defined by the folkways of the larger culture. Responses in the face of illness, tragedy, crisis, and death that are entirely appropriate in any other social situation would be received as jarring in the hospital, since they might deter the hospital functionaries from their need to define these events as their domain of work, of routine, and of day-to-day experience.[13]

The hospital has cast aside the rules governing the exposure of the human body, although gestures are institutionalized to maintain their appearance. Apparent changes in mores about nudity observable in some cultural segments and in stage display have not reached the intimate encounters in the hospital. The sociologist who accompanies a physician or nurse to the patient's bedside must deal with his own response to the events associated with examination procedures. If he is embarrassed, he is sure to communicate his embarrassment to either practitioners or patients and thus jeopardize his research effectiveness. If, conversely, he is successful in becoming part of the group, he is likely to be handed a stethoscope by a physician so that he too can listen to the fascinating tones in the patient's chest. Such "success" requires continued delicate consideration of all the audiences looking on.[14]

The hospital is a place in which most people can be recognized by what they wear; uniforms and laboratory coats abound. While some attire is worn for functional purposes, most of it, in fact, is worn as a label. While I would offer no general advice to the researcher on what to wear and when to wear it, I would caution him to apply his sociological skills to a careful adaptation of the garment of his choice. I have seen laboratory coats worn in such a way that they signaled the stranger – the interloper – to all initiated comers. Little cues, such as degree of starch or acid marks, are recognized as identifying the department of the wearer. Physicians in one large metropolitan hospital felt that the proliferation of white laboratory coats was such an inroad on their own identity that they voted to switch to gray ones.

13. The excellent study by David Sudnow, *Passing On: The Social Organization of Dying* (New York: Prentice-Hall, 1967), describes the various devices by which the unusual is cast into routinized behavior patterns. Sudnow points out how, even within the hospital, death can become routine in some patient care units while remaining a special occurrence in other hospital areas.

14. Researchers report various ways of coping with such situations. It appears that whether the stethoscope is refused or accepted, passing this test depends on the ease of the sociologist in responding to the invitation.

The hospital, like all institutions, is replete with special meanings attached to facts, behaviors, and relationships. The way the stethoscope is worn, the precision of obeisance to procedures and policies, and the placement of a person during rounds are indications of status. Even facial expressions can become defined as culturally expected behavior. Interviews with patients are full of repeated references to the smiles of nurses, with which they communicate their willingness to care for patients and to perform tasks that in the broader culture are defined as demeaning, dirty, and unpleasant.

Changes in the real world of the hospital reveal themselves to the sociologist frequently through changes in traditions and expected behavior rather than through formal and deliberately developed policies. For example, the changes in the status of nurses can be observed at the charting desk, where nurses do not stand up anymore when doctors approach, and at the elevator, where during the last ten years the intra-institutional supremacy of the physician has given way to the courtesies claimed by women in society at large.

The researcher will do well to be sensitive to observed relationships and to determine whether gestures belong to interpersonal or to interstatus categories. The banter and perisexual gestures frequently associated with the relationship between physicians and nurses need careful observation before they can be properly interpreted.[15] By becoming attuned to the institutional definitions and expectations of behavior, the sociologist will be protected from formulating erroneous conclusions that merely serve to reinforce the popular mystique of the hospital.

WORLDS OR STAGES

While there are many ways in which the researcher can structure the framework and the methodology of his investigation, it might be useful to suggest one possible conceptual distinction determined by the nature of the data to be collected. To a significant degree, the hospital is a federation of occupations, most of which are organized into distinct departments. An increasing number of these occupational groups claim or strive for professional status.

The fact that medicine, which for many writers has served as the prototype of the professional model, looms large and ever present has fostered an aura of imitation and contagion. While nurses, dieticians, and social workers are veterans on the scene of occupational battles, newcomers such as rehabilitation technicians, oxygen therapists, and medical assistants have only recently entered the fray.

---

15. A recently arrived British nurse was observed rejecting the arm of a physician who placed it around her waist while looking over her shoulder at a patient's chart. When the surprised doctor asserted that he "didn't mean anything by it," she testily retorted, "If I let somebody put his arm around me I want him to mean something by it."

With the development of functional domains, there occur degrees of social closure that give rise within the hospital to what one might call the worlds of the participant occupational groups. These worlds are characterized by their own norms, conduct, subtle but ever present differentiation and gestures, symbols, and argot. They also develop membranes that need to be penetrated if participant research is to be conducted effectively. It might be said that a large proportion of the research conducted within the hospital setting deals with the social concerns of these worlds. In choosing one or several of these worlds of work, the sociologist combines, of course, institutional research with studies of occupations and professions.[16] Even studies of the institution itself frequently take on what I call a world orientation. Many of these studies select the administrative process or structure as the focus of research. The world view of the hospital, therefore, seeks to isolate systems, whether they are visible by virtue of occupational label or whether they need to be analytically identified by reference to formal organization.[17]

While the notion of hospital worlds is oriented to component groups with common occupational and organizational bases, another frame of reference comprises the stages on which the various task and function systems of the hospital occur. The foremost ones are, of course, the locations where patient care takes place. Here we must cease to think of the domain of any one of the hospital's component groups unless we use the patient care area merely as an extension of the study of one of these worlds, such as medicine or dietetics. The metaphor of the stage offers to the researcher a way of comprehending the processes, the functions, and the tasks that have to be performed, i.e., the repertory that comprises the dramas to be played. Members of all groups in the hospital become actors, relating to each other in overt and covert ways, and it is here that the observer can catch his first glimpses of the cast of characters and the nature of the script. The world view of the hospital leads to a research orientation that seeks to identify the component subsystems of the hospital and to study the forces that mold them, whether they are located within the hospital or are part of a larger societal institution. The

16. A large number of studies combine institutional research about the hospital with study of one of the component occupations. This is particularly true of nursing, but also applies to other professions. See J. Ben-David, "The Professional Role of the Physician in Bureaucratic Medicine," *Human Relations,* 11 (1958): 255–74; Ronald G. Corwin, "Role Conception and Career Aspiration: A Study of Identity in Nursing," *Sociological Quarterly,* 2 (April 1961): 69–86; Morris J. Daniels, "Affect and Its Control in the Medical Intern," *American Journal of Sociology,* 66 (1960): 259–67; George Devereux and F. R. Weiner, "The Occupational Status of Nurses," *American Sociological Review,* 15 (1950): 628–34; Mary E. W. Goss, "Influence and Authority Among Physicians in an Outpatient Clinic," *American Sociological Review,* 26, no. 1 (February 1961): 28–39.

17. See Perrow, "Goals and Power Structures."

stage concept, by contrast, is institutionally, functionally, and territorially bound and enables the researcher to focus on the consequences of contact and interaction between worlds and their members and to look for interworld accommodation and conflict.

By no means should the notion of the stage be limited to the patient care area itself. Administrative offices, the dining room, elevators, the corridors, and waiting areas can all be fruitfully used as stages. I once used a small elevator, limited to hospital personnel, as a vantage point for observing the kinds of recognition given by members of various hospital worlds to functionaries from other segments of the hospital. Similarly, observation in the dining room of a large metropolitan hospital during the early 1950s revealed slow changes in the seating patterns of Negro nurses as the RN staff moved toward racial integration.

And the stage concept has further uses. The many worlds of the hospital cause its people to define others at various times as fellow actors or as audiences. Thus the researcher should look for distinctions between behavior that is center stage, backstage, and offstage. Again the patient care units are the most dramatic examples of the utility of this distinction, since the patient himself is likely to be defined as audience (though not always); this accounts for differences in behaviors, expressions, and even attitudes manifested in the service areas or anywhere away from the patient unit.

It is also worthwhile to mention that the hospital is like a theater in which many actors never go home. Though this pattern is diminishing, hospitals typically provide living quarters for nurses, house staff, and a number of other employees. It might be worthwhile to distinguish between offstage behavior within the occupational role and off-duty behavior that is accessible to the sociologist, since much of it occurs in close proximity to his research site.[18]

Methodological Considerations

ASKING THE RIGHT QUESTIONS

Two of the many aspects of sociological question-raising deserve some mention here: the level and the theme. I am using the term "level" to refer to the degree of specificity or generality that the researcher applies to his hypothesis. Is the hospital a laboratory in which the investigator wishes to test general sociological hypotheses to which the peculiarities of the hospital's business are merely incidental? Does he wish to study the applicability of such sociological concepts to the special world of the hospital? Or has he chosen a case approach to the hospital as a specific

18. Habenstein and Christ, *Professionalizer, Traditionalizer, Utilizer*, pp. 48–52.

data basis for the possible development of generally applicable propositions?

In her dissertation, Rhoda Goldstein applied to nursing the generally accepted notion that Negroes and Jews are objects of research in the investigation of minority-group problems.[19] She could have also chosen to ask: What are the minority groups that are specific to nursing? This would have been a different level of question and a different study. Her finding that Jews do not constitute a minority-group problem in nursing, since there are practically none in this occupation, made one kind of contribution to sociology. Had she chosen to cast her question on the level of exploratory specificity, her study would have revealed that men and Catholics share with the Negro the status of minority group in nursing.

Everett Hughes suggested in his lectures that in studying institutions, the sociologist might do well to select those aspects of an institution that take on special meaning in the context of that institution's business, and which therefore are, so to speak, under the magnifying glass of emphasis and importance.

By selecting what I call the themes of research, the sociologist chooses substantive issues that, once studied, become part of the conceptual resources of the discipline. The fate of idealism in medical education[20] is an example of the sensitive discovery of a major theme, its identification, and its subsequent availability for the sociological analysis of other situations in which this issue might not be so obvious.

The pursuit of initial hypotheses should not be so rigorous and inflexible as to preclude unanticipated findings. In the process of discovery of new relationships, new questions are formulated and old ones modified. The very fact that the hospital harbors so many complex substructures provides opportunity for the sociologist to sharpen his questions and to test them. During a necessary initial period of exploration the researcher might do well to provide various significant others in the hospital community an opportunity to react to his research questions and to determine whether they are perceived to be valid, applicable, and answerable within this institution.

OBSERVATION AND INTERVIEWS

A sociologist, clipboard in hand, stands at the door of a patient's room conducting a study of patient care processes. His eyes, quarter trained by his developing sensitivities to health and illness, observe a marked

19. Rhoda Lois Goldstein, "The Professional Nurse in the Hospital Bureaucracy" (unpublished Ph.D. dissertation, University of Chicago, 1954).
20. Howard S. Becker and Blanche Geer, "The Fate of Idealism in Medical School," in *Patients, Physicians, and Illness,* ed. Gartly Jaco (New York: Free Press, Macmillan, 1960), pp. 300–308.

change in the patient's appearance. A moment of crisis seems to be occurring. Should he interfere or should he maintain his observer's stance of nonintervention? This issue, in varying degrees of severity, will unavoidably arise whenever research is conducted in the hospital.

No simple answer can be given, though most of those who have been involved in such situations tend to agree that the role of the observer cannot be maintained when a real threat to the life of the client is involved. This is partly due to the moral issue surrounding the question of human life, partly due to the almost inevitable problems of sympathy and empathy,[21] and partly due to the interesting sociological consequence of physical presence.

No matter how well established the nonresponsibility of the researcher may have become in the eyes and minds of the practitioners, this absolution from the obligations deriving from physical presence is not linear, but curved in accordance with degrees of severity and crises. However, the sociologist had better beware! What in one instance may be an appreciated as well as expected protection of the life of the patient and the job of the nurse can at other, apparently identical moments be viewed as an inappropriate and friction-creating interference. During many hours of personal observations, however, I have only twice been confronted with a situation in which I felt the necessity to depart from the role of observer.

Another point of caution is reached with the distribution of data gathered by means of observation. Typically, observations are organized in sampling periods. The kind of question that has been asked needs to be carefully examined before the kind of sampling done in hospital research can be determined. Particularly in those studies addressing themselves to processes in the patient care unit, the multiplicity of contributing behavior patterns and the variations in their distribution must be taken into account. The observations in the patient care unit will catch partly the world that is confined to that unit, partly segments of medical behavior governed by significantly different behavior distributions, and, thirdly, visitations from the other worlds of the hospital such as the laboratories and the technical and service departments. A sampling procedure based on assumptions primarily applicable to the patient care unit itself may fail to account reliably for distributions whose essential determination resides offstage.

In many ways, with the possible exception of physicians, the population of the hospital offers fruitful and usually cooperative subjects for interviews. The problem is more likely to be in finding time for these encounters than in gaining cooperation. While nurses have generally

21. Peter Kong-ming New, "The Personal Identification of the Interviewer," *American Journal of Sociology,* 62, no. 2 (September 1956): 213–14.

been found to be among the most cooperative subjects of sociological research, they are typically so busy and indispensable during their work hours that they find it difficult to absent themselves on their own for purposes of an interview. It might be easiest for the researcher to make arrangements through the nurses' department head or supervisor and thus to legitimize the interviews.[22] On the other hand, the individualistic tradition of the medical staff makes it generally advisable to make individual arrangements with physicians, although clearance by the appropriate officers of the medical staff may be necessary.

Interviews with patients frequently involve gray areas of jurisdiction. While in most hospitals the research on patient care units requires only clearance by administration and by the nursing department, this arrangement stops short of direct discussion with the patient, particularly in institutions serving private practitioners. Consent of the attending physician is necessary before patients can be interviewed.[23]

Generally speaking, patients welcome the opportunity to talk to someone who listens with personal interest. Sociologists should be careful not to be seduced into a quasi-medical role by the patient's frequent search for certainty about his condition, his treatment, and his prognosis.[24]

Discussions on almost any topic in the hospital must be examined for their normative component. Unlike the functionaries in universities or other service institutions, doctors and nurses are frequently seen as deserving of gratitude and admiration for devoting their lives to the service of mankind. These norms tend to influence data whether obtained by interview or by questionnaire. Careful probing is necessary to determine whether praise results from role expectation or whether it is an expression of an achieved response. Criticism is likely to be veiled or censored. Generally speaking, patients have been noted to veil their negative feelings by ascribing critical comments to physicians attending other patients.[25] For this reason, I have been leery of patient question-

22. Habenstein and Christ, *Professionalizer, Traditionalizer, Utilizer,* pp. 11–16.

23. An interesting example of the difference between individual and collective behavior occurred when we sought permission to interview patients at a meeting of the department of medicine. Our request to the assembled staff for cooperation was greeted with silence and refusal to act. Our subsequent approach to individual physicians for permission to interview their patients yielded only one refusal in eighty-three cases.

24. Coser, *Life in the Ward.*

25. While interviews can test for the normative component in patient responses, questionnaires suffer the continuous risk of capturing responses that reveal the good-patient norm rather than individual variations. See Hans O. Mauksch and Daisy Tagliacozzo, "The Patient's View of the Patient's Role" (progress report of a research project, Presbyterian-St. Luke's Hospital, Chicago, March 1962), pt 1, "Analysis of Interviews." In the second, unreported phase of this study, which sought to quantify patients' responses to medical and nursing care, it became obvious that in a seven-point scale of patients' attitudes, the zero point would not reflect the dividing line between praise and dissatisfaction. Probing revealed that any patient response that was less than "very satisfactory" was likely to contain a degree of criticism. This suggests the possibilities of methodological experimentation that could establish criteria for shifts in questionnaire responses caused by prevailing normative expectations.

naires; I consider them less capable than sensitive interviews of penetrating behind expected attitudes.

Also, it might be useful to remember that questions that suggest negative responses can be severely threatening to the patient, who is under strong pressure to maintain the good-patient model and to believe in the efficacy of his doctor. Patients also seek to protect their nurses; thus supportive, nondirective interviews may penetrate deeper than specific inquiries about sensitive issues. To interview human beings during various stages of pain, toxicity, and inpairment requires sensitivity.[26] Nevertheless, interviews with seriously ill patients shortly after their admission with a heart attack have been accomplished without damage to the patient. In fact, it even was our experience that after our study became known, patients called our office requesting to be interviewed. Some physicians reported beneficial consequences of the interview experience, and occasionally some whose patients were not included in our study seemed to feel slighted.

RECORDS AND REPORTS

Among human institutions there are probably few that produce as many written documents as the hospital. Records are kept by nurses, the admissions office, the business office, and the medical staff. Most of these records are official documents of the institution. The physician, in addition to his entries in the patient's chart and his medical staff reports, keeps private records on his patients. Hospitals report to public agencies such as local, state, and federal offices; to local and regional commissions such as hospital-planning commissions; and to a variety of occupational and industrial associations, notably the American Hospital Association. It is possible to conduct research exclusively in this wealth of records.[27] Yet this abundance of data output has to be carefully examined for the nature of its categories, the meaning of its terms, and the source of its information.

A special kind of record is the patient's chart. It is meant to be a repository of significant events affecting the care and progress of the patient. Yet careful observation of the events surrounding charting will yield interesting parallels to the police blotter. Not all that actually occurs is recorded, nor does all that gets recorded really occur. Unlike the police blotter, however, the patient's chart can reveal feedback effect from the record to the real world. Not only is the chart a reflection of events; the events of patient care are, to a significant degree, influenced by the policies governing charting. Behavior that is to be recorded is

26. Raymond S. Duff and August B. Hollingshead, *Sickness and Society* (New York: Harper & Row, 1968), pp. 18–25.

27. Seymour Warkov, "Irregular Discharge from Veterans Administration Tuberculosis Hospitals: A Problem of Organizational Effectiveness" (unpublished Ph.D. dissertation, Yale University, 1959).

likely to take precedence over behavior not entered in a report, regardless of relative clinical merit. Nevertheless, some investigators feel that the patient record is preferable to observation as a source of data.[28]

There are many locations within the hospital where records are kept and reports filed. Patient records are normally stored in the medical record library of the institution. The degree of retrievability of these documents varies greatly among institutions. At best, there is a computerized access system with a choice of several access codes. At worst, the records are merely sorted by case number. Efforts to automate the hospital record system are proliferating, although in most places these are only experimental beginnings.[29]

The researcher should keep in mind that the various structural segments of the hospital may have developed their own records but that there may be reports in the hands of others of which they are not aware. Thus in one large metropolitan hospital I happened to discover that there were three committees active on the revision of records, each unaware of the activities of the others. One was sponsored by hospital administration, one was sponsored by the medical staff, and the third was a fascinating in-group effort by the computer staff to present a *fait accompli* to the hospital.

Though the first reaction to this lack of consistency in communication and continuity may at first scare the inquiring sociologist, he might consider that these very differences in data organization, categorization, and selection are in themselves an important opportunity for gaining additional knowledge and insights into the crucial modes of thinking and perceiving that govern the hospital worlds. I am, of course, emphasizing here the use of the records and data themselves rather than supporting any conclusions offered in these reports.[30]

The same encouraging comment about the ease of data-gathering which has been made earlier applies here, too. Once the researcher has achieved entry and legitimation, once he has established that he is not trying to find fault or to look for an exposé, he can probably expect cooperation. This applies not only to the hospital but also to the various other health agencies where data can profitably be pursued.

28. Warren Thomas, "A Model for Predicting Recovery Progress of Coronary Patients," *Health Services Research*, 3, no. 3 (Fall 1968): 185–213.

29. W. A. Spencer, C. Valbonna, and L. A. Geddes, "Requirements and Applications of Automation in Hospital Functions," *Journal of Chronic Diseases*, 17 (June 1964): 469–81; W. V. Slack, G. P. Hicks, C. E. Reed, and L. J. Van Cura, "A Computer-Based Medical History System," *New England Journal of Medicine*, 274 (January 27, 1966): 194–98; M. S. Blumberg, "Hospital Automation: The Needs and the Prospects," *Hospitals*, 35 (August 1, 1961): 34.

30. Milton I. Roemer, A. Taher Moustafa, and Karl E. Hopkins, "A Proposed Hospital Quality Index: Hospital Death Rates Adjusted to Case Severity," *Health Services Research*, 3, no. 2 (Summer 1969): 96–118.

Written data about certain aspects of the hospital are not confined to the agencies that are manifestly concerned with hospital business. Police records as well as interviews with policemen are fruitful sources of knowledge about certain aspects of the hospital, particularly the emergency room. One group of medical students, in studying an emergency room in each of two cities, discovered after eliminating other factors that the apparent differences in efficiency, speed, and climate between the two emergency rooms were due to the behavior and involvement of the police rather than to institutional factors.[31]

Caution is advisable in using such sources about the hospital as magazines, newspapers, and some of the trade books in print. The drama, the newsworthiness, and the social concern surrounding the hospital give rise to written material that emphasizes the extreme, seeks to expose, and in a sense extols either end of the range from good to bad.[32] In view of the almost continuous searchlights that scan the hospital in search for the great or the horrible, it is to the credit of social scientists that they have been able to establish, at least generally, their place as serious investigators in the hospital community.

The literature that exists about the hospital is probably one of the most difficult thickets to negotiate. The sociologist should be aware that literature concerning hospitals is found in the categories of the social sciences, medicine, nursing, hospital management, and engineering, and in the ever growing number of journals representing the new hospital occupations. Each of these literatures has its own indices and sometimes radically differing modes of categorizing material. Serious pieces of work do occur in the most remote corners of this maze of print.

Utility and Feedback

The sociologist who conducts research in the hospital is almost certain to be confronted with the issue of research pure versus research applied. The strong goal-oriented culture of the hospital and the public and professional pressure stemming from the mandate to improve individual and collective health envelope all activities within the hospital with the question: "What good will this do?"

31. William W. Beckett, Jr., Alfred J. Bosche, Jr., Bruce K. Brookby, James A. Gerst, Thomas L. Huffman, Edward W. Szoko, Judith Travostino, and Drew J. Winston, "The Emergency Room" (unpublished class project in human ecology and behavioral science, School of Medicine, University of Missouri, June 1969).

32. Typical of this dilemma is the reception of the book by Milton Gross, *The Doctors* (New York: Random House, 1966). It is considered by the medical community to be an exposé. Dr. Franz J. Ingelfinger, "The Arch-Hospital: An Ailing Monopoly," *Harper's Magazine*, 237, no. 1418 (July 1968): 82–87, a review-article discussing Duff and Hollingshed, *Sickness and Society,* is of interest in that the reviewer raises the question of legitimacy.

Sociologists who have conducted research in the hospital can be found all along the continuum of this issue. There are those who adamantly assert their unconcern with utility and who profess to limit their relationship to the hospital to its use as a data base and as an incidental matrix for the pursuit of their inquiries. There are others who have become so identified with the goals and values of this institution that their activities are primarily governed by the desire to assist the health professions and the institution in meeting their objectives. The largest number of researchers are probably scattered somewhere in between.

For the new researcher, studies undertaken in the hospital might well serve as a profitable exercise in the sociology of sociology as well as in the sociology of research. At this time we are hearing the call for relevance of the social sciences, a call articulated sometimes by brain and occasionally by brawn. The hospital might well serve as a serious testing ground for the compatibility of the scientific pursuit and involvement with social goals. To what extent the dichotomy of pure and applied research is a real one or one that applies primarily to poor research of either sort is something for the investigator to contemplate.

The investigator in the hospital will discover that there are languages that are appropriate to the interdisciplinary stages of patient care and others that are spoken in the separate worlds of the health professions. Though different, both are equally valid. Likewise, the sociologist conducting research in the hospital might consider the appropriateness, validity, and morality of developing and maintaining two thought and language systems, one that is appropriate to the maintenance of the sociological stance and provides his link with his own discipline, the other to establish and maintain a mode of communication with his host culture. This comment does not recommend a mode of cooptation, but rather a semantic and role device for communicating sociology effectively.

Such communications will be frequently called for. By virtue of his research activities the sociologist is a free-floating agent in an institution that is otherwise characterized by fairly ritualized and predictable relationships. He will be tested for his ability to keep secrets and confidences. It is not uncommon for the sponsoring group, particularly if it is hospital administration, to expect the sociologist to report occasionally. It is essential to establish the confidentiality of the sociologist's own findings and observations. At the same time, occasional reports to all groups are usually beneficial, particularly if they can contain concrete suggestions that could improve either the care of patients or the current problems of the group to whom the report is made.

The reporting researcher might beware of the pressure to produce results, findings, and benefits too quickly. While the biological sciences and medical research pride themselves on their tradition of slow and deliberate progress from experiment to experiment and from basic investigation to controlled application and evaluation, the sociologist is all too frequently expected to recommend sweeping policy changes after the most cursory collection of data. If there is anything in which firmness is advisable, it is in the continuous assertion of the limitations of the applicability of findings and the probabilistic nature of social knowledge. The sociologist has to remind his audience that the right to fail and to return to the drawing board is not limited to physical and biological science investigations.

Although the preceding pages contain many warnings and cautions, the conduct of research in the hospital offers to the sociologist genuine professional and personal rewards. Not the least of these is the sense of broadening and expanding the intellectual and scientific resource base of one of society's major institutions. At a time when most academic disciplines are in the process of questioning the significance of their own contributions, the hospital offers to the sociologist rich opportunities to observe and to test the significance of sociological propositions and precepts that may seem old hat in a graduate sociology seminar. If his eyes are open and his ears tuned in, he will find himself in the midst of an intense sampling of all modes of human interaction and he will be impressed with the many researchable questions that offer themselves to him. While doctoral students in sociology departments search all over for topics for their dissertations, the hospital, like other real-life situations, can keep the researcher well fed with new ideas.

In the last analysis, sociological research in the hospital might well be evaluated by three criteria: the quality of the research itself; its impact on the host world; and its contribution to sociology in the form of new questions, concepts, and methods.

Studying Legislators

For several reasons, it is most difficult to interview successful politicians, a significant majority of whom are legislators (including congressmen and aldermen). First, the public and the press stereotype them, and the legislators — willy-nilly, though usually after a good deal of thought — have tended to go along with most of the sterotypes. With his own biases likely to be formed by the general climate of opinion also, the sociologist is likely to emerge from an interview with a legislator with a collection of the same stereotypes he could have collected from the daily newspaper. His respondent has usually been satisfied to see the interview turn out this way, unless he has discerned that his interviewer is a person of great perceptiveness and will not use the interview to damage him very much as a public figure.

Secondly, the legislator is a tremendously busy man; the pressures on his time are almost unbelievable, even though he usually schools himself to appear calm and unhurried. He can rarely afford to give any time to a scholarly interviewer, who has no claim on his attention and nothing to offer him. For this reason, the researcher must plan his approach to the legislator very carefully.

Third, because the public record of the legislator is easily accessible without an interview, the social scientist is likely to be seeking information the legislator regards as confidential, and it may be difficult to induce him to part with it. Assurances of confidentiality, anonymity, etc., which the social scientist uses in all interviews, have to be especially sincere and effective when he faces a legislator. The legislator has much more to lose by disclosure of personal, confidential information than has the ordinary citizen.

204

There is a fourth factor here that may either help or hinder the interviewer. The legislator is likely to be an alert, lively, reasonably intelligent person with a better than average education. In the United States Congress, a large proportion of the members could even be called intellectuals. This means the legislator-respondent is likely to have previously thought of the question the interviewer asks him. He may have taken a private or public position on the matter, which does not always encompass all his thoughts on it. He thus may be able to come up quickly with a thought-out answer to the question, but it may not be the answer the interviewer is seeking.

I am talking about the typical legislator—the man who thrusts himself into the public eye, who can never escape public attention while he is in politics, who has run successfully for election and will seek election again, and who has formulated opinions on a wider range of public issues than have most citizens but is aware that his constituents have varying opinions on some of those issues. We shall ignore unusual types: the congressman who was appointed to fill out a term and has no intention of running in the next election; the Wayne Morse type, who speaks out vigorously on any and all matters, regardless of what his constituents may think; the legislator from one-party district, who has practically no chance of getting serious campaign opposition no matter what he says or does. My observations are based on direct experience with interviewing congressmen in 1961 on the Medicare Bill,[1] and as a member of the Minnesota legislature during the 1963-64 term, on continued acquaintance with Minnesota congressmen and legislators, and on some published reports of the experience of others in interviewing legislators.[2]

Access

The interviewer should carry on his person a letter of identification that he is a qualified social scientist, that he is engaged on a study for such-and-such a purpose, and that he is employed by X University or research institute. Even if he is not asked to show this, it can do no damage to volunteer a means by which the legislator can ascertain the interviewer's legitimacy. Legislators are generally quite conscious of the sociologist's concept of legitimacy.

The interviewer should interview his own representatives first, explaining to them carefully the purposes of the study. Seldom will one be refused an interview by one's own representatives. If the interviewer

1. The results of this study appear in my book *The Power Structure: Political Process in American Culture* (New York: Oxford University Press, 1967), chap. 12.

2. Charles O. Jones, "Notes on Interviewing Members of the House of Representatives," *Public Opinion Quarterly,* 23 (Fall 1959): 404–406; James A. Robinson, "Survey Interviewing Among Members of Congress," *Public Opinion Quarterly,* 24 (Spring 1960): 127–38.

can obtain a letter of introduction from them, it will aid him materially in approaching other legislators. If he has performed ably with his own representatives, he might even get them to use their meager secretarial resources to help set up appointments for him. This is valuable for much more than the time it saves the interviewer: it assures him of a much better chance of gaining the appointments. If one has great difficulty in making appointments with state legislators, he can try to catch them in the corridors, but this informal approach will not work with the busier congressmen. Other legislators to interview early, for the help they may provide in gaining access to others, are the formal leaders, the majority and minority leaders and the whips, or whatever their assistants are called in the particular legislature you are studying.

It would be next to impossible to interview legislators when the legislative body is not in session, as they are scattered then and hard to reach. Only a mailed questionnaire is feasible at that time. Even though they sometimes attend conventions and meetings together, these occasions are with few exceptions not good times to reach them, as they have the public on their minds then. During the session, the early part is by far the best time to approach them. When the session is just beginning legislators are willing to take on assignments that they will reject out of hand later on.

Even though a legislator will be more generous with his time early in the session, it is not wise to ask him for more than fifteen or twenty minutes. If the interviewer needs more time than that, he should avoid indicating how much time he actually needs, and just trust to luck and the momentum of the interview to carry him through. If the legislator finds the interview interesting, he is likely to provide the necessary time, if not at the initial session, then at a subsequent one.

If the interviewer has much time and wishes to probe deeply, he can usually attach himself to the staff of a congressman or to the staff of a legislative committee or caucus, and from this vantage point he can observe a great number of things that he could not find out by interviewing. With permission, he can even follow a congressman or legislator around and find out how he functions. The difficulty of this procedure is that it will inhibit contacts with other legislators, and therefore one should use it only in a team effort or in the last stages of the research. But it is a valuable technique: it often offers access to conventions, caucus meetings, closed committee meetings, and "smoke-filled rooms" from which the researcher is usually excluded. One can make contacts at these places with many knowledgeable persons in politics who are not legislators: party workers, administrative officials, a great variety of staff experts, pressure-group representatives and other lobbyists, and so on. These can often readily be interviewed, either formally or in informal conversation. Of course, in attaching oneself to the staff of a congressman or legislator one has to choose well: it is best to choose a member of the majority party with high prestige and power. Some of this rubs off on the staff of the legislator and usually aids the interviewer, except perhaps when he tries later to interview members of the opposing party. In studying anything political, one almost has to have a partner who will cover the opposition. A good rule is : One researcher at least for each political party. A politician is willing to credit the researcher with objectivity—as long as he is not seen too often with members of the opposing party.

Questions

Legislators are such busy persons that they usually do not suffer fools gladly, although most of them are schooled in courtesy. Questions addressed to them should be intelligent ones; beware of talking down to legislators. No one is well informed about everything, however, so explanations may sometimes have to be made before a question is clearly understood. Of course, experienced legislators are likely to know much more than freshmen about the sort of thing the interviewer is likely to be discussing, and the interviewer can readily ascertain in advance how much experience a legislator has had.

While some legislators immediately use first names, it is unwise for the interviewer to try to establish a primary relationship straightaway. The interview must inevitably retain the character of a secondary relationship, and the interviewer should seek the role of Simmel's stranger, charcterized by impartiality, objectivity, anonymity, and confidence, rather than any role of intimacy. Intimacy will not be achieved anyway, and one can be made foolish in a pseudo-intimate relationship. So even when he is addressed by first name, the interviewer should address the legislator by title or by "Mr."

The interview should be straightforward; the tricks of interviewing should be used sparingly and cautiously, if at all. Legislators are schooled in seeing through sham. They also want to be very clear about the purpose of the interview, so the interviewer should prepare himself thoroughly to answer questions on his purposes.

Most legislators will see little benefit in a study that seeks to probe their opinions on a specific issue, unless the interview brings new information. They have already taken, or are about to take, a public position on the issue. They know that any position they take will create some enemies, and they see little value in offering justifications that will possibly rub salt in the wounds of their enemies. Certain topics are to be avoided in any interview: what another legislator said during an interview (although it's all right to refer to what he said in a public statement), corrupt practices and legislative ethics, favors to constituents and campaign finances. But legislators love to talk about the politics of an issue, or of the whole session or legislature — that is, the possibilities, probabilities, and alternative strategies for a bill or a program. They find the ever shifting vicissitudes of politics fascinating, and this fascination is often one of their main motives for serving in the legislature. They take a rational gambler's attitude on the chances of passage of any particular bill, and they love to show off insight into ways in which a bill's chances of passage can be changed.

Subgroupings

The characteristic traditional divisions among politicians — Republican versus Democrat, liberal versus conservative, educated versus uneducated, etc. — may be important to the interviewer as he approaches a legislator. In general, he can more easily gain rapport with an educated legislator than with an uneducated one, with a liberal than with a conservative (because the latter tends to suspect university social scientists of being liberal, usually correctly).

THE SKILLED AND THE UNSKILLED

While all legislators enjoy talking about the politics of legislation, some know a lot more about it than others. If the interviewer gets a skilled and experienced politician to speak openly, he has tapped a rich vein of information and insight. While most legislative leaders are skilled politicians, there are many nonleaders who have the same skills and insights, and might be more willing to talk. I suppose the ideal person to interview on the politics of legislation, or the tactics and techniques of getting a bill passed or killed, is an experienced legislator who is not a leader and yet has great skill and insight. These are rare, but every legislative body seems to have one or two. They can be located by asking others, or by looking up records of success in getting legislation enacted, of length of service, of leadership positions.

THE PARTY-ORIENTED AND THE INDEPENDENT

The American party system is so weak that once a man is elected to public office, he may not have to do anything more for his party or have his party do much for him. This situation varies according to the party structure in each state. In general, the more patronage there is, the closer will be the relationship of legislator and party. Where the party rests heavily on volunteer service, the legislator can build up his own private group of volunteers or organization, and does not then relate closely to the party. Even in Massachusetts, where the Democratic party is said to be strong and controls considerable patronage, the senators Kennedy built up their own private organizations and were not close to their party. In general, the legislator close to his state party will more often reflect the ideology of that party than one who is not. The latter will feel freer to follow national trends or his own whim in regard to issues. By whim I mean a position deviant from the party's.

A deviant position may not be entirely a personal matter, although on the congressional level it is likely to be; it may be the position of some other person or group that has bought the legislator. There are three conditions under which a legislator may be bought: (1) He may be bribed on a specific piece of legislation. This is a rare occurrence in most legislatures, for if he is found out, it will probably mean the end of his legislative career. (2) Some vested interest may have paid for his campaign. In this case, he is beholden to the vested interest on all issues concerning it, but not on others. (3) He may be an attorney—as 20 to 45 percent of state legislators are and agrees to represent interests that are buying his legislative services in the guise of hiring his legal services. This is the most common form of buying a legislator, and accounts for the poor reputation of lawyer-legislators among their fellow legislators, despite their high level of skill. Of course, there are many lawyer-legislators who are not bought in any way. In any case, it is to be noted that legislators are only partly bought, and on many issues are free to support their party or an individualized position. In general, the legislator close to his party, and one who is strongly supported by his party for reelection, is less likely to be bought. The political party is the chief countervailing force to the economic interests operating in politics in the United States.

ADMINISTRATIVE AND COMMITTEE STAFFS

If the interviewer has great difficulty in making appointments with congressmen (as he does during any time but the beginning of the session), he would do well to think of interviewing the congressmen's administrative assistants, and even sometimes the chiefs of staff of important committees. These men are knowledgeable as most congressmen, and often are more willing to talk to research interviewers. State legislators rarely have administrative assistants, and chiefs of staffs of their committees are not nearly so knowledgeable as their counterparts in Washington, so one has to continue to work at getting to the legislators themselves at the state level.

Records and Information About Legislators

There is a trememdous body of records available about legislators. In the national Congress, the daily *Congressional Record* records all discussions and speeches and votes. There is a *Congressional Digest* with poorish bibliographical sketches of all congressmen. One can usually get copies of committee hearings and reports, and copies of bills. Publicity releases of the congressmen and those of lobbyists are generally available for the asking. At the state level, the researcher can see the daily records of actions taken on each bill, usually with individual votes. He can see or get copies of committee reports and bills. There is usually a "blue book" on the legislature or the whole state government, and many informal brochures on the legislatures prepared for lobbyists and visitors. Almost any legislator will be willing to turn over to him the voluminous "junk mail" that arrives at his desk each day—committee reports, administrative agency reports, lobbyists' brochures, and other propaganda. The researcher has access to more printed and mimeographed paper on any given day than he can possibly read. No legislator could read one-tenth of the printed material that reaches him each day, not to speak of the letters, which he is usually more willing to read (but most of which he must also turn over to an assistant). Like the legislator himself, the researcher must learn quickly how to pick and choose among all these documents, and there is no sure-fire technique for selecting well.

One might also want to read the information on legislators put out by other groups. Newspapers do a varying job, but sometimes offer valuable information to the researcher. The difficulty is that no newspaper story can be regarded as either accurate or complete. As I noted earlier, newspapers also tend to force politicians into stereotyped images. Campaign literature on both sides is valuable, even for its distortions, which are inevitable. Sometimes pressure groups keep records on legislators, and may make them accessible to a researcher, but usually these are worth no more than what the researcher can more easily find in the public record (he won't get access to anything confidential). One thing the researcher must keep in mind when studying legislators: He is studying public persons, about whom most of the general information is readily accessible.

The very plethora of public information seems to be related to the paucity of private information. Considering how articulate most legislators are, and how hungry they are for public esteem, singularly few autobiographies of legislators are ever published, which suggests that they do not keep diaries or journals. At most, a congressman may publish an account of his experience with a certain bill or committee, most of which has already been reported in the public records. The paucity of "inside story" writings by legislators needs an attempt at explanation: (1) They are extremely busy men who rarely retire early and seldom have time to keep diaries; (2) the only information they have that is not fully available to the public anyway is secret information, which it might prove embarrassing to someone to reveal; (3) like all professionals, they are not keen on revealing professional or trade secrets; (4) most of what they do is so simple and so public, that an inside story would add little to the public record; (5) the politician faces the stereotyped image of himself as superficial in knowledge, shallow in conviction, and possibly venal in interests; he despairs of breaking this stereotype, doesn't bother to do anything about it, and trusts that history may deal kindly with him.

Thus very little of the information published on legislators is of the case-material variety. Exceptions occur, of course, and some political scientists have studied specific campaigns or specific pieces of legislation and have delineated the roles of specific legislators in these settings. But most writings of political scientists—published in their many excellent books and in journals like the *American Political Science Review* and *Public Opinion Quarterly*—deal with legislators or legislatures or legislation *en masse*, as an aggregate to be studied statistically. Beginning with the Eagleton series in the late 1950s, there have been noteworthy case studies too, and any sociological investigation of legislators or legislatures would surely want first to survey the many excellent studies published by political scientists. I believe we sociologists have made serious errors in our studies of power structure and the power elite by jumping into research without reading first what the political scientists have published on these topics.[3]

Not infrequently legislatures make studies of themselves, but only on matters of procedure and administration. They provide most direct information to the sociologist of large-scale organization, who wishes to compare legislatures with businesses and other institutions. At the same time, to understand fully a group's behavior, one must first learn the institutional framework within which it operates, and these studies of the legislature as an institution should thus be valuable as background material. There has been a great deal of discussion concerning legislative procedures and reform activity in recent years.

Participation

In a sense, it is quite easy for a social scientist to participate in the outer realms of the legislative world. With just a little bit of safe introduction, from his own representatives, for example, he can attend committee hearings, general sessions, some of the corridor or lobby activity, and so

3. Certainly Floyd Hunter and C. Wright Mills paid little attention to political science studies before publishing their influential works *Community Power Structure, The Power Elite*, and *Top Leadership, USA*.

on. This is a valuable initial activity for the investigation, and he can often make appointments for interviews through contacts made here. When he is ready to go to the next deeper level of the culture, by attaching himself to the staff of a specific committee or specific legislator, he must choose wisely, for he cuts himself off from areas naturally inimical by reason of the conflict nature of all politics. If he attaches himself to a member of the majority party, as he is most likely to do, since this offers the widest range of experiences and important contacts, he cuts himself from the minority party and from dissidents within the majority party. There is a deep inner level of politics that the investigator is not likely to get into unless he takes an actual job on the staff, and even then he will not see everything that happens to a legislator.

One place the investigator should make a special effort to follow the legislator is into his constituency — out of the marble halls into the streets and the local meetingplaces. Here he will see a different legislator, an ordinary friendly person who listens and talks to everyone, never putting on airs. He may be surprised to find how deferential the legislator — even the top-level congressman — appears in the local ward clubs back home. It isn't currying favor so much as being willing to listen, willing to modify his own opinon on the spot, and willing to do the little favors that party workers expect in exchange for their many services to the legislator at campaign time. In most ways, a legislator will be much more responsive to a researcher if he aids his election campaign a little bit.

Ideally, the investigator ought to begin his work early in the campaign, and start by aiding many candidates (but of one party only) in several districts. After the campaign he then has an "in" with several legislators and can interview these immediately, and plan with them his strategy for interviewing and observing at the capitol when the session opens. His main interviews and general observations should take place during the first two months of the session. As things get busy, he can join the staff of a committee or a legislator for the most intensive experiences, and carry on with his observations right through the most frantic month of the session. With luck, he may have made himself so useful to his legislator or committee chairman by then that he is employed on the staff (either for pay or as a volunteer — this latter is not unknown among political science graduate students who want the experience). When the session is over, he may know one legislator so well that the legislator will talk to him quite frankly, in full confidence that his remarks will never be identified. Thus a good study of a legislator and his session requires a full year, and the investigator should select carefully the man to whom he attaches himself.

Linguistics

Language is no problem in studying legislators or legislatures. Straightforward, grammatical English is not only preferred but essential, in order to avoid any hint of condesension. Only a few technical and specialized words—drawn from the law—need to be added to the interviewer's vocabulary. Argot is limited to two or three words, such as "croaker" to refer to a camouflaged item in a general bill, which has been inserted in the hope of lulling the legislators into enacting a measure they would not ordinarily pass. Avoid using sociological jargon, and remember never to mention bribery or legislative ethics—legislators are sure no outsider understands what the terms mean.

The World of the Legislature

The legislator's world is different from what the sociologist is likely to suspect. Unless he comes into this world from the usual lower channels of ward-club politics, he is not likely to appreciate it, and if he fails to recognize its unique dimensions, he should not carry out his study. In the first place, it is a world of self-aware importance. The legislators believe deeply that what they are doing is important, and they create a sense of excitement about it. For most state legislators, their lives—as farmers, small businessmen, trade-union officials, lawyers, or whatever—in their local communities would be pretty dull if they were not also in the legislature. Second, they gain great prestige with the folks back home by being in the legislature; when home, they are leaders in their community, no matter how modestly they behave. Third, they are impressed with their own importance and prestige, and therefore tend to behave with dignity. Evidence of competition and deviance tends to be hidden, and is revealed only by the sharp tongue of gossip—which is constant in the corridors.

Certain values are highly prized in the world of the legislature: a sharp mind (a "lawyer's mind"), specialized knowledge (often that of an economist or sociologist or educator), willingness to work hard, tolerance of opponents of the less able, a friendly though not necessarily intimate attitude toward others are qualities that will permit a man to go far in a legislature. Of course, experience aids especially the first two of these values, so the legislator gains in respect as he gains in experience. The young man who is willing to learn by asking sensible questions of his seniors, who studies bills before he criticizes them, who can defend his own bills with cogent arguments and facts, and who generally behaves with dignity and good sense is likely to go far up the scale in the legislature, provided he doesn't threaten his seniors by getting there too fast.

There is a lot of tension is most legislative work, the pace is very fast, and one can easily make a mistake in a vote. Each legislator watches the votes of a chosen few leaders in each major subject area in an effort to avoid mistakes. He knows that he cannot know everything about every bill, not even about every major bill, but he would find it hard to explain this to his constituents. He is pressured between the pedestrian world of his constituency and the heady world of the legislature. So he regularly lets go and relaxes. There are frequent drinking parties and dinners where liquor flows freely, literally, for legislators. These are in the capital city, and hence away from the constituency for the most legislators, and they occur during off hours and in places newspapermen are not supposed to frequent. Although lobbyists abound as hosts, their special interests are seldom mentioned. The lobbyists even keep most of the legislative staff out of such parties (partly to save money, and partly to increase the legislators' sense of freedom). These informal gatherings, where many legislators get drunk, but not drunk enough to tell any secrets or to pass out, are occasions to pick up much informal information about techniques and strategies of legislation — if the interviewer could ever get into them. The lobbyists never say anything about the behavior of their guests, but I suspect they watch for any sign of weakness or deviance and use it quietly later on to gain their votes. The only other place for the legislator to relax is in his own home (if his family doesn't make too many demands on him) or his hotel room (where his wife or next-door neighbor may also bother him).

In sharp contrast to the lobbyists' evening parties at the capital city, the home community makes quite different demands on the legislator, and has different expectations for his behavior. Here he is expected to behave like all the others, only more so: he is first among equals; he has prestige, but he owes it to the work of a good number of friends at election time. He must work at home, too, mending fences (that is, soothing those whose favored bills he has voted against), keeping his ear close to the ground (that is, listening for signs of opposition), returning favors (intervening with government administration in minor ways in return for help during election campaigns), and otherwise preparing himself for the next round of legislation.

I haven't tried to explain the process of getting a bill passed, or a major bill amended or killed. These processes are reported in standard political science textbooks, but they indicate how tremendously complicated the professional lives of the legislators are. There are many worlds of the legislator, and the interviewer should be aware of which one he is observing at any particular moment.

References

Eulau, Heinz, William Buchanan, Le Roy Ferguson, and John C. Wahlke. "The Political Socialization of American State Legislators," *The Midwest Journal of Political Science* 3 (May 1959): 188–206.

———— "Role of the Representative—Some Empirical Observations on the Theory of Edmund Burke," *American Political Science Review* 53 (September 1959): 742–756.

Finer, Herman. "The Tasks and Function of the Legislator." Pp. 379–384 in *Theory and Practice of Modern Government* (New York: Henry Holt, 1949).

Fox, W. T. R. "Legislative Personnel in Pennsylvania," *Annals of the American Academy of Political and Social Science* 195 (January 1938): 32–39.

Hacker, Andrew. "The Elected and the Anointed: Two American Elites," *American Political Science Review* 55 (September 1961): 539–549.

Hjelm, V. S. and J. P. Pisciotte. "Profiles and Careers of Colorado State Legislators," *Western Political Quarterly* 21 (December 1968): 698–722.

Huitt, Ralph. "The Congressional Committee: A Case Study—The Roles of Congressional Committee Members," *American Political Science Review* 48 (June 1954): 340–365.

———— "A Case Study in Senate Norms," *American Political Science Review* 51 (June 1957): 313–329.

Lockard, Duane. "The Tribulations of a State Senator," *The Reporter* (May 17, 1956): 24–28.

MacRae, Duncan, Jr. "The Role of the State Legislator in Massachusetts," *American Sociological Review* 19 (April 1954): 185–194.

Matthews, Donald R. "U.S. Senators and the Class Structure," *Public Opinion Quarterly* 18 (Spring 1954): 5–22.

McConaughy, John B. "Certain Personality Factors of State Legislators in South Carolina," *American Political Science Review* 44 (December 1950): 897–903.

Prewitt, K. "Political Socialization and Political Roles," *Public Opinion Quarterly* 3 (Winter 1966–1967): 569–582.

Ruchelman, L. I. "Profile of New York State Legislators," *Western Political Quarterly* 20 (September 1967): 625–638.

Shils, E. A. "The Legislator and His Environment," *University of Chicago Law Review* 18 (1951): 571–584.

The Study of Southern Labor Union
Organizing Campaigns

The thought of my dispensing advice on field-study procedures brings to mind imagery of a grizzled prospector demonstrating the use of his pick and shovel and pan to operators of a modern gold dredge. Modes of inquiry that were already of questionable status when I was taking faltering steps of research apprenticeship appear now to be completely out of fashion. My data-gathering experience has been largely restricted to participant observation, in several of its various forms. Should I, a procedural anachronism, hold up my primitive research tools for inspection?

At the moment, however, as far as research involving union-management conflict in the South is concerned, what else is there but my pick and shovel and pan? The behemoth of inquiry, equipped with grant, computer, interviewers, and technicians, hasn't appeared on the scene of industrial conflict below the Mason-Dixon line. The machinery is in vogue, but the subject matter isn't. The heavy stuff won't roll in until the study of union-management relations becomes respectable. As to an approximate date for the rise of respectability, I wouldn't hazard a guess. In the meantime the war between the two perennial adversaries beckons to the lone researcher with bewitching promise. As the shuffling sourdough might put it, "There's data in them thar hills! And maybe theory, too!" I have poked around a bit, and, urged to talk about my searchings, I'll tell what I've been trying to find out and the trails that I've followed. Perhaps such an account will prove refreshing, if not instructive.

Buford Junker has offered a fourfold classification of subtypes of participant observation, from the "complete observer" to the "complete participant," with the two intermediate categories of "observer-as-participant," and "participant-as-observer."[1] Since acceptance of, or at least reference to, this typology has become fairly general, I shall place my own fieldwork procedures within the Junker scheme. I recognize two of the categories, "complete participant" and "participant-as-observer," as providing bins of comfortable fit for research approaches with which I am familiar, with the latter as descriptive of the pathway to data that I have been following in my study of southern labor union organizing campaigns. The main distinction between the two subtypes seems to lie in the matter of research-role concealment. The participant-as-observer not only makes no secret of his investigation; he makes it known that research is his overriding interest. He is there to observe. To mention a second distinction that I regard as important, the participant-as-observer is not tied down; he is free to run around as research interests beckon; he may move as the spirit listeth.

The complete participant, on the other hand, as far as the study of industrial situations is concerned, is stuck with the work. With an emphasis on observation, the participant-as-observer may lend a hand on occasion to push a desk across a room, or a tongue to seal envelopes; the complete participant may find his nose so incessantly pressed to the grindstone of work routines that he has little time or opportunity to observe the social interaction going on around him. A benign nod might be tossed in the direction of a complete participation role as drummer in a hot rock-and-roll combo, as taster in a winery, or as commander of a flagship in peacetime. But there are manifold activities, particularly those of interest to an industrial sociologist, in which participation can be stupefactive. As one who has put in many stultifying hours in concealed dedication to sociology in the lower depths of factory work, let me express frank enthusiasm for the participant-as-observer role. In my experience its advantages outweigh its disadvantages, and I favor it against the third approach listed by Junker, that of observer-as-participant. The chief distinctions here lie in the quality and quantity of contacts with respondents. Whereas "the observer-as-participant role is used in studies involving one-visit interviews,"[2] "numerous brief contacts with many persons,"[3] and "relatively more formal observation

1. Buford Junker, *Field Work: An Introduction to the Social Sciences* (Chicago: University of Chicago Press, 1960).

2. Raymond L. Gold, "Roles in Sociological Field Observations," *Social Forces,* 36 (March 1958): 221.

3. Marion Pearsall, "Participant Observation as Role and Method in Behavioral Research," *Nursing Research,* 14, no. 1 (Winter 1965): 38.

than either informal observation or participation of any kind,"[4] the participant-as-observer role calls for informality of relationship with a few key informants or guides over a long period of time, and perhaps more intensive immersion in the minute details of the processes being studied.[5] The first is primarily an "outsider" role,[6] the second an "insider" role.

Junker's fourth category, the complete observer role, I have not had occasion to employ. I do not see how it could be maintained in the study of union organizing campaigns in the South. The larger mass meetings, conducted by union officials for the recruitment and morale-boosting of those eligible for union membership, might be open to those who would observe from the concealment of the mass; but in the general meetings of the size that union leaders of my acquaintance have been able to muster, such concealment would be difficult to sustain without correlative establishment of a complete participation role in the workplace involved. I do recall the case of an enterprising white student of mine who played the complete observer at a gathering of a local chapter of the Black Muslims by crawling under a pile of boards heaped at the back of a rickety meeting hall. However, the likely consequences of detection being what they were, this student limited occupancy of his observation post to a one-night stand.

I had become habituated to the participant-as-observer role long before I knew it by that name. Before reading Junker's work, I had become resigned to the cumbersome designation "continuous observation and interviewing in context," though until this moment there has been no printed announcement of my own awkward terminology. I now make a further distinction, a subclassification, in regard to my preferred research role, in the hope of clarifying as I complicate. I refer to a differentiation of perspective that has, I think, special relevance for the study of social conflict. One perspective entails observation from and participation with both sides of the conflict; the researcher stalks with the Hatfields and ambushes with the McCoys. The other perspective provides a running view of the war with the compliments of one of the two combatants. These distinctions cry for naming, and various designations come to mind. I have settled, for the time being, on "fence-riding" for the dual, or split, affiliation. "Tightrope walking" might do just as well, with "riding a tiger" crudely apt, but too heavily freighted, perhaps, with distracting imagery. I have thought of "above the battle," which carries agreeable connotations of professional elevation, removing all suggestion of precarious, undignified, or otherwise uninviting position. It also car-

4. Gold, "Roles in Sociological Field Observations."
5. Pearsall, "Participant Observation as Role and Method."
6. *Ibid.*

ries a gargantuan load of wishful thinking: maintaining effective research communication with conflicting groups over an extended period of time is a ticklish undertaking. If the researcher seeks to hoist himself too far above the battle, he may encounter stratospheric conditions where data run disappointingly thin. If he plunges into the thick of things, hobnobbing in easy camaraderie with both Hatfields and McCoys, he may at any time, particularly during periods of acute hostility, be perceived as too chummy with the opposition; as a consequence he may be drummed out of both clans. I have found that fence-riding can be a nerve-racking experience, even in a northern industrial situation where collective bargaining has been established and where union-management relations go on from day to day in apparent harmony.

The alternative perspective available to the researcher who would essay a participant-as-observer approach to the study of organizing campaigns I have given a provisional label: "Ernie Pyling." Ernie Pyle, it may be remembered, was a news correspondent who followed American troops, including front-line fighting units, during World War II.[7] Like Pyle, I have during recent years followed the troops, representing one side of the union-management conflict that rages in the South. Since the focus of my investigation has been primarily on the organizing campaign, with my interest in the strike incidental to overall organizing efforts, and since unions initiate and conduct the campaigns in the role of attackers, the observational perspective that I have chosen would appear to be the logical one to take. It would be unrealistic, I am sure, to attempt a fence-riding approach in a conflict so permeated with strong passions and gut-deep estrangement, where both sides go all out to win and play for keeps. I have encountered nothing in my reading to induce me to drop the presumption that reciprocal hostilities between union and management were just as intense in times past in the industrial areas of our North and West. Maintaining effective research communication with both sides in situations characterized by a reluctant willingness of management to "live with the union" is difficult enough. Where the two antagonists have not even achieved a stage of incipient accommodation, possibilities of fence-riding would be slim indeed. I am willing to entertain, far back in my mind, the possibility that someone else, someone with the right dual connections carefully developed and maintained, someone recognized by both sides as possessed of impeccable neutrality and trustworthiness, or someone of exalted status or overwhelming charisma, might be able to conduct a study of labor union organizing campaigns in the South with a participant-as-observer approach *and* with the sustained cooperation of both adversaries. Certainly, one who has been Ernie Pyling with the union forces would not be given the

7. See Ernie Pyle, *Here Is Your War* (New York: Pocket Books, 1944).

opportunity to acquire data accessible only through a management group. As far as possibilities for application of other research procedures are concerned, it would appear likely that some type of polling or interviewing technique would have a better chance of winning dual cooperation. Yet here too I am inclined toward pessimism. The word that I get, indirectly and from a variety of sources, is that the management of southern industry does not look with favor on the study of union organizing regardless of research procedures contemplated. University professors of my acquaintance, who possess detailed familiarity with the mores of both business and academe in the South, have said, "You don't study unions down here." Puzzled students have told me of the refusal of relatives, highly placed in southern industry, to discuss with them the managerial point of view on unions. Some of these students were not members of my classes; nor can I claim blame as a source of their curiosity. One writer, a contributor to national magazines, called on me when she heard that I was studying unions. "I wanted to see what you looked like," she said. "You know, this just isn't done in the South."

At this point I must make two confessions. The first is that my choosing a taboo subject for research was not due to any deliberate boldness on my part. The investigation wasn't planned. I stumbled into it quite by chance. I blush now at my naïveté at my first encounters with union officials and pro-union workers. Secondly, I must admit that conversing with working stiffs is for me a matter of taking the line of least resistance. The union organizers of my acquaintance are for the most part only improved varieties of old-fashioned blue-collar drudges, and having experienced somewhat the same beatitudes and stringencies of condition, I find a pleasing measure of fellow feeling in our otherwise professional relationships and correlatively an ease in informal communication. My academic career has been, in a sense, an appendage to an earlier horizontal progression through a series of miscellaneous low-caste occupations. During my graduate student days, research in a factory gave me an opportunity to escape from my reference group to spend the afternoon observing and interviewing the machine-tending hoi polloi. In the bowels of the factory we were all dropouts; I was the dropout who went on to get a Ph.D.

During recent years there has sprung up in our centers of higher learning and research a group of students who seem to have the inclination, if not the background, to interact informally with the great unwashed. However, their interest in the working class, employed or unemployed, centers on the development of action programs, not field study. Graduate student rosters of southern universities may include a few potential Ernie Pylers; however, under present-day pressures to speed up processes of qualifying for niches in the academic woodwork,

candidates for the Ph.D. cannot spare the time for observational procedures that may get them involved for many months in the field with no
assurance that their gleanings can be shaped and tidied into dissertation
form. For those who find themselves thus cramped for time to follow a
possible research interest in union-management conflict in the South,
there are alternative sources of data to draw upon, such as the library,
the files, and use of more formal techniques of interviewing. Recourse to
these and possibly additional options meets with rather severe limitations. During one campaign I employed a fixed-choice questionnaire
with results that were not disappointing. However, this undertaking
represented but one phase of a larger effort, and it was not carried out in
conformity to acceptable standards of survey research.

I see no problem of entrée for the researcher who elects to study
union-management conflict from an Ernie Pyle perspective if he is willing to make his observations from the union side of the fence. I have
found, at all levels of union officialdom, doors wide open to the study of
organizing campaigns. Although my contacts with union organizers and
officials have not been widespread, owing to the character of my research, which has been intensive rather than extensive, I am led by the
invariably friendly reception that I have received to the presumption
that union leaders in general, at least on the southern scene, welcome
the spotlight of the sociologist. They feel, I gather, that they have much
more to gain than to lose by investigation and its possibilities of con-
sequent publicity. This is not to say that the open-door policy represents
a despairing "What have we got to lose?" attitude. It is true that some
unions have been taking campaign beatings with almost monotonous
regularity and for a long time; but other unions rack up victories in a
majority of their campaigns, and they too are likely to give the researcher a friendly reception. In fact, a representative of one union took the
initiative in inviting me to have a look at some union victories. The
researcher cannot, of course, expect a union to offer a ringside seat to
witness the exchange of punches that commonly takes place in labor-management relations after the union has won the right to representation and a contract, and collective bargaining has been instituted.
Permission to watch collective bargaining sessions, or other types of
infighting that are conducted on company property, would have to come
from management as well as from the union. But I discovered to my
initial surprise and subsequent embarrassment that under certain circumstances the managerial invitation may be graciously though unenthu-
siastically extended when gentle pressure is applied by an apparently
ascendant union official. I have been ushered into the offices of managers of fairly large business establishments, to their obvious discomfort
and mine, along with plant employees and union stewards, to watch the

union business agent handle employee grievances, beating company officials into the ground, figuratively speaking, while doing so. Although this sort of approach to observation of in-plant aspects of union-management conflict can indeed be productive of abundant, sometimes astonishing data, its use would appear to be limited to a relatively rare set of circumstances.

Opportunity to observe my first organizing campaign came quite unexpectedly. An organizer for the Textile Workers Union of America, who had heard of my interest in industrial relations from a friend of one of my former associates at the University of Chicago, called at my office at Duke University one spring day to ask me if I knew of any Duke students who might be willing to work a few hours for the union, for pay. He wanted men to help distribute leaflets at the site of a prospective organizing campaign, about ten miles from the university. Our encounter netted no student help for the organizer (this was prior to the development of a New Left movement at Duke), but in the course of our conversation the organizer suggested that I might like to attend a mass meeting that was to be held to kick off a campaign for employees of a textile mill located in the foothills of the Blue Ridge. It sounded like an interesting outing, and I showed up, on a rainy Sunday afternoon. The meeting was brief, held in the soggy out-of-doors on a dirt crossroad near a baseball park. My new acquaintance and members of his workers' organizing committee had been unable to obtain indoor facilities in the mill town or in other towns of the surrounding area. The scene in the rain impressed me — the opening prayer, the earnest speakers, the intently listening mill hands, men and women, and the nearby ball park with a roofed-over grandstand, dedicated to local heroes who had fought for justice and freedom in World War II, but denied to some of those heroes who were standing in the rain.

The campaign lasted the rest of the spring, all summer, and into the autumn. The union got beat, the first of a long, unbroken series of defeats that I was to witness or to hear about. I watched the process, from the April kick-off meeting to a November dismantling of the goal posts, by averaging every other weekend at field headquarters. Since my organizer-sponsor had been laying the groundwork for another campaign for several weeks before taking his final lumps in the first one, I was able to make the switch from one observation post to another with no problems of clearance. I would have experienced no difficulty in establishing myself in the second situation anyhow. During the course of the first campaign I met some visiting dignitaries, officials of the union at the vice-presidential level, who came down from national headquarters in New York or over from regional headquarters in Charlotte to contribute speeches designed to improve morale and to appraise the progress and prospects of the campaign. Also, early in the summer, I had attended a union conference at regional headquarters, and there, over a period of two days, I made the acquaintance of other union officials and many of the southern organizers. I learned, from these extended contacts, that my sponsor was highly esteemed by his superiors in the union hierarchy, but that he was also regarded with mixed feelings as a man of unconventional organizing ideas. Now, knowing him over a longer period of time, I am inclined to the belief that my Ernie Pyleship was launched as one of his innovations. At any rate, if my experience may be considered as indicative of what other sociologists might reasonably expect, neither establishment nor maintenance of access to observation posts for close scrutiny of union organizing processes poses any notable difficulty.

It is my feeling that if major hindrances to a durable and productive field-study relationship with southern union people are to be encountered, they will be found in the behavior of the researcher. I suspect that organizers, and workers too, would rather quickly tire of a would-be Pyler who had been oversocialized to a teaching role, didactic style, to the extent that he would feel comfortable in human interaction only while lecturing the other fellow. Such a need to hold the floor would be especially handicapping, I think, if it were accompanied by mannerisms indicating a self-conception creaking with status. A prevailing inclination to listen, heightened by genuine interest and curiosity, and suspended only long enough to ask for further relevant information or to raise pertinent questions, would carry one best, I am sure, over the long haul.

Besides a tendency to let the other fellow do the talking, I have had one other important thing going for me in my study of union-management conflict. Early in my first campaign I began to arrange my searchings around a central question: How can we account for the union's success or failure in organizing campaigns? This question, of course, was of vital practical concern to the organizers, and it tended to be sure-fire in eliciting the interest of workers in my research. How to win was not just a problem to the union officials, it was *the* problem. For the dedicated it was all-consuming. For those with minimal devotion to the cause—that is, the organizers called "pork-choppers"—it was at least the heart of a job. No matter how deep or how superficial the occupational motivation, the question was always good for thoughtful discussion, sometimes animated argument when the experts found themselves in disagreement. And there was frequently disagreement when the question was tossed into a group—if not over basic matters, then over the fine points.

Those who remained relatively silent in group disputations would impress upon me later a point that they had failed to make, one that they had been reluctant to put forth in the group situation or one that had come to mind after the discussion had ended. I could also expect to hear again in private the analyses and expansions thereof of those who had been most loquacious or argumentative when the discussion was on. The question appears to be a simple one, but the answer becomes complex. The way for blue-collar and ex-blue-collar people to present complex matters clearly and convincingly to their fellows is to bring forth concrete examples, that is, to talk about a specific campaign that they have experienced. And since the success/failure question has a perpetual relevance to the work at hand, it could be introduced, in one form or another, at just about any time, on the job or during off hours. Such shop talk never seemed importunate. It was in season at field headquarters, driving along county roads to the home of some prospective union member, with groups that lingered on after the mass meeting, at meal-time in the Greasy Spoon, in the hotel lobby at regional conferences, or over a beer anywhere.

During recent years the big question has bifurcated to include a twin problem of deep concern: how to win a contract for collective bargaining after winning the certifying election that decides campaign victory or defeat. The additional topic for discussion does nothing to impede or to retard the continuous interviewing and observation in context; it augments it. I feel certain that I would not have received the same gratifying quality of acceptance during the early phases of my study had I seized upon and belabored a question of slight intrinsic interest to the union people. After friendships were developed and trust was established, the nature of the subject matter of inquiry became less important, I feel, for the development and maintenance of my relationships. The situation is becoming one in which I no longer volunteer explanation of my research purpose as I move from one obersvational post to another; and rarely am I asked, as new faces appear, what I am doing. I seem to move from situation to situation over bridges of organizer interacquaintance. Perhaps the questioning goes on during my absence, with organizers vouching for my trustworthiness to each new group of workers. However, I suspect that my welcome in union circles might have deteriorated rather quickly had I shifted my orientation from topics of vital interest to my respondents to questions of little or no appeal.

In general, the organizing campaign, as I am familiar with it, represents an attempt by a group of international labor union officials to induce the employees of a given industrial or commercial establishment to give an explicit indication of their desire to form a local chapter of the union served by the men who do the urging. This evocation of avowal takes time, from several months to a year or more. Several determinants have a hand in dragging out the process. For one thing, the explicit indicating must follow certain procedures instituted by the National

Labor Relations Board. Arrangements are made, in most cases, for conducting a union certification election by secret ballot. This election normally terminates the campaign; its results spell victory or defeat for the union. Also, NLRB officials will insist on seeing, before calling for the vote, evidence that at least 30 percent of the employees involved have expressed their desire, by petition, for an election. The organizer in charge of a campaign usually takes upon himself the responsibility of acquiring the necessary proportion of signatures, and this may take a few weeks. However, the organizer will not pass on to the NLRB the minimal 30 percent of possible signatures that it takes to get the election wheels rolling until he has received some form of assurance that the union has a good chance of winning, that pro-union ballots will be in the majority, preferably by substantial majority. This assurance may be hard to come by, may take many months in the getting, and may never be obtained if the organizer feels that he must have in his possession petition cards signed by 50 percent, 60 percent, or 70 percent of the eligible voters before he extends an election request to the NLRB. It may take less time to come to the decision that a union victory is a good bet if the organizer seeks other signs of good omen, such as the size, morale, and effectiveness of an organizing committee that he has developed among strongly pro-union workers. It takes time, of course, to shape up such a committee and to assess the results of its work. If management, as a counterorganizing tactic, should fire the organizing committee, or a substantial proportion of its membership, then the organizer has to shape up another committee if he is to go on with the campaign. One organizer had two committees shot out from under him before losing his certification election. Finally, the campaign may be prolonged by managerial action that is legalistic as well as legal. Company officials may delay the setting of an election date by requesting a special hearing to reach decisions on matters connected with delineating the electorate. In the view of union organizers, calling for a hearing represents delaying tactics on the part of management, which seeks additional time to allow its employees to reconsider their urge to union membership.

Management, of course, provides the eligible voters with ideational material for their second thoughts. Just as the organizer and his staff encourage workers to sign petition cards and to vote for the installation of a union, company officials exude counteracting discouragement. As the union officials organize, management officials disorganize. In fact, the campaign involves the attempts of both sides to organize relationships with the potential electorate and to disorganize relationships built up by the opposition. Furthermore, the organizing efforts of the two adversaries may reach far beyond the employees of the mill or factory in question. Both attempt to build supportive linkages with other groups and agencies in the community and over a wider canvas in state and nation. Most strikingly, the community gets drawn into the struggle, with management characteristically gaining the most effective help. The campaign thus gets spread out over a network of intergroup relations while it extends over stretches of time.

The election administered by the NLRB is the concluding event of a series that gives the organizing campaign a typical form. Possible and actual variation of doings and happenings within a general context of tactics, occurrences, and conditions engenders uncertainty of outcome. The union may win an election that its officials expected to lose; more often it loses when victory has been predicted. Many campaigns wind up with defeat or triumph by very close margins. As the campaign spins out, as things happen, as conditions develop, as the union employs routine tactics or tries something different, as management counter-attacks, each successor in the stream of events is assessed by the organizer and his group at field headquarters as to nature and degree of influence on the progress and outcome of the campaign. These appraisals are grist for my curiosity mill, which grinds away on the question: How may we explain success or failure? They direct my vision, point out to me what I should see and take into account, and supply me with hypotheses for rumination, selections, and reforumlation. When I notice something hitherto undiscussed, the experts at hand offer explanation. I come to understand what I see. By watching the campaign roll on in its full development and in its particulars, I get a better grasp of what the experts are talking about when they relate experiences of other times and places. I come to understand what I hear. I get steeped in the lore of campaigning. I acquire an acquaintance knowledge for ease of mentation within the imponderabilia of the occupation of union-organizing. I establish a base in the tacit knowledge of the craft. I get pictures in detail, from which abstractions may be constructed with minimal distortion, so that a union official with decades of experience can say, after reading one of my theoretical efforts, "You've got the picture." Thus I might claim that the participant-as-observer role provides me with both the "act-meanings" of *Verstehen* and the tentative "action-meanings"[8] requisite for the development of theory.

Since my teachers and informants are not passive spectators of campaign processes, but practitioners trying to utilize their skills and various other resources to overcome great obstacles to attain their end in view; since these practitioners apply alternative ideas, sometimes new and highly imaginative ones, in the attempt to solve their problems; and

8. Abraham Kaplan, *The Conduct of Inquiry* (San Francisco: Chandler, 1964), pp. 358–63.

since I observe such activities over the organizer's shoulder and in his very shadow, so to speak, I might also claim an adumbrative "learning by doing" method of inquiry, given strong recommendation by John Dewey[9] and Mao Tse-tung.[10] To call it "incipient experimentation" might be stretching the claim too far, but I do see these observational procedures as efficacious preliminaries to field experiment.

I offer brief depictions of types of situations in which the Ernie Pyling technique can be used for observing characteristic activities of the organizing campaign. In most of these situations the researcher not only sees and hears what is going on within range of his eyes and ears; he gets reports on what is happening beyond the limits of his perception. He gets common-sense interpretations of these events, both near and far, and he can initiate or intervene in conversation for heightened apprehension and comprehension of observation and idea.

Hanging Around Headquarters

Perhaps the most fruitful hours of fieldwork, in regard to the organizing campaign, are spent at field headquarters, usually located in an office in a union hall or in a suite of motel rooms, and not many miles from the factory under organizing attack. If the location is a union hall, it may be the property of a sympathetic labor union that has won its campaign and has settled in the community. If it is a motel room, it will be in an establishment where the proprietor is not so hostile toward unions that he will not tolerate the protracted residence of organizers and the almost continual coming and going of pro-union workers. The organizer in charge of a campaign spends a great proportion of his time in his office, which serves as the center of a web of communication. If the target of the organizing attempt is a large mill, the union may assign several more organizers to assist the man in charge; these assistants drop in from time to time to report the work done in the field, that is, their successes and failures in contacting workers in their homes for petition-card signatures or their progress in developing groups of "actives" as organizing committees to participate in phases of the organizing process. The assisting organizers also engage in exchanges with their chief involving appraisals of the campaign situation and in discussions on tactical problems and possibilities. Pro-union workers drop in, too. There is a day-long stream of callers, arriving singly, in twos, threes, and large groups, fitting visits to their work schedules. They bring the news of the hour from the mill and the community, informing the organizer of ominous, promising, or

9. John Dewey, *The Quest for Certainty* (New York: Minton, Balch, 1929).
10. Mao Tse-tung, *Selected Works* (Peking: Foreign Languages Press, 1965), vol. 1, pp. 295–309.

amusing events and answering his searching questions. These callers serve as extra eyes and ears for the organizer; through them he keeps tabs on what goes on in the mill, department by department. He is ever on the alert for materials that can be shaped into issues to be played up in leaflets or at mass meetings to advance identification with the union and disaffection toward management. So the stretchout has hit the weave room? So the spinners are unable to understand how their piece-work pay is computed and think they're being cheated? So the superintendent has been calling the loom fixers to the office for questioning and brainwashing against unionism? So the second hands have been saying that the company would never work with a union, hinting that the mill would be shut down and leased out as a warehouse if the union won the election? So the forelady in sewing has been very nice to the girls lately? So they're starting to hand out the sweet stuff, repainting the rest rooms and installing new toilet bowls? So the company president has sent out a love letter to his blue-collar employees, telling them of his hopes and plans for better days together if everyone continues to pull together for that brighter future? So the food-cart service is getting worse every day, the Brunswick stew isn't fit for the hogs, and Sonny Pickens dug around in his potato salad today until he found a spider, held it up, and shouted triumphantly, "I found it!" thus indicating to everyone that there was sure to be something wrong with the company-dispensed lunch?

The organizer finds out what is going on in the workplace, in all detail of possible relevance to his organizing effort; and, privileged to sit in on the têtes-à-têtes, so does the researcher. If the foreman lets his female employees hold prayer meetings on company time to keep them happy and nonunion, if supervisors are cracking down on employee conversation to reduce possible union talk, the researcher hears about it from the lips of the workers involved. If he wants to discuss these or other matters with the visitors, he may. He'll meet them again, at the office or at meetings, and they'll converse with him freely, having noticed that the organizers speak without constraint in his presence.

If the organizer looks for a high proportion of signed petition cards in relation to the number of eligible voters, he may keep a very careful accounting of the process of card-signing, referring almost daily to his file of contact cards. On each card, headed by employee name, job designation, department, and home address, he may note date of contact, name of person who did the contacting, and a few lines of appraisal of the employee's union orientation, including the yes or no of his petition-card signing. With a select group of trusted actives, representing the various mill departments by work shift, the organizer may go over his contact cards. In private conferences with individuals or small groups the organizer may receive help in casting about for possibilities of inducing the unsigned to come into the fold. From the thoughtful discussions will come a consensus, either that further effort should be expended on the refractory or slippery ones or that further effort would be futile. By listening to these discussions the researcher discerns a variety of pressures, interests, and circumstances that serve as counter-influences to appeals made by union adherents, and thus may bear on campaign outcome. The following excerpts from my field notes, taken down verbatim during assessments of the unsigned, offer an example of the appraisal process and the type of opportunity given the researcher to observe and record it. In this particular instance, head organizer George Forstal (all names are fictitious) and two of his staff, Mike and Lucille, discuss with a committee of four textile workers some card-signing possibilities in the napping department:

> *George:* We should sit down and go over the names of those who haven't signed. We should talk about what kind of people they are – how to approach them, who their brother or father is, who they ride with. We need one more card from Napping B [second shift of the napping department] and we'll have a majority.

One worker suggested the name Garver, asked George if he had signed. George said no.

"Then he told a lie," said a second worker. He added, "My brother is quitting Thursday. He's going to school, the Hilltop Bible School."

> *1st worker:* Your brother's a minister, isn't he?
> *George:* (referring to names again): Adkins. Doesn't he roll blankets?
> *3rd worker:* He's gone [out of Napping B].
> *George:* The way they move around!

Other names were discussed – Chester, Graham.

> *3rd worker* (in reaction to the name Graham): I don't believe he'll sign.
> *Lucille:* Yes, I believe he will sign. I talked to him. He just didn't understand what the union is all about.
> *2nd worker:* He's the kind of guy that will find out things from you and tell others.

*   *   *

> *George:* Sparks? Whitaker's working on him. Somebody said his wife was the key.
> *4th worker:* I don't know.
> *George:* Earl Waddell?
> *2nd worker:* Can't do anything with him. He's got one of those pie-eating jobs.

George then mentioned Jack Scott, a "colored fellow."

> *3rd worker:* If you get Gaither, you get Scott. Scott does what he says.
> *George:* Some of the boys have been deviling Jack, and they've got him scared. They've been sticking union cards in his pocket, so they show, and then asking him where he got them.

During most of my observation situations thoughout this campaign, I was able to take notes with pencil and pad as I watched, listened, and conversed. The fact that George did not disapprove of this note-taking made it all right with those who called at union headquarters. Occasionally at some of the larger gatherings and formal meetings questioning eyes would be directed my way; but always George's lack of concern over my activity seemed to allay suspicion of my motives. I would replace pad after pad as they filled up with my own special shorthand and grind down pencil after pencil with the small plastic pencil sharpener that I carried with me.

Observing Mass Meetings

But I did not venture to take notes openly in all campaigns and all situations. In my observation of mass meetings conducted by George Forstal I did not hesitate to bring out pencil and paper for verbatim recording. But during a campaign led by an organizer I shall call Wren I watched and listened with folded arms during the weekly mass meetings held in a hall provided by another union. The following excerpt from my observations, within an hour after the close of one meeting, indicates the type of material gathered at mass meetings when I did not consider it advisable to flash a pencil.

Wren now called on Jones to talk. "I see that the colored workers are well represented tonight. It looks like Brother Jones has been doing a good job. Brother Jones, do you want to say a few words?"

Jones, a large, raw-boned Negro who had served as a organizer for another union in another area, and who now volunteered his services to help with the organizing of the few colored workers of the target mill, stood up from his seat in the rear of the hall. "I just want to say that I agree with what you said a hundred percent. You've all got to get out and sell people on having a union. I've been in union work for twenty-one years, and I know that people stay home and don't attend meetings. And they're going to go and stay home after you have a union here, and only a few of you will go to the meetings. You are the leaders, and you will keep it going."

Jones went on: "There are two stages, the way I look at it, in getting a union. The first stage is the drive, where you get out, as you did, and get enough cards to petition for an election. The second stage is the stage you are going into now, and that is the contest stage. You are in a contest with the company to win the election. It's a contest over who's to decide things in the plant from now on, whether the bosses and their stooges are going to go on deciding everything themselves, or whether you are going to have some say in what happens to you, some say about your wages and hours and working conditions."

Jone's voice, when he started to talk about the "contest," rose in increasing emotionalism, and he was shouting loudly when he spoke of the bosses and their stooges and deciding things. His voice resumed a moderate tone now, as he referred to the Scriptures.

Jones said that there was a passage in the Scriptures that he thought was appropriate here: "As a man thinketh, so is he." He also cited another line, which I am unable to recall. I did not get too clear a connection between this line and what Jones then said, that they were right in what they were trying to get for themselves, and since they were right they could win.

"You can be a success, because you are on the Lord's side in this, and the Lord's side is the side to be on [voice raising again]. Even if they argue that they're not making much money, that there's work enough for only four days a week and this is not the time to organize a union, remember that they're making money whenever they run. They're making money out of our work even if they run three, two, or even one day a week. They don't operate unless they can make money. The bosses make a profit on all that you do, and it's up to you to get your share, just as much as you can get."

Jones was now shouting enough to raise the roof. I noted that the white people in front of me looked a little restive, as if wishing that Jones would finish and sit down. I noticed a sort of restiveness in myself, perhap an embarrassment for the speaker and an empathy with the audience. I was wishing that Jones would finish and sit down, or at least talk more moderately. It was if he were abusing his invitation to "say a few words" by launching a long, loud speech. (Jones took longer in his talk than I indicate in the telling.) I noted, however, that some of the Negroes were obviously enjoying Jones's harangue. They were grinning and making gestures of strong approval.

Other Observation Situations

Other types of observation situations of the participant-as-observer variety included those afforded by accompanying organizers on house calls at the homes of mill workers for the purpose of obtaining petition-card signatures, making trips to the mill gates at shift-change time to watch organizers hand out union leaflets to homeward-bound workers, and joining worker crowds at picket lines during strikes, with the special excitement at shift change when carloads of nonstriking workers, with the protection of city, county, and state police, and would drive through the lines to the accompaniment of shouts and jeers from the strikers. These three types of situations provided, of course, ample opportunity for interviewing in the form of conversation.

In one campaign involving six plants of one company, I attended the special meetings held each week at a central location for the dozen organizers involved. These meetings, conducted by a union vice-president, centered around reports of the organizers on events of the week in their respective campaigns and discussion of tactics to foster the progress of the organizing drive. In this situation I was privileged to sit back from the conference table and take verbatim notes.

My strike-watching opportunities included not only headquarters and picket-line observations in four strikes conducted for the purpose of pressuring company officials to bargain collectively after certification elections had been won; they also included observation in a miscellany of situations connected with a long strike of considerable magnitude, drama, and significance for the southern future of an international union. This strike found me in daily courtroom attendance in a small town. Several union officials of my acquaintance and four active millworkers were given prison sentences for conspiring to dynamite an electric power substation. The problem of note-taking in a courtroom where the judge was lavish with his contempt-of-court citations and sentences was solved by the screening provided by the heads and torsos of several cooperative millworkers.

Interviewing

As I have already noted, my application of the participant-as-observer role to the study of union-management conflict involved continuous interviewing as well as observation. This interviewing, conducted as informal conversation, varied from direct questioning on a great variety of specific topics of timely interest to nondirective exploration of perception and feeling.

In two of the campaigns of the six-plant drive I launched programs of formal interviewing of employees with the use of four-page questionnaires. In the first of these interviewing attempts I approached my respondents without the seal of approval of the organizers. In the second situation an organizer accompanied me to each house to make the introduction and to provide assurances that I was OK, that I was really from Duke, was not a stooge of the company, and would hold confidential what was told me. In the first situation the fearful workers expressed their suspicions by either refusing to talk with me or providing false answers to my questions.

The following offers a sample of responses received from the non-sponsored questioning of one Medford Sprinkle, who was first asked to accept one of five statements that came closest to expressing his feelings about having a labor union in his mill:

  (a) We are very much in need of a union in our mill.
  (b) Conditions in the mill aren't too bad, but I think a union would help a lot.
  (c) I can't see that it makes much difference whether we have a union or not.
  (d) A union might help us a little on a few things, but generally it would do more harm than good.

(e) All that a union would bring us is a lot of trouble.

Sprinkle was unable to pick a position. He handed the five cards back to me, saying, "I haven't any opinion about the union. I haven't been thinking about it. I haven't had time to think about it." He then explained that his mother had "taken sick" a month ago, and that he spent his spare time visiting her. "I go over to my mother's when I get up in the morning, and don't get back till two o'clock, when it's time to go to work."

Sprinkle's answers to some of the succeeding questions were recorded as follows:

Q. 3: Sprinkle was unable to suggest any good things or any bad things that might come of having a union. He repeated his lack of opinion, spoke again of his sick mother.

Q. 4: Sprinkle said that none of the influences listed had any influence on him. Of newspaper articles he said, "I've seen nothing in the paper about the union." Sprinkle didn't know what locally prominent people said about the union, nor did he know what nationally prominent people said. He hadn't talked the subject over with relatives, neighbors, or friends. When I asked him about talks with neighbors, he said "I haven't been anywhere. Just to my mother's." He said, in a sort of summary here, "I haven't heard any talk about the union at all."

Q. 8: He said that an organizer called on him once during the campaign. "A guy was here, but I wasn't home." Sprinkle couldn't give any opinions about the organizers because he hadn't met any of them.

Q. 19: He took *(a)* position here, indicating he felt that the foreman in his department was well liked by the workers. Sprinkle commented, "He's too good for his own use. Nobody could dislike him. He even worries about the help. I was raised with him and went to school with him."

I discovered, after this survey was abandoned, that Sprinkle was not only in surreptitious communication with the organizers as a strongly pro-union worker, but was regarded as possessing potentialities for leadership.

In contrast, Mattie Reece provided frank answers to the formal questioning when I called at her home a few days after being introduced to her by the organizer in charge of the campaign. After completing the questionnaire, Mrs. Reece went on to talk freely about the stretchout in the weave room:

If the union falls through, we haven't ever seen such hard times as we'll get. I can't keep my job going now. I can't get looms fixed. I can't get running. The second hands [supervisors] show no interest. A second hand said that it's easy now, but if the seconds [defective weaving] don't come down, it's hard to tell what we'll get later on. I figure he meant after the union is gone.

In a big meeting they asked about the restroom ventilation. Some girls had complained that it was too hot to change clothes in there. They asked me how it was in the restroom. I said I didn't know. I said I don't get to stay long enough to find out. Some days I can't get the time to go in. I punish myself. There's not time to go in there. I go straight in and out and don't take the time to comb my hair.

The other weavers are in the same fix. There's no time to eat. I've worked day in and day out without stopping to eat. The dope wagon [lunch cart] comes in and half the looms are standing. Many times I just take coffee or milk. It's that way with the other weavers, too.

When I first came to work, twenty years ago, I could go to the waterhouse [restroom] and talk or rest five minutes. Now there's no time for anything. Grady Spicer told me that if he goes to the waterhouse the second hand comes in there watching him.

It's killing us all. My health is affected. I'm so nervous some days. . . . Everybody is on pins and needles. They're afraid to say anything, or do the least thing wrong. It's a continual strain for everybody. They're all afraid they'll lose their jobs, and if anybody needs a job, I do.

John Crawford, loom fixer with fifteen years' seniority, also previously assured of my trustworthiness, had no hesitation in telling of his turning from anti-union to pro-union:

I changed my mind about the union. I was for the company. I even went to the union hall and talked for the company. . . .

They used to call me in the office. They asked me what I thought about the union . . . all such as that. In the first campaign [five years earlier] they wanted me to talk for them. . . . They wanted to know how I was going to vote. I told them that before this they said it was going to be secret. They said, "Crawford, if you go with the wrong crowd, you'll suffer with the wrong crowd." That was my second hand and the big boss in the office. . . .

When I came here, weavers had thirty-six looms. Now they've got eighty-eight or ninety. When I came here there was one weave room and three smash hands. Now there are two [smash hands per weave room]. Fixers have a whole lot more looms. They had forty-two or forty-three when I came. Now it's sixty-two looms to keep repaired. . . . You don't stand around and laugh and talk, not even at dinnertime. You eat your dinner at your workbench. . . . When you get more than you can do, it's hard on your nerves. I come in at night jittery.

Documentary Materials

Although the participant-as-observer relies, in the main, on watching, listening, and conversing in the gathering of his data, he may have access to a variety of documentary materials that have bearing on his chosen problem. In my own study of labor union organizing I find that each campaign produces a plethora of printed matter, including mimeographed and typed materials. The union disseminates occasional messages to members of the work force in the form of one-sheet leaflets, distributed at the mill gates. It also mails out letters. One could obtain a rough idea of the progress of a campaign by perusal of the union publications as they are issued. Also available is the company campaign literature, offered less frequently in the form of printed booklets and letters from the company president, mailed to a body of employees with the potential electorate obviously in special view. The company literature, always brought to the attention of the organizers by pro-union workers, can readily be obtained by the researcher. Likewise, copies of strongly anti-union periodicals, mailed to workers directly from the publisher during the organizing campaign, are readily available. The researcher can always find a pro-union worker who is willing to give up his copy of *Militant Truth,* a four-pager that seems to appear at irregular intervals when needed. With Bible and American flag riding the upper corners of page 1, this periodical is unwavering in its attack on those fraternizing conspirators: Reds, atheists, race-mixers, carpetbaggers, and labor union bosses. In addition, mimeographed or typed materials intended for a more restricted distribution are sometimes obtainable. A worker may take advantage of a careless supervisor or solve the problem of lock and key to smuggle out sheets of advice or instructions on counterorganizing. Such materials will be photocopied for quick return to the foremen's desk or file, and copies may be reduplicated.

Duplicates of several lengthy documents involving the hearings of fired workers before the Employment Security Commission have come into my possession. One such document, having special relevance to the progress of an organizing campaign, reveals the question-and-answer details of a hearing given a fired millworker before an agent of the ESC. In this instance the terminated employee, a loom fixer with over fifteen years' seniority, was handed a penalty of nine weeks, meaning that he would not be able to draw unemployment compensation until nine weeks had elapsed. The decision of the appeals deputy carried further meaning, as an obvious warning to other employees, that those who received disaffectionate discharges need not hope to cushion their drop from the payroll with the timely support of weekly checks from the government. To accomplish this, a company attorney brought witnesses before the deputy to testify that the fired worker had violated a company rule prohibiting sleeping on the job. The critical question was: Did the discharged employee lose consciousness when he closed his eyes while taking a smoking break in a booth provided for that purpose? In the following excerpt from a copy of the transcript of the hearing, the company attorney presses the question:

Q. Well, will you say now that you did not lose consciousness while you were in the smoking booth?

A. I don't believe I did.

Q. Well, are you sure?

A. Well, I am pretty sure that I didn't, for Henry Settle walked in and said slip over and I slipped over.

Q. Yes, sir, but you could have been out for a little while while you were . . .

A. It would have had to been a little bit if I was.

Q. But you say you could have been out for a little while?

A. Well, I'd say that I was nodding. I won't say that I was conscious all the time, and I won't say that I wasn't. That's about the only way I can say it — but . . .

Q. Well, then you would have to say that you could have been unconscious for part of the time, isn't that right?

A. Well, I don't . . . No, I won't say that.

Q. Well, you said you didn't know whether you were all the time or not, didn't you?

A. I don't know. . . . You asked me there if I was or I wasn't and so I will say that I was conscious, for when Settle walked in and said slip over, I did.

Q. Yeah, but I am talking about before that time.

A. I was conscious I would say all the time I was in there.

*   *   *

Q. And of course, you admit that you did have your eyes closed and everything?

A. Yeah, my eyes was closed.

Q. Do you know how long they were closed?

A. No, I was gone from my job approximately ten minutes but I don't know how long.

Q. Well, it could have been as long as five minutes?

A. I guess so, I don't know, I wouldn't say that. I wouldn't say exactly how long my eyes was closed.

It was decided that the fired fixer had lost consciousness during his smoking break; so in addition to losing his job, he had to wait nine weeks for his unemployment compensation.

Of supplementary use to observing participants who seek to describe, understand, or analyze the southern labor union organizing campaign are various compilations of data that are readily available to anyone. Found in libraries, these materials may lend themselves to special studies, statistical or historical in nature. The annual reports of the NLRB, available in law libraries, offer statistics on cases involving unfair labor practices. Classifications are according to size of establishment involved, industry, geographic area, and outcome of hearing. These reports also provide statistics on representation elections by number, labor union involved, size of bargaining unit, number of employees voting, industry, geographic distribution by states, and election outcome. Additional data available in these reports include number and outcome of decertification elections and results of appeal of Board decisions to the courts. The written decisions of the NLRB and the court judgments made in cases that were appealed from Board decisions are available in bound volumes dating back to the Board's inception in 1935.

A handy guide to all formal decisions handed down by the NLRB in disposing of unfair labor practices issues and union representational matters is the *Labor Law Reporter,* a comprehensive digest found in law libraries. For each case of unfair labor practices the *Reporter* offers quotations from the statement of the trial examiner, the Board's areal representative who investigates and passes judgment. Judgments of the national Board, given when the trial examiner's decision is contested by employer, employee, or union, are also given in the *Reporter.* The following provides an example of the type of material published. The statement presented here is that offered by a three-man board; the judgment was made in recent months after a trial examiner's decision, favorable to a southern local of the Teamsters, was contested by the employer:

> The main issue of this case is the charge that employer violated Section 8 (a) (3) and (1) of the Act by laying off and discharging employees because of their union activity. A more novel issue is whether employer caused to be published a document threatening to close its plant because of union activity, or whether the group publishing that document was an agent of employer.
>
> Employer made no secret of the fact that it was opposed to the union campaign in its plant. Within the first weeks of the campaign, employer made several anti-union speeches to the employees, and then laid off or terminated many of the employees.
>
> About the same time, a meeting of community businessmen was held at a local bank and addressed by employer. In the course of its remarks employer indicated that it was opposed to organization of its employees by a union. After employer left the meeting, several of the businessmen formed an ad hoc committee called the Committee of Interested Citizens for Continued Progress. Within a few days the committee published a "fact sheet" that was distributed through the community and asserted that employer would close its plant unless the employees rejected the union.
>
> Shortly afterwards, employer made a public statement to the effect that every citizen had a right to express his views and that employer was not responsible for the committee's publications and views. However, employer did not deny or repudiate the committee's publication, and in effect suggested that the committee was performing a civic duty when it issued the publication. This was a tacit acknowledgment that the assertion in the fact sheet was true. Therefore, while there is no real evidence to show that employer instigated formation of the committee or publication of the fact sheet—and hence no showing that the committee was employer's agent—employer's response to the publication did convey the impression that the publication was correct and employer would close plant rather than go union. This response undoubtedly had a coercive effect upon the employees, and violated Section 8 (a) (1) of the Act. By the same token, it helps to show that

employer's mass layoffs and discharges in the first week of the union drive were discriminatory, and in violation of Section 8 (a) (3) and (1) of the Act.

The committee has also been charged with violating the Act in connection with the publication of the fact sheet. But no agency relationship having been established between employer and the committee, there can be no such finding.[11]

The Bureau of Labor Statistics offers annual summary tables on work stoppages, with data on number of work stoppages by industry group, by state, by metropolitan area, and by major issues involved. Also listed are statistics on average days lost by stoppage, number of workers involved, percent of total employed involved, and percent of total work time of man-days idle.

The Duke University library has a collection of manuscripts donated by a former southern regional director of a textile union. These records, once kept in the files at union regional headquarters, might interest historians of southern labor-management relations. They cover a fourteen-year period, from 1927 to 1941. I have been informed by union officials that local unions keep in their files all materials pertaining to organizing campaigns, including leaflets, letters, NLRB judgments, and court decisions. "Nothing is ever thrown away," said one union business agent. When the files fill up, the more ancient materials are sent to a central collection point for continued preservation. Unlike materials stored in libraries, however, contents of union files are not offered for public perusal. One may explore the union's archives only at the discretion of union officials. I have been offered access to files in several instances, but as yet have not taken advantage of this opportunity. Company officials undoubtedly preserve their own records of organizing campaigns in similar fashion. It is possible that access to such files might be accorded those who do their Ernie Pyling from the company side of the fence. It is also possible that unaffiliated researchers might be permitted to examine some of the organizing campaign materials stored by the antagonists. Since the police of municipality, county, and state get involved from time to time in matters connected with organizing campaigns, such as strike activity and surveillance of organizers, there may be materials stored in files that would be of value to students of labor-management conflict.

Evaluation of the Participant-as-Observer Role

I can offer only a cursory evaluation of the role of participant-as-observer in field investigation, owing to limitations of space and my own research experience. I find that the observing participant has

11. "NLRB Decisions," *Labor Law Reporter 1968-1 CCH,* p. 29857.

certain rather obvious advantages in comparison with the complete
participant and the participating observer. There are also, I have discovered, certain handicaps or problems connected with my favorite role,
some of which may have special connection with the study of social
conflict from the minority side of the fence. In addition, I have arrived at
the tentative conclusion that my Ernie Pyling approach shares with
other kinds of participant observation some necessary functions of social
research that are inadequately performed with nonparticipatory procedures of inquiry.

First of all, as I indicated earlier, I would give a high joy-in-work
rating to the role of participant-as-observer in comparison with other
field-study techniques with which I am familiar. I appreciate the freedom
of movement, the ability to go where the action is, lacking in the role of
complete participant, as well as the freedom from boring work. It may
be possible for the complete participant to overcome the usual problem
of limited range of observation by selecting a job that places him at the
hub of interaction. In one fortunate job placement in a large expensive
restaurant I was assigned duties that kept me close to the chef, at the
very center of the web of communication. As kettle-washer for a man
who dirtied a lot of cooking paraphernalia, I could unobtrusively take it
all in as I scrubbed pots and stoves and refrigerators and mopped floors.
The chef was the beloved leader of the kitchen crew, in hostile relationship with white-collar management. In important respects the situation
was similar to my activities in union research, when I attached myself to
the organizer in charge of a union organizing campaign. Still, there were
the long hours at my own tedious work role, my inability to press the
chef and members of his staff with out-of-work role questions, and the
ever present danger of being caught applying stubby pencil to pocket
notebook. Running around with organizers has been far more exciting.
The comparison may be a bit unfair here, with research procedures
entangled with subject matters. The work of the organizer seems in-
trinsically more interesting than that of the scullion or the factory hand.
Perhaps I would find complete participation as an organizer even more
absorbing than participation as an observer in an organizing campaign.

A possible disadvantage of my favorite research role appears to lie in
the combination of an Ernie Pyling data-gathering approach with the
substantive area of social conflict. This handicap would in all likelihood
be shared by any research procedures that involved participation with
one of two warring parties; the researcher finds himself persona non
grata with the opposition. This kind of consequence should be given
serious consideration by the prospective Ernie Pyler, especially in situations such as union-management conflict, where the stakes are high, a
heavy line of societal cleavage is maintained, and one side possesses a

preponderance of power, with ramifications of the ascendancy extending through many aspects of life. In the South "union" is openly recognized by a majority of the people, including nearly all of those who count, as a dirty word. In other regions of the United States too, I am led to suspect, the influential circles of business, industry, and the professions regard labor unions as unacceptable in both practice and principle. No matter how conservatively they are led, the potential challenge of labor unions to concentrations of power is there. Early in my research on union campaigns I was warned by a managerial representative of one of our large industrial organizations that my association with union organizers might cut me off permanently from rewarding relationships with managerial America; and a University of Chicago Ph.D. failed to acquire a teaching position in a small southern college when he expressed a desire to live near me in order to share my research interests.

In addition to other reputed weaknesses of participant observation, the likelihood of bias in the gathering of data by Ernie Pyling procedures must concern members of the sociological fraternity. Granting that there is danger of bias in all research, because we can't keep the researcher out of his equations, and that the probabilities of distortion are increased when affiliatory feelings are involved, I would suggest that the ultimate goal of scientists, theory that works, will eventually provide its own correctives. Aware of the pragmatic necessities of the logic of science that we all must face eventually, the social researcher who seeks to make contributions that will further the development of his craft and add building material to the house of knowledge will take care to separate his emotional attachments to people and causes from the hypotheses he is testing. It is not likely that the sociologist who has spent years in his investigations would insouciantly risk seeing his work go down the drain by allowing prejudice to sway scientific caution. In my view, perhaps a naïve one, the challenge and excitement of creativity involved in concept and theory construction affords an overwhelming counterforce to any motivation to express a substantive bias.

Relatively minor problems do pop up from time to time during the course of an investigation involving participation. For the most part these special difficulties are mere embarrassments. For instance, as an observing participant trying to preserve the modicum of dignity expected of a university researcher, I have been put to the poise test by male factory workers who call out in loud voices to female workers, "Here he comes, girls! Watch out—don't let him get behind you!" It is also difficult to carry on unruffled in the midst of a picket-line crowd when an organizer announces loudly for the benefit of three or four state policemen who are monitoring the situation, "Professor Roy is with us today to witness this travesty of justice!" When shift change brings arrival and departure of carloads of strikebreakers through the picket line amid the jeers, catcalls, and threatening gestures of the strikers, and an organizer calls out, "You can yell at the scabs too, Professor!" — then I am not only embarrassed by the presence of state troopers, but also made slightly uneasy by the hard stares of some of the strikers, who note for the first time that I have not been yelling at the scabs too. In fact, I am chronically faced with small decisions in regard to degree of participation. It is not difficult to avoid the kind of participation that might have appreciable influence on the outcome of a campaign, but sticky situations involving the appearances of affiliation keep coming up. In labor-management conflict in the South there are no neutrals. People are on one side or the other, and to the pro-union worker, already feeling somewhat paranoid from his perceived persecution, the nonsupportive stranger might well be a company spy. Organizers seem to understand and accept the research function; they are pleased to help the researcher get the facts. It is the occasional mill hand, or group of mill hands, that creates temporary embarrassment. I say temporary, because I have always been able to count on the intervention of an organizer to allay the suspicions of workers.

During the early days of one very bitter strike I looked around while eating a hamburger in a small restaurant near the picket line to find myself hemmed in by a semicircle of staring, angry eyes. Recognizing in the encircling group the faces of several inflexible members of the M Squad, an auxiliary of enforcers for the striker cause, I headed, sensibly, for union headquarters, two blocks away. There I exchanged ol'-buddy greetings with the organizer in charge. He explained my presence to the half-dozen M squaders who had silently escorted me to the hall, and later, with inappropriate cheerfulness, he informed me of the plot to assault me, checked and finally abandoned when I made a beeline for the union stronghold. I have endured anxious moments at mass meetings and at committee meetings when jittery workers have announced "There's a spy in our midst! The bosses know everything that goes on in these meetings!" In most instances, however, no one questions my presence, and the organizer will assure me privately after the meeting that I am not the suspect and that "any time over five people get together, one of them is a spy."

During the past year I have had to put up with a new sort of uneasiness. I have been observing the organizing of a local union composed largely of Negro women, and since Negro women in the South characteristically do not own automobiles, I am asked by organizers to help with the transportation problem after evening meetings. I am, of course, glad to build up acceptance of my research role with such minor services. However, occasionally my last passenger is an attractive young woman who lives across town from the next-to-last drop, or several miles out in the country. I can imagine what the situation might seem like to passing motorists, or to pedestrians if I acquired motor trouble or a flat tire. At such times I am torn between my desire to get the young lady to her home as quickly as possible and my fear of attracting the attention of the police if I go over the speed limit.

A more serious sort of anxiety swept over me one night last year during my observation of interaction between scabs and strikers at a midnight shift change. The crowd of strikers was small at that hour. The second-shift strikebreakers had driven on past them, through the usual verbal onslaught, but with the ample protection of four armed state patrolmen. One of the strikers, assigned the job of counting the cars, announced to the others that there were a dozen or so automobiles unaccounted for in the night exodus; they must be still in there, waiting for the strikers to leave. The strikers decided to pretend to depart, thus drawing off the state patrolmen, who would be only too glad to conclude a trying day. By circling back after the police had left, the strikers could handle the remaining scabs in more relaxed fashion. The police left, as predicted, and we didn't have long to wait before the first of a line of cars appeared. When the rocks started to fly, I found myself in an awkward situation. What if the police weren't as dumb as the strikers thought they were, saw through the ruse, and returned to pack us off to jail? What was I doing, at my age and with all those diplomas, shoulder to shoulder with a bunch of men throwing rocks at a bunch of other men in the middle of the night? I didn't have time to go to jail. I had to get back to Durham no later than the next day, back to my classes, to my eager students. Should I make a brisk dash for the cover of yon cornfield before the police returned? Could I make it, before getting shot, if they should return immediately? Surely the first car in the caravan of dented bodies and fenders would have reached a telephone by now. But if I streaked for the cornfield, the strikers would see it, and such behavior would mark the end of my study of union-management relations in these parts, perhaps in the entire South. Maybe it would be better if I were to start throwing things myself, before the strikers noticed my inactivity and interpreted it as anti-union behavior; for there was no organizer on the scene to explain sociological research. I made my decision. Sweating freely — it was a warm night — I ran back and forth with the strikers, stooping and swaying and swinging my arms in a balletic imitation of a man throwing rocks. Finally the last car screamed around the bend in the road. With my companions I made a rapid but dignified dash for my own automobile. The cops did not show up.

On the positive side again, the participant-as-observer shares with the complete participant the strong advantage of being able to penetrate the veil of public relations that is such an impediment to the one-shot interviewer, with distortion of response especially characteristic of situations where forthright answers to the questions of the inquisitorial stranger might lead to unpleasant consequences. A bit of dramaturgy may be encountered from time to time, most of all in the early stages of an investigation; but in the ordinary course of events acceptance comes, trust deepens, the guard drops, the researcher can move about freely to interview as he wishes, and he can get honest answers to his direct probing.

The opportunity to build a relationship of trust with the organizer, and with others deeply involved with the organizing process, may lead not only to effective interviewing, but also to effective observation. The organizer, as a skilled practitioner possessed of acquaintance knowledge, knows more than he can tell.[12] By moving over the campaign scene and living through the campaign process with the organizer, trying to see what he sees as he in turn tries to explain it all, the researcher can, to a degree, acquire a vicarious grasp of his mentor's know-how. He can fill in the contextual details in their spatial configurations to get, in Susanne Langer's words, "the picture."[13] And, by maintaining his interviewing and observing relationship over a period of time, he can see a moving picture with its axial strand, the story, which gives the changing contextual configurations of episodes their meaning.[14] The observer of organizing campaigns may thus gain an apprehension of the perceptions, or "act-meanings,"[15] of those who participate in the intersubjective world of labor-management conflict. From his *Verstehen* of the common-sense meanings of everyday life, the fieldworker may be able to offer "comprehensive gross descriptions"[16] of human behavior that ring true when read back to participants of his special world of investigation.

The researcher will also know more than he can tell when he essays verbal description of the campaign; but since he is a scientist, his problem goes beyond that of accurate representation. The researcher's task is to transcend his acquired acquaintance knowledge to establish the inferential linkages, or, as Kaplan would term it, the "action-meanings,"[17] that constitute scientific explanation. While accepting Dewey's counsel that "acquaintance knowledge is frequently *not* knowl-

12. See Michael Polanyi, *The Tacit Dimension* (New York: Anchor Books, Doubleday, 1967), pp. 4–11.

13. Susanne K. Langer, *Philosophy in a New Key* (New York: Mentor Books, 1948), pp. 87–88.

14. See John Dewey, *Experience and Nature* (Chicago: Open Court Publishing Co., 1925), p. 307.

15. Kaplan, *Conduct of Inquiry*, p. 360.

16. Arthur F. Bentley, *Behavior, Knowledge, Fact* (Bloomington, Ind.: Principia Press, 1935), p. 322.

17. Kaplan, *Conduct of Inquiry*, p. 331.

edge in the sense of being warrantably assertable,"[18] and Kaplan's warning that "familiarity helps us see an explanation, but it does not necessarily help us have one,"[19] I press the claim that the *Verstehen* of acquaintance knowledge, acquired by participant observation, provides the soundest base, as well as the most fruitful source, for the engendering of action-meanings in human affairs. I would stress, with Alfred Schutz, the function of common-sense constructions of the reality of everyday life as "thought objects" in the determination of human behavior,[20] averring that such *a priori* conceptions in perception — or "symbolic pregnancies"[21] — provide salient constituents in the kind of problematic situations[22] that sociology must face. In the closing pages of his *magnum opus, The Philosophy of Symbolic Forms,* Ernst Cassirer notes that "in its beginnings the theoretical concept clings to perception as though to exhaust it, as though to gain possession of all the reality it contains."[23] And in a summary statement he says:

> The history of exact science teaches us over and over that only such concepts as have grown out of the very source of thought have ultimately proved equal to experience. We may say, with an image borrowed from the language of chemistry, that sensory intuition acts as a catalyst for the development of scientific theory. It is indispensable for the process of exact concept formation.[24]

18. John Dewey, *Logic: The Theory of Inquiry* (New York: Holt, 1938), p. 152.
19. Kaplan, *Conduct of Inquiry*, p. 331.
20. Alfred Schutz, "Common Sense and Scientific Interpretation of Human Action," *Philosophy and Phenomenological Research*, 14, no. 1 (September 1953): 3.
21. Ernst Cassirer, *The Philosophy of Symbolic Forms*, (New Haven: Yale University Press, 1957), vol. 3, *The Phenomenology of Knowledge*, p. 202.
22. Dewey, *Logic*, pp. 107–108.
23. Cassirer, *Philosophy of Symbolic Forms*, vol. 3, p. 451.
24. *Ibid.*, p. 416.

Problems in the Ethnography of the

Urban Underclasses

We started the study of an all-Negro public housing project in St. Louis, Missouri, in 1963 with warnings that middle-class whites or blacks would not be able to obtain any but the most superficial information; that we would be lied to, conned, threatened, and turned on; that we would be physically and emotionally in danger; that no matter how well we thought we knew people, we would never be able to get them to tell us their truth. As outsiders we would not be trusted. We would be defined and treated as representatives of the welfare establishment, something that was to be feared and retreated from, exploited or fought. Finally, we were reminded that no matter what we did, we would never personally know the constraints of American poverty or racism.

Now at the end of the study of the public housing project and a second study of a working- and lower-class white neighborhood, we believe that most of these initial allegations are essentially incorrect.

This paper is based in part on research aided by grants from the National Institute of Mental Health (grant MH-09189) and from the Office of Economic Opportunity (contract OEO-1241) to the Social Science Institute of Washington University. We have depended heavily on the field experience of Boone Hammond, Joyce Ladner, Ethel Sawyer, David Schultz, Robert Simpson, and Martha J. Yancey, who worked with us in the Pruitt-Igoe research, and Alvin W. Wolfe, Barbara W. Lex, Shulamith Decktor, Mary Farvar, De Wight Middleton, Constance Pennacchio, Sidney Selvidge, Jr., and Ronald Stutzman in the study of the Soulard area.

245

This is not to say that we did not encounter barriers. We were lied to, threatened, and all the rest of it. Yet over time, with sensitivity and patience by residents and fieldworkers, we were able to collect what appear to be meaningful observations. During a period of racial upheaval, violence in the streets, and urban crises, middle-class academicians entered the core areas of Los Angeles, Chicago, Washington, New York, and many other cities, established meaningful friendships, obtained information, and returned to report their findings. They were no doubt changed by their experiences, but essentially unhurt. The striking similarities among the findings of the many studies suggest some validation of the results.[1]

We are not sure it is possible to codify ethnographic methods. The strategies employed, the subgroups to be included, the questions asked, the roles observers take, and the kinds of information collected depend not so much on abstract methodological principles as on the unique character of the community and of the problem being investigated. One might even argue that in order to know how to study a community, one must know it so well that the proposed study need not be done.

The Negro community we nevertheless ventured to study is located in two adjacent public housing projects near the St. Louis downtown area known as Pruitt-Igoe. It has a local reputation as a pathological den of thieves, prostitutes, and drug addicts. The crime rate is said to be fifteen times that of the city in general. It represents an extreme case of the labeling process applied to an institutionalized community.

The white community we studied, known as the Soulard area, is a private housing neighborhood with the lowest median family income of any census tract in St. Louis containing 90 percent whites. Since its median family income was still considerably higher than that of the Negro public housing community, and its reputation was considerably less gamey, our initial aim of collecting comparative data on lower-class white and black communities proved impracticable.

Intensive field observations were carried on in the all-Negro public housing project for three and one-half years, as contrasted with a single year in the white area. Two of the Pruitt-Igoe researchers also studied the Soulard area. Both projects involved teams of graduate research assistants and faculty members. In Pruitt-Igoe both white and Negro students were used; only white students were used in the Soulard. Anthropologists and sociologists were included in both research teams.

---

1. See, for example, Elliot Liebow, *Tally's Corner* (Boston: Little, Brown, 1967); Kenneth Clark, *Dark Ghetto* (New York: Harper & Row, 1965); John Horton, "Time and Cool People." *Trans-action* 4, no. 5 (April 1962): 5-12; and Gerald Suttles, *The Social Order of the Slum* (Chicago: University of Chicago Press, 1968).

Unsolvable Problems

There are at least three general problems that remain in a kind of limbo between being recognized and being attacked without being solved. They have pervaded out fieldwork, and much of this essay is at least implicitly aimed at specifying our attempts to solve them.

First we believe that it is impossible for middle-class academicians, white or black, to know, in the personal sense of being fully enmeshed in them, the constraints imposed on the lower class. Even though we lived there, felt the heat, the cold, the anxieties, the highs, the lows, the lack of control, and so on, *we knew we could leave.* Going native, constraining ourselves to be without money, remaining for long periods of time, walking the streets with unemployed men, begging dimes on the corner for wine, or waiting in clinic lines with worried mothers and wounded children did not close off the single safety valve of being able to leave when the going got too rough.

This is perhaps the single major limitation of lower-class ethnographies. It can be argued that the underlying factor determining the life style of the lower class is the lack of control over life chances. The social scientist who is supposed to understand and subjectively interpret the adaptations, life style, values, etc. of the poor is in the position of not being able personally to assume the major underlying premise of lower-class life.

The second unsolved problem is not unique to ethnography; rather it revolves around the nature of the scientific process and the use of previous knowledge, understandings, theories, or stereotypes when collecting new information.

Our experience suggests that observers who go to the field without formulating intellectual or theoretical problems to solve are likely to waste a great deal of time while collecting rather careful ethnographic data. We also found that those who enter the field with clearly defined theoretical statements and problems are not so likely to discover new relationships, characteristics, or variables. The ethnographer's previous understanding of the lower class, whether it comes from Claude Brown, Malcolm X, Kenneth Clark, Daniel Moynihan, or Robert Merton, may be inappropriate for the community being studied. Knowledge of existing literature is crucial to ethnography; it clearly sensitizes the observer; yet commitments to narrow theoretical or ideological positions has a blinding effect on observations being made and reported.

We have found the general strategy suggested by Alvin Gouldner in one of the early research staff meetings particularly helpful. Gouldner suggested that we should pay particular attention to the complaints made by our informants. Properly viewed, complaints are symptoms of systemic tension, points in the social system where systemic linkages are under strain. Complaints, when viewed in this manner, provide indications of the social system indigenously perceived. This proved to be a useful heuristic device in the early stages of the study. While it did assume that there was a system, or views of a system held by our informants, it made no assumption about the specific character of the system being studied.

The third unsolved problem revolves around the honesty of fieldworkers. There are at least two dimensions: emotional and intellectual honesty with oneself, and presentational honesty with one's informants.

The methods of participant observation require researchers to break the tenets of a methodology based on the dualistic model of knowing provided by the natural sciences, i.e., one that separates the knower from the known. Ethnography is likely to require that the fieldworker enter unfamiliar and anxiety-generating situations. Such anxieties and emotions influence one's observations; they affect one's willingness to enter similar situations and obtain access to data; they affect the perceptions of the observer; and finally they affect, often implicitly, the interpretation and reporting of data.

Although we have only impressionistic evidence of the relative effectiveness of some twenty graduate-student fieldworkers, one underlying characteristic of good fieldworkers appears to be the ability to surrender oneself.[2] Such a surrender requires the management of anxiety and ability and willingness to expose the self to problematic situations.

Finally there is the problem of honesty with informants. Ethnography requires that observers establish social roles acceptable to informants. Perhaps the greatest temptation facing fieldworkers is to permit themselves to be pushed by informants into roles other than social science observers. While it is possible to collect data while playing such roles, there are serious limitations in the nature of the data that are available. Such a strategy raises ethical issues that are difficult to resolve. There are practical problems raised by presentations of essentially false selves. Out experience suggests that it is difficult for anyone to act consistently out of character. The inconsistencies and contradictions that occur raise suspicions and reduce the level of trust.

These problems of honesty are crucial. They are not solved by simple edicts, nor are they entirely solved by the specific methodological strategies we discuss below. Their solution seems to rest in a commitment to knowledge.

2. See Kurt H. Wolff, "Surrender and Community Study: The Study of Loma," in *Reflections on Community Studies,* ed. Arthur J. Vidich, Joseph Bensman, and Maurice R. Stein (New York: Wiley, 1964), chap. 7.

Obtaining Access to the Community

Unlike formal organizations, lower-class neighborhoods do not have a top echelon from which one must obtain permission to enter the community in order to do research. The powerlessness that has typically characterized such neighborhoods makes it possible to evade the initial barrier of a formal organization. At the same time, obtaining access to such areas and their various subgroupings may be more difficult. One does not have the advantage of an organizational chart identifying subgroups that might be included in the study. In a ghetto one must discover subgroups and strata as the investigation proceeds. Neither does the researcher have the sometimes dubious advantage of being introduced to an informant with the statement: "The management [or union] has expressed interest in this research."

Establishing and developing relationships in a slum is not so difficult as it is anxiety-producing. The first rewarding contacts come quickly, yet as Barbara Lex and Alvin Wolfe point out, additional data and contacts are strongly influenced by the first.[3] Researchers become identified with a particular segment of the community by its members, and there is a tendency to stick to first informants and their friends. It is relatively easy to meet the friends of one's informant. This may happen either purposefully — i.e., the observer asks his informent to introduce him to his friends — or casually, when the researcher is accompanying the informant during his everyday activities. The number of informants increases from a single family or individual to include the members of a relatively homogeneous network of friends and/or relatives.

William F. Whyte's *Street Corner Society* and Elliot Liebow's *Tally's Corner,* unquestionably representing some of the best ethnographic descriptions of underclass settings, are ethnographies of such networks. The degree to which they are representative of the larger community in which they are situated, or a larger sample of such informal groups, is left to speculation and rather casual comparison.

This problem of single researchers becoming hooked into single networks was less evident in the public housing project, where local networks were apparently not so strong as they are in many lower- and working-class neighborhoods. Networks were strong in the white neighborhood. One of the students made his initial contact with his landlord, who also owned a neighborhood bar. Other contacts followed, including the owner of a small grocery store, an apartment-house owner, a foreman in an automobile factory, and two other skilled craftsmen.

3. Barbara Lex and Alvin W. Wolfe, "The Effects of First Contacts by Researchers in Urban Field Work" (paper presented at the annual meeting of the Central States Antropological Society, Chicago, April 28, 1967).

The image of the community based on his field notes is that of a stable working-class population that has lived in the same neighborhood for at least ten years, has a strong sense of community, and fears, above all else, the recent influx of rural migrants into the neighborhood.

A second student made her initial contact with one of these migrant families. While she found it more difficult to increase her sample by following their network of friends, a description of the neighborhood and the city based on her data is strikingly similar to Louis Wirth's in "Urbanism as a Way of Life."[4] Her data imply that the neighborhood is made up of relatively isolated families, exploiting and being exploited by the city.

Still a third student concentrated her ethnographic efforts on the study of the remains of a Syrian community. Her descriptions of the relatively shady political involvement, ethnic identification, patterns of social mobility, and sense of community are similar to Whyte's description of the West End of Boston.[5]

These three quite distinct networks representing quite different life styles were observed in a small, clearly bounded urban neighborhood. One of the striking substantive findings of our research is that, contrary to the expectations we had formed from previous research and descriptions of lower-class worlds, these lower-class communities may contain a great variety of life styles, cultural traditions, and ways of coping with strikingly similar existential conditions. The single researcher using a limited series of contacts in such a community is likely to be limited in the nature of the conclusions that he draws.

Caretaker Contacts

Community service agencies or caretakers may be used to obtain access to lower-class communities. Rather than arbitrarily knocking on doors, meeting possible informants in bars, in stores, or on corners, it is possible to do as Whyte did[6] and have local service or welfare organizations introduce the researcher to the community. Researchers are likely to find it easier to explain their research to such community caretakers, who in turn can introduce them to members of the community and vouch for their credibility in the process.

We have found that the use of such service personnel, while providing easy access to the community, has a limiting effect on the range of available informants. An illustration of this problem can be seen in the

4. Louis Wirth, "Urbanism as a Way of Life," *American Journal of Sociology,* 44, no. 1 (July 1938): 8–20.

5. William F. Whyte, *Street Corner Society* (Chicago: University of Chicago Press, 1955).

6. *Ibid.*

case of the families and individuals used as respondents in the study of racial integration of a settlement house in the white neighborhood. The settlement house, located on one edge of the neighborhood adjacent to an all-Negro residential area, became racially integrated a few years before our research began. One student interviewing families introduced to her by the settlement house staff collected data indicating that there was little or no interracial hostility among the families. This initially surprising conclusion can be understood by the fact that the families interviewed were those who continued to use the settlement house after it was integrated. Additional interviews conducted among families selected independently of the settlement house showed great concern about integration and hostility toward Negroes.

Researchers become identified with the caretaker who introduces them to the community. Families met through the department of welfare, housing authority, or police were suspicious of our claims to be autonomous researchers. Not surprisingly, such informants gave us information, both primary data on themselves and descriptions of the community, that were consistent with the rules or values expressed by the caretakers.

Sex Role and Segregation

Not only do participant observers become identified with caretakers or networks of friends, but within single families it is sometimes difficult to maintain close relationships with adults of both sexes. The study of women, particularly in female-based houses, may be limited to interviewing and observation in homes and apartments. Women make relatively few excursions into the street. The study of lower-class men requires leaving the warmth and protection of "home." The study of both sexes presents special problems to the participant observer.

Elizabeth Bott suggests that some lower- and working-class families are likely to be characterized by conjugal separateness.[7] Rainwater has suggested that relationships between men and women are likely to be less integrated in lower-class families than in other classes.[8] Irving Zola implies in his study of gambling that lower-class men are likely to segregate their leisure activities from their families.[9] We have found evidence that lower-class men are also likely to separate their role as worker (as opposed to provider) from that of family head.[10]

7. Elizabeth Bott, *Family and Social Network* (London: Travistock Publications, 1957).
8. Lee Rainwater, *Family Design* (Chicago: Aldine, 1965).
9. Irving Zola, "Gambling in a Lower Class Setting," *Social Problems,* 10 (1964): 353–61.
10. Alvin W. Wolfe, Barbara Lex, and William L. Yancey, "The Soulard Area: Adaptations by Urban White Families to Poverty" (St. Louis: Social Science Institute, Washington University, 1968), chap. 7.

These substantive findings, suggesting that the male's role set is likely to consist of highly segregated roles, have methodological implications. Members of a man's role set may include the family of wife and children, his girl friend or mistress, his peers on the corner, and his work group of boss and co-workers. The male's presentation of self, as husband, lover, friend, or worker, may be quite different in each of these situations. While each of these roles may have its own rewards, the system is maintained by its atomization, i.e., the segregation of roles. The problems of the participant observer are not solved by telling him to go with the male as he plays each of these roles and at the same time to maintain relationships with the various members of the role set. We doubt if this can be done by a single researcher. In one case when an observer suggested to a man whom he had met in his home that they go to the corner together, the respondent replied, "I don't think that would work. Some of the guys may not like you snooping around."

A rather extreme example of the development of separate roles is seen in the case of one man in his early twenties who had at least two clearly distinct roles. On one side of the city he was known by the name given to him by his family; on the other he had given himself a different name. When he visited his mother he wore coveralls or work clothes and presented a conservative, almost Uncle Tom image. On the other side of town he wore the clothes of a pimp or cat, and was the manager of a stable of prostitutes working out of a bar he tended. His mother got occasional glimpses of his second self when he came home with a new scar or bandage, but she apparently believed that he was making a living as a waiter. We obtained data on this particular man by having a male researcher go with him to a bar while a female researcher stayed at home with his mother collecting data on his more conventional world.

These are role problems that are encountered principally when the fieldworker establishes close relationships with his informants. If the above strategy is followed, it appears necessary to have at least one researcher for each of the major subgroups within the community. Obviously there are other research strategies, and it is not necessary to get in-depth data on every subgroup within the community. Gerald Suttles' recent study in Chicago clearly indicates that a researcher following a more detached role (approximating that of the phenomenologists) is able to collect interesting and meaningful data on several groups without becoming involved or identified with any one of them.[11] By emphasizing the pure observer role it is possible to observe in a greater variety of situations and groups.

11. Suttles, *Social Order of the Slum.*

Caretakers and Clients

Current research continues to document the complicated though profound relationship between the life styles, adaptive strategies, and structure of lower-class cultures and the policies of welfare and community services. Interviews with functionaries of such agencies provide a series of lay hypotheses concerning the nature of the community. These data not only are useful as a source of hypotheses and descriptions of the community that might be examined further; they also may be viewed as important aspects of welfare ideologies, i.e., rationales for the specific policies and practices of control services. Interviews with caretakers provide information about the rules and regulations that residents of the community must know and overtly conform to in order to obtain the services provided. For example, from the manager's discussion of the income levels that supposedly force upwardly mobile families out of public housing, one is led to hypotheses about the demographic character of a public housing community. Longitudinal examination of family characteristics revealed, however, that very few families have been forced out of Pruitt-Igoe because of incomes higher than the maximum limits.

Welfare and community services provide social researchers with specific data on families using those services. In the case of public housing, one can obtain censuses of the population. Departments of welfare, schools, police, hospitals, and clinics, all provide at least some data relevant to most underclass areas.

The study of community caretakers might also involve observation of the control-service process within the organizations *per se*. With the cooperation of agencies researchers may take some official-looking role that provides a relatively unobtrusive observation post. Such research strategies have provided important data and theory, yet our experience suggests that middle-class academics have difficulty accurately interpreting the subjective understanding of the agency from the perspective of the lower-class client. Graduate-student observers repeatedly concluded their observations in such service agencies with comments such as "Bureaucratic in character and not appropriately programmed for the life styles of the lower class"; yet when we interviewed the indigenous clients of these same agencies we were somewhat surprised at the reported positive reactions to the bureaucratic treatment and relatively lengthy waiting period required to obtain the agencies' services. As we soon came to understand, people growing up in the lower class are socialized into this kind of treatment; they not only expect to receive it, but are somewhat dismayed by occasional informal and personal treatment. The discrepancy between the reactions of middle-class and lower-class observers not only suggests major differences in the constraints or life chances under which the two groups live, but also illustrated the more general problem of using middle-class observers in lower-class settings, and suggests the use of lower-class informants, particularly when research is focused on subjective interpretations of actions or events.

Social Roles for Observation

Participant observation is different from the heuristic models prescribed by the physical sciences and their interpretive philosophers. Rather than being separated from the observed, the participant observer engages in a face-to-face relationship, frequently becoming a part of the groups being studied, affecting and being affected by them.

A central element in the method of participant observation is the nature of the role the observer establishes. It becomes an important determinant of the nature and quality of the data accessible to the observer. He must accommodate himself to the role, work with the ever present problems of maintaining a role that provides him the freedom to observe meaningful behavior, and when he has completed the study be able to leave the situation with, in Buford Junker's words, "himself unhurt, free to report, and turn information to data for a contribution to his social science."[12]

We have found that researchers who are able to integrate the role of observer with roles that are available within the organization or group being studied are best able to reduce the obtrusion that occurs. This is perhaps easiest in institutionalized public settings—the housing authority, the department of public welfare, the hospital—where it is possible to sit at a desk as a functionary of the organization. The presence of such an observer apparently affects the behavior of organizational members, particularly during the initial periods of observation, although it has but an indirect effect on the clients.

In more informal situations, either in such public settings as a playground or street corner or in more private settings such as an alley or home, the availability of the more unobtrusive observation roles is sometimes quite problematic. The initial presentation of the researcher to the community is likely to have a rather limited effect on the nature or character of the role that is finally established. Although the researcher may introduce himself as a "social scientist doing objective research," it is difficult to maintain such a role. The lower and working classes are apparently unfamiliar with the role of social science researcher. Partic-

12. Buford H. Junker, *Field Work: An Introduction to the Social Sciences* (Chicago: University of Chicago Press, 1960), p. 11.

ularly during the early period of our investigations, before we knew a great deal about the groups being studied, we had relatively little control over the roles into which we were cast. Rather than accepting our definition of ourselves, informants implicitly placed us in roles with which they were familiar and into which we apparently fitted.

We found that among some of the white lower- and working-class families the mention of the university or of university students resulted in our being associated with self-styled students who had earlier attempted to sell magazine subscriptions in the neighborhood. In the public housing project the only whites who visit apartments and ask long series of questions are welfare functionaries. Even though we were quite explicit in explaining that we were from the university and had no association with the housing authority or department of welfare, it was frequently several months before we were treated as something other than social workers.

Respondents perform for researchers. The kind of performance depends largely on their understanding of the researcher's role. Thus we found that unemployed men, thinking that researchers were social workers, performed in a manner that convinced the researchers that they were seriously looking for jobs and that their unemployment was out of their control. Frequently men commented, when discussing unemployed friends, "He won't go downtown, he might find a job there." Similar performances took place within households in the early part of the research. Mothers rarely punished their children in any way but verbally. It was only later that more unconventional patterns of behavior developed – after the researcher had become accepted in the group being studied.

Such obtrusions and corresponding performances are not unimportant data to the social scientist. One of the major conceptual difficulties now confronting research on poverty is the degree to which the poor are aware of and committed to conventional norms. Although these performances demonstrate little about commitment, their success indicates an awareness of conventional structures.

Not less obtrusive, although less recognizable, are the more informal roles into which researchers are cast. For example, two of the students working on the housing project research had been ministers before coming to graduate school. When they mentioned this to their respondents they were quickly cast in the role of minister or charity worker. We inadvertently reinforced such paternalistic role assignments by occasionally bringing food or secondhand clothes or loaning money to our informants.

The role-related resources the researcher brings to the research setting may have a major effect on the data collected. Additional money, while providing alcohol or food, unquestionably facilitates the respondent's changes in behavior. Automobiles had a major effect on the data we were collecting among young men. The researcher's automobile provided informants with means to leave their home environment. But data collected under such situations are not likely to be representative of a group without an automobile.

We were also defined as thrill-seekers—people who had come to see the high life. Very often we were given this role when one informant introduced us to his friends. Not unrelated to the role of thrill-seeker is that of a pushover, i.e., someone who has come to the slums for fun and has money that he is willing to spend or can be readily conned out of.

It does not result in a complete loss of effort when the researchers accept the social roles provided by the informants. One researcher found that each time he passed through a group of children, they would beg a nickel from him. He had to decide whether he should simply ignore the kids and run the risk of being alienated from them and their families, or give each of them a nickel everytime he walked past. Not thinking highly of either of these alternatives, he found a third response: he used the situation as an opportunity to explore the behavior of begging or conning by relatively young children. He made the kids talk him into giving them money, and was therefore able to use the role of pushover to his advantage. Similarly, the researcher who is defined as a social worker by informants has access to information concerning the relationship between social workers and lower-class persons.

But there are several negative consequences of completely accepting indigenous roles. One of these is the observer's loss of control over areas that may be studied. He is so constrained by the social role given to him that the areas of information that he may study are limited.

Advantages of Living in the Community

Most anthropologists would not think of doing research on a community or subculture without living in the community being studied. Still it is possible to collect meaningful data without living in the ghetto. Herbert Gans lived in the West End of Boston, but Liebow did not live on Tally's corner. In Pruitt-Igoe participant observers spent between ten and thirty hours a week in and around the community, although they did not live there. We lived in the white area being studied, while at the same time we had obligations as students and professors. In neither case was full time spent on the research. Our experience suggests that if researchers are not spending full time on their research, they should *not* live in the community being studied. When we went to Pruitt-Igoe, we went there to work — to make observations and to interview. When we went to Soulard we were going after a day's work at school, and therefore we found ourselves less actively and perhaps less effectively engaged in the collection of data.

There are distinct advantages to living in the community being studied. It provides ready means of establishing relationships with informants. On meeting their neighbors, observers may introduce themselves as researchers and simultaneously identify themselves as members of the community. Living in the community provides a rather clear means of integrating one's role as observer and participant in the community.

Another advantage of living in the community being studied is the immersion in the common everyday constraints of living in the neighborhood. While these may determine much of the nature of the community, they may be so basic that they are commonly assumed and therefore not reported by informants. One finds them out as he begins to suffer their consequences. For example, we were not aware of the amount of dirt and heat experienced by residents of Pruitt-Igoe until we rented an apartment for staff meetings and interview settings and found it was necessary to keep the windows closed in order to keep the apartment clean. While this kept out the dust, it made the heat unbearable, and we finally bought an air conditioner. (It was the second air conditioner in the entire project.) Living in the dilapidated houses of the white slum provided further important information on the cold, the heating bills, and the powerlessness of a tenant whose landlord refuses to repair a sink or refrigerator.

Going Native

The participant observer often purposely becomes totally involved in the situation being studied. In the lower class the use of casual dress and casual speech with a bit of southern accent frequently aids this process. But at the same time there are ethical and legal issues that must be faced, particularly when one studies a marginal population. There are at least two related problems that the participant observer must confront when studying the lower class or any marginal group. One of these involves a political decision while the second is a personal decision. Both can be viewed as ethical issues.

The political issue involves the legal status of the social science researcher. In the case of Pruitt-Igoe, all of the names of the participant observers were given to the local police at the beginning of the research. We anticipated that we would become involved in marginal activities and were thus concerned with the consequences of being arrested.

Although we were frequently present with groups participating in deviant behavior, we were not arrested, and therefore were not forced to face the issue directly. Although the question of what would be done if we were arrested was left up to the individual researchers, the informal norm in our research group was that we would suffer the consequences of the arrest, just as our informants would. This decision was based on heuristic as well as ethical considerations. To be arrested would provide important information concerning the relationship between the police and the lower class. More than this, one who copped out would no doubt have little chance of returning to the deviant group. Luckily we were never forced to test these assumptions.

The second issue revolves around interpersonal relationships with one's colleagues. One of the most striking things that we discovered was that the labeling process applies not only to deviant behavior, but also to those who study it. Apparently it is assumed that people who study deviance must have more than a professional scientific interest in it. As we were told, "Anyone who's studying homosexuals must be a homosexual himself—why else would he be studying it?" This is a personal risk that the researcher must take if he decides to study deviance.

We see the important heuristic advantages of direct involvement of researchers in the behavior being studied, yet we doubt that a participant observer who attempts to develop a role that he is uncomfortable in playing will be successful either in playing the role or in collecting relevant information. In this as in other problems facing the participant observer, the decision must be individually made on the basis of one's own reactions to the situation.

Whether by his design or otherwise, the observer is likely to be invited by his informants to participate in marginal activities. It is possible to refuse such an invitation and maintain one's research relationship with informants. Ethel Sawyer, at the beginning of her study of a lesbian community, was pressured by members of that community to become engaged in homosexual relationships. She explained to her informants that she would not be able to do research on the community if she became personally involved with any of its members, because to become identified with one person in such a competitive community would be sure to disrupt relationships with its other members. She also indicated in a neutral way that her inclinations lay in the other direction. While her explanation did little to stop the lesbians' advances, it did serve to elicit acceptance of her refusal.

Another researcher, a young man this time, after studying a family for over a year, was approached by an attractive woman in the family with an invitation to sleep with her. The researcher faced a real dilemma: if he refused, he would either be considered a "spoiled square," one who thought himself above the standards of the community, or be thought to dislike this particular woman. He explained, in effect, that he and she were now good friends, and that going to bed together would be sure to change the relationship — it might be that they could not be friends after that. Besides, her husband might find out, and clearly he would not like it. He also explained that he would become engaged in a more personal relationship than would be helpful for the research. Settling the matter along these lines was neither an easy nor a short process; indeed, it took several days. But with tact and persistence the researcher was able to reinforce his role as a researcher interested in the entire family.

These interpersonal problems not unrelated to the legal issues, has been identified by S. M. Miller as overrapport[13] — establishing such a close social relationship with informants that the nature of the information is both limited and biased. Participant observers often spend several months with families, establishing and building relationships with them as informants. Researcher and informant may move from a work relationship, in which the researcher is primarily interested in gathering data, to personal friendship. While developing close friendly relationships with informants does provide access to information of a personal sort that would not otherwise be available, at the same time it produces problems when one attempts to move back from friendship to a research relationship. As Miller points out, "friendship connotes an all-accepting attitude; to probe beneath the surface of long-believed values would break the friend-to-friend relationship." Thus when friendship becomes too strong, researchers find it difficult to ask questions at all; and in the most extreme cases, some of our observers refused to transcribe information obtained. As one student said, "I wasn't working then and what she told me was personal. It was just a conversation between two people."

We are not arguing here that researchers should become machines who simply enter situations, make observations, and interview informants without becoming involved in the social aspects of the situation. The relationship between the participant observer and the informant combines elements of both work and friendship. A fieldworker must achieve the spontaneity of friendship with an informant and still maintain enough control of the situation to obtain the desired information and relate that information to other data — a difficult task. Miller suggests that the field worker "should try to make clear that he is interested in the number of people in the particular situation, and that his research activities are his prime reasons for being present." This is a key to solving the problem.

13. S. M. Miller, "The Participant Observer and 'Over-Rapport,' " *American Sociological Review*, 17 (February 1952): 97–99.

Kinds of Questions and Interviewing Techniques

There is a considerable number of interviewing techniques available to participant observers. The most successful in terms of the amount of apparently valid information obtained is a technique that we call a guided conversation. Rather than being provided with a series of specific questions to be answered in the course of an interview, researchers were instructed to obtain unstructured information on a series of topics. These ranged from husband's occupational history through relationships with neighbors, problems with the housing authority and landlord, concerns with housing and neighborhood, concerns with children, and problems with welfare, school, and police to attitudes about the city.

Interviewers or participant observers began interviews with general open-ended questions and then, depending on the nature of the response given by the informant, followed up with additional questions related to specific areas. When respondents said something interesting, ambiguous, or surprising, the interviewer asked additional questions to explore the area in depth. There are two consequences of this type of interview. First, the interviewer's freedom to direct the conversation into any channel that opens up makes it possible to obtain information about subjects that were not seen as significant by the researcher before the interview, and in the early parts of an exploratory study such unstructured interviewing seems to be particularly fertile. But second, it sometimes encourages an informant to give more information than he in fact has.

We have found that informants become sensitized to the quality and type of information that interviewers desire. They become trained to answer questions quite specifically and in detail. While interviewing is a kind of conversation, and frequently is most fertile when conducted in a conversational style, it breaks some important informal rules governing conversational behavior. In normal conversations there are rather clear limits as to the amount of detailed information that can appropriately be discussed, revealed, or dwelled upon. One of the tasks of the participant observer is to communicate to this respondent that these rules of conversation do not apply—that is, that it is appropriate to go into detail. Rather than being concerned about boring the interviewer with details, the respondent must be made to feel it is this detail that most interests the interviewer. Over time and with persistence informants began answering questions with increasing specificity. Thus when, after six months of fieldwork with one family, the researcher asked the mother about the identity of a young girl who had visited the home, the mother replied, "She's the youngest daughter of my sister by her first marriage." Earlier in the relationship she had referred to the girl as "my niece."

However, there is danger in unstructured interviewing. Through the use of relatively subtle cues, the interviewer may oversensitize the informant to the extent that he, the informant, is encouraged to produce information on a subject whether it is true or not. One researcher began asking specific questions about the use of marihuana and heroin in the neighborhood. Beofre the interview was completed the informant had developed a rather complicated story of his involvement in the heroin traffic into St. Louis. The researcher returned home that evening excited about his "great data" and worried about whether or not he should destroy the tape holding such sensitive and incriminating information. Before the study was completed it became clear that the entire story had been made up, and close examination of the transcribed interview revealed the powerful shaping process that had taken place in the interview. It is possible that less obvious biasing takes place in many open-ended interviews – a bias resulting from the interaction cues provided by interviewers.

Respondents as Lay Social Scientists

When the relationship between informant and researcher had become so close that it was difficult to ask personal questions, it was possible to restructure the situation by suggesting to the informant, "Now that you know me and what I'm doing down here, why don't you take the part of a sociologist and tell me about the community?" Such a technique provides a context apart from the personal realm of the informant. By structuring the interview in this way we were able to increase its spontaneity, and afterward we were frequently able to ask more personal questions of the informant again. However, it is difficult for the researcher to make direct inferences from such secondary data. For example, several informants in such situations mentioned boys and girls having sexual intercourse in stairwell halls and laundry rooms, but never in the three and a half years that we walked through the buildings of Pruitt-Igoe did we observe anything of the kind in any of these semi-public places. (This does not, of course, mean that it never happened.) Similarly we collected stories of persons trapped in elevators, falling down elevator shafts, and being hit by objects thrown from the building. Again, in all the years of participant observation in the community, none of these things was observed by researchers, although they were occasionally reported in the newspaper and apparently did happen.

These experiences suggest that there is a distinction between events that happen only occasionally but gain a great deal of publicity and become particularly salient, and those that happen so frequently that they may not be seen as significant enough to report.[14] It is crucial that researchers be aware of *both* the frequency and the salience of events. While dramatic events may not be reported accurately, they are important aspects of the reality experienced.

Discrepancies between direct and indirect observational data may themselves suggest something about the group being studied. Events that happen daily but are not reported by informants are likely to be the world known in common and taken for granted. Those that happen frequently and are reported frequently are likely to center around the major tasks or activities of the group. Those that happen relatively infrequently but are widely reported suggest something of the boundaries of the group. In the two communities we studied in St. Luois there were apparently crucial boundaries over which community members had little control. We are suggesting that while the participant observer may have difficulty obtaining conclusive evidence concerning the frequency of events, this difficulty, or discrepancy between direct and indirect information, may itself provide important insights into the community being studied.

Informants may also be used as a source of hypotheses and indigenous social theory. That is, it is possible directly to involve informants in the development of research questions and to use them to check the validity of the data being gathered and the conclusions being drawn. Again caution should be used. Just as it is possible for an interviewer to communicate to a respondent the kinds of information he wishes, he can also communicate his own understanding of proper indigenous social theory. Such informants do not have training in the scientific methods and are quite likely to slant information so that it is consistent with their understanding of their academic friends' view of the world.

Folklore, Slang, and Lay Sociology

One of the principal sources of information on a slum community, particularly the Negro community, is found in special argot or slang, music, folklore, newpapers, and occasional self-studies.

In our studies of the housing project we developed a rather lengthy dictionary of slang used in interviews, on the local Negro radio station, and in local Negro newspapers. Fieldworkers were instructed to note the use of slang, its meaning, and the context in which it was used. Frequently the meaning of words was not clear out of context of the

14. See Gideon Sjoberg and Roger Nett, *A Methodology for Social Research* (New York: Harper & Row, 1968), p. 164.

interaction. If one assumes that Arabs' concern with camels and Eskimos' concern with snow is reflected in the many terms that these groups have developed to deal with and classify these phenomena, one can also use the special slang of the ghetto as an indication of some of the focal concerns of its inhabitants.

Folklore is more difficult to gather than slang. In the case of the Negro ghetto, much of the folklore is not readily apparent to the casual onlooker. Only after we had established considerable rapport with some of our better informants was it possible to tape-record rather lengthy epic poems — "The Monkey and the Lion" was one — or groups of teenagers "playing the dozens."

In most urban areas there are newspapers published by and for Negroes. While these may not describe the specific neighborhood that one is studying, they do illustrate, as Kenneth Clark[15] suggests, some of the important polarities in the life of the Negro community. One finds these papers filled with slang and stories of ghetto notoriety — sexual exploitation, crime, occasional police heroics — as well as rather staid liberal editorials on civil rights and poverty.

In many urban areas there are also radio stations specializing in the rather distinctive musical styles followed by the blue-collar Negro and white. Students of urban subcultures may profit from systematic study of the style and content of the music listened to and purchased in these communities. Since disk jockeys and jazz musicians are generally known to be creators of Negro slang, systematic linguistic analysis of disk jockeys' patter might also provide fertile cultural data.

Finally, there are documents written by members of the community being studied. We have found some few attempts at writing novels, although most writing efforts take the form of autobiographies or diaries. In general, none of these appear to be serious attempts to create literature, but rather reflect the slum dweller's attempt to make sense of his life. The housing project community, with the aid of an Office of Economic Opportunity community organizer, produced its own self-study. Such documents are likely to provide some indication of the slum dwellers' perspective on themselves and the larger society.

In addition to these existing documents, and following the suggestion of Derek V. Roemer, we hired several teenagers to write daily diaries.[16] We found them quite willing to record their activities, yet the diaries were kept in such a cursory manner that it was necessary to use them as interview guides rather than as primary data.

15. Clark, chap. 7.
16. Derek V. Roemer, "Adolescent Peer Group Formation in Two Negro Neighborhoods" (unpublished Ph. D. Dissertation, Harvard University, November 1968).

Danger and Sensitivity to Social Realities

In addition to the psychological anxieties and confusion that result from participant observation in a poverty-stricken community, current popular literature on slum communities suggest that outsiders going into the community are vulnerable to physical harm. Pruitt-Igoe had such a bad reputation that we were told by members of the community itself as well as by outsiders that we were fools to stay down there after dark, and that there was no question that one of us would be harmed if we continued to do the research. In the entire three and a half years of intensive participant observation in that community and the year in the white slum, there were relatively few instances of verbal hostility and only one instance of clear physical threat. (The latter occurred at two o'clock in the morning when the researcher was with an informant on a street corner. Both were high on wine and the informant had gotten into a knife fight with another man.) Our experience indicates that, given a relatively normal level of interpersonal sensitivity to situations, researchers may enter lower-class communities without being harmed.

There are at least two sources of interpersonal threat and danger that may be encountered in participant observation. We have chosen to label these "anonymous" and "presentational." The first, anonymous danger, is present in any situation in which one is more than ordinarily vulnerable to threat from a stranger; walking through Central Park after dark, for instance. While the anonymity of Central Park after dark is difficult to cope with, the urban researcher may reduce anonymous danger by becoming known to the residents of the neighborhood he is studying.

The second source of danger, stemming from the way the researcher presents himself to his informants, is largely under his control. To say that he should not act in a manner that angers his informants or seems to pose a threat to them is to belabor the obvious. Beyond this the urban researcher must become sensitive to dangerous situations and the manner in which his behavior is being interpreted by persons he encounters. During the first weeks of our research in the public housing project, one of the more aggressive researchers had the idea that one way to make friends in the Negro community was to buy drinks for persons in bars. After he had done this twice, the bartender approached one of the other members of the research staff and said, "Tell thay guy to stop buying drinks for everybody and leaving his money on the bar or he'll end up with a cap [bullet] in his ass." By buying drinks and leaving money around he was not only acting in a very different manner from other members of the community, but also communicating to every person in the bar that he had considerable money, thus making himself an inviting target. We learned very quickly not to carry a briefcase or wear a tie in the housing project. These middle-class artifacts are taken to indicate that one is either collecting insurance payments, collecting bills, or repossessing installment-purchased household goods.

We do not mean to minimize human dangers. Rather we mean to communicate the importance of being aware of and sensitive to dangerous situations, and the relationships between danger, presentation of self, and human interaction. The best insurance against physical harm is the establishment of friendships in the community. Such friends watch out for researchers, warn them of inadvisable behavior, and keep them out of or away from vulnerable situations.

Negro and White Researchers in a Negro Community

As we mentioned earlier, we were told before, during, and after the Pruitt-Igoe study that it was impossible for white researchers to know and discover the reality of the black ghetto, not only because whites would never be able to know what it was like to be a Negro in American society, but also because they would not be trusted by their informants. Informants would con them and make fools of them, they would be in danger, and whites had no business studying Negro ghettos anyway.

While there was considerable variation among both white and Negro students' ability to collect data in Pruitt-Igoe, many white students were in fact able to go into the community and establish rather close relationships with some of its members. Although they were deceived, especially during the early phases of the research, their data are consistent with those collected by Negro researchers. Most Negro researchers had a much easier time establishing relationships and collecting unconventional data than did white researchers. Our experience suggests that white researchers may spend twice as much time before they find deviant information—e.g., that a family is making income not reported to the housing authority. Negro researchers not only had the advantage of not being readily labeled as outsiders but also were better able to communicate, using both slang and common understanding in a way that white researchers had difficulty doing even in the last phases of the research.

White observers had little means of obtaining feedback on the nature of the data they were collecting. A major contribution of Negro observers was discussing with white researchers the relevance and validity of the data the whites were collecting.

We have also found a rather important reciprocal function for white researchers studying a Negro community. It is impossible for the participant observer to observe and be cognizant of everything that occurs in a research situation. One of the major problems facing the participant observer is that events become so commonplace that they are not viewed as being problematic and therefore are not seen as significant. A Negro researcher who comes from a poor family of thirteen, for example, may not see this size as being problematic, and he may not wonder that towels, toys, and other objects are not in their "proper places," that eating habits are somewhat irregular, that parents do not insist that all sit down and say grace together. These things may be so familiar to him that they do not become a part of his observations. (On the other hand, he could doubtless give us valuable insights on any middle-class white family that permitted him to study it.)

Toward the end of one night in the field when money was short but thirst unquenched, one white researcher pawned his watch to buy wine at the suggestion of the men he was with. It suddenly occurred to him that one of the important functions of expensive jewelry and clothing was as a kind of savings account. One could wear these items and thus show the wealth that one controlled, and at the same time have a source of cash if other money was not available. He suggested this hypothesis to a Negro colleague. The response was "Well, of course! You mean you didn't know that?"

It is not surprising that our dictionary of slang was created by a white and a black researcher working together. The white researcher took special interest in words that the Negro researcher used when talking to informants in bars. He would make notes, listing words that he was not familiar with, and after the three-way or four-way conversation he would ask his Negro colleague what the words meant. The Negro researcher was frequently not aware of using some of the expressions. Together they were able to accumulate a rather extensive list of Negro argot words.

Our point is that while Negro researchers are likely to have access to information that may not be available to white researchers, there are characteristic features of lower-class Negro life that Negro researchers are likely to take for granted and therefore not report. These things are largely unknown to the white middle-class American (the middle-class Negro will probably be familiar with them even though they may not form part of his personal life), and his náiveté has its advantages. What the Negro researcher overlooks or takes for granted, the white researcher sees as problematic — something to be explained.

There are other problems faced by Negro researchers studying the ghettos. Ethel Sawyer, one of the Negro researchers involved in the Pruitt-Igoe studies, suggests that these problems stem from the close identification of the Negro researcher with the community being studied.[17] There are two consequences of this identification. The first of these can be viewed as "withholding tendencies." More specifically and more bluntly, the Negro researcher must ask, "How much of this, if any, should I record, report, or even bother to write about?" The Negro researcher, aware of the public stereotype of the Negro community, faces the problem of reinforcing this negative image when he reports observations of deviant or unconventional behavior.

The second problem Sawyer identifies is the degree to which Negro researchers feel they should reveal to the white world what is unique about Negro ghettos. That is to say, a Negro researcher may ask himself, "Should I expose what is distinctly ours?" One might view the culture of the Negro American, at least a large part of it, as a distinctive means of coping with whites *per se,* whether through argot, "game," Uncle Tomism, or other adaptations. The question facing the Negro researcher is whether or not sharing this information through professional publications will have detrimental consequences to his own valued image of Negroes.

These problems are not unique to Negro Americans or Negro researchers. On the one hand, the participant observer is commissioned to move into a group, establish rather close relationships with its members, and perhaps become identified as a member of that group. On the other hand, he is expected to remain objective, not to become emotionally involved, and at the same time to understand relevant subjective perspectives. Thus the participant observer becomes directly involved with a group but at the same time remains an outsider. Issues of loyalty to those with whom he has close relations are likely to become an issue for him.

Problems of Reactions of the Observer

Whether the participant observer becomes directly or indirectly involved in the situation he is observing, participant observation is an individual process and the reaction of the individual interviewer or observer to the situation being observed is an important source of information to be used, as well as a source of bias that must be dealt with.

Involvement of researchers in the ghetto community has a staggering effect on their ability to think in an objective manner about sociological aspects of the data. Individual researchers closely involved with the community being studied have difficulty filtering out the total mass of data and qualifications placed on data, a parsimonious theoretical model.

17. Ethel Sawyer, "Some Methodological Problems in Studying Socially Deviant Communities" (unpublished paper, Social Science Institute, Washington University, 1967).

A participant observer who becomes close to the group he is studying is likely not only to begin participating in its activities, but also to become engaged in the competition for scarce objects. He thus runs the "risk of personal attacks, frustrations, and an interpersonal involvement"[18] that while unquestionably providing information may also result in confusion, a distortion of vision, and even retreat.

Kenneth Clark's identification of these problems and discussion of possible antidotes is extremely relevant. He suggests that the involved observers should have a parallel person who would

> test the observations, insights, and conclusions of the primary observer. Such a person would have to be more detached than he but at the same time fully cognizant of the problems and processes of the situation. He must be of equal professional status and capable of the same level of, if not more, penetrating insight and intelligence. He must be protected and removed from direct competitive involvement with the community and with the primary observer himself. He must be a person whose confidence, even more important, in whose critical judgment and integrity, the observer has total confidence.[19]

The structure of academic life, with its relatively clear differences in competence and status of students and professors, provides one ready solution to this problem. Our experience suggests that considerable envy is likely to be generated when some members of a research team are not directly involved in data collecting; yet a professionally competent person removed from the field, who will read field notes and discuss them with researchers, is likely to be of major value to a project. His detachment from the individual idiosyncrasies of data collection will aid him in identifying general social patterns as they emerge.

Advantages of Team Research

The ethnographic method of participant observation was developed for the study of relatively homogeneous and small societies and communities. The application of the method of participant observation to the urban world of the working and lower class requires that a team of researchers study a single community with individual members of the team focusing their attention on specific subgroups within the community. The organization of research teams should be a reflection of the nature of the community being studied. Thus some researchers focus their attention on families at home while others may focus their attention on teenage males and/or females, others on younger children at play, others on married men following conventional roles, and still others on married or separated men in more unconventional roles.

Some social scientists argue that ethnographic studies should be done

18. Clark, *Dark Ghetto*, p. xvi.
19. *Ibid.*, p. xviii.

alone or in very small teams of two or three members. For example, Charles Valentine argues that because participant observation is a highly personal task and because the quality of the data will depend on the quality of the relationship between informant and researcher, the maximum amount of time should be spent directing one's attention to the nature of the relationship, rather than attending to relationships with other members of a team of researchers.[20]

We obviously prefer the team approach. Clearly it is one direct means of solving the problems we have been discussing. At the same time our experience with team research indicates that there will be conflicts among members of large teams of researchers. These conflicts stem from at least three sources; personal idiosyncrasies, theoretical and ideological differences in approaches to data, and the nature of the observations being made. While conflict stemming from personal differences is of little use to anyone, differences in ideological, theoretical, and observational perspectives became the major basis for the development of awareness by members of the team of issues confronted by our research. The principal differences centered around the question of disorganization and organization of lower-class life. When Jules Henry or Alvin Gouldner reinterpreted the limited observations made by students in a manner that did not reflect the students' understanding of the field data, he forced students to think through assumptions that were being made, and to collect data relevant to the issues being discussed.

Conflict among observers is a productive process when it illuminates the limitations of the nature of the generalizations being made by a single researcher in his network of informants. By providing what Gouldner terms "hostile information,"[21] i.e., data that are inconsistent with the generalization being formulated, other members of the research team force him to look further both into his own data and into the contingencies involved in its collection. Thus he is constrained to move beyond the mere description of a community and begin asking analytical questions.

20. Charles A. Valentine, *Culture and Poverty* (Chicago: University of Chicago Press, 1968), Appendix.
21. Alvin W. Gouldner, *Enter Plato* (New York: Basic Books, 1965), p. 271.

Index

271